SOCIAL POLICY REVIEW 28

Analysis and debate in social policy, 2016

Edited by Menno Fenger, John Hudson and
Catherine Needham

First published in Great Britain in 2016 by

Policy Press
University of Bristol
1-9 Old Park Hill
Bristol BS2 8BB
UK
t: +44 (0)117 954 5940
e: pp-info@bristol.ac.uk
www.policypress.co.uk

North American office:
Policy Press
c/o The University of Chicago Press
1427 East 60th Street
Chicago, IL 60637, USA
t: +1 773 702 7700
f: +1 773-702-9756
e:sales@press.uchicago.edu
www.press.uchicago.edu

© Policy Press/Social Policy Association 2016

British Library Cataloguing in Publication Data
A catalogue record for this book is available from the British Library.

Library of Congress Cataloging-in-Publication Data
A catalog record for this book has been requested.

ISBN 978-1-4473-3179-7 hardback
ISBN 978-1-4473-3181-0 paperback SPA members' edition (not on general release)

Contents

Notes on contributors

Philip Brown is Professor of Social Change, Director of the Centre for Applied Research in Health, Welfare and Policy (CARe) and Director of the Sustainable Housing and Urban Studies Unit (SHUSU) at the University of Salford, UK. He has led and delivered a wide range of projects for the private and public sector, charitable bodies and European Commission. Philip's areas of interest are broad and encompass social exclusion, migration, homelessness, fuel poverty, and regeneration.

James Caiels has been active in health and social care research for over 12 years. His recent work includes the Personal Health Budgets Evaluation study funded by the Department of Health. He is currently lead researcher on the Engagement strand of the Quality and Outcomes of Person-centred Care (QORU) Policy Research Unit, developing methods to improve the participation of hard-to-engage people in research.

Karen Christensen is Professor of Sociology at the Department of Sociology, University of Bergen, Norway. She has been a visiting researcher at City University, London, and King's College London, and is currently the Head of Department of Sociology in Bergen. During her career she has researched and published in areas such as modernisation of social care services, new welfare service relationships, care policy practices, disability and independent lives, comparative social policy and migration impacting on care work.

Gordon L. Clark is Professor and Director of the Smith School at Oxford University, is Sir Louis Matheson Distinguished Visiting Professor in the Department of Banking and Finance at Monash University and is a visiting professor at Stanford University. His most recent books are the co-authored *Saving for Retirement: Intention, Context and Behaviour* (Oxford University Press, 2012) and *Sovereign Wealth Funds* (Princeton University Press, 2013).

Stephen Crossley is a PhD student in the School of Applied Social Sciences at Durham University. His research is funded by the ESRC and examines the construction of 'troubled families' as a social problem and the operationalisation of the Troubled Families Programme. Prior to commencing his PhD, he worked with local authorities and voluntary sector organisations in housing, neighbourhood and public policy roles.

Peter Dwyer is Professor of Social Policy and currently Director of Research in the Department of Social Policy and Social Work, University of York, England, UK. His teaching and research focuses on issues related to social citizenship, inclusion/exclusion and welfare and migration. He currently leads a large, collaborative, Economic and Social Research Council (ESRC) funded project on welfare conditionality (see www. welfareconditionality.ac.uk).

Menno Fenger is Professor of Governance of Modern Welfare States at the Department of Public Administration and Sociology, Erasmus University Rotterdam. He also is Co-Dean at the Netherlands School of Public Administration. His research focuses on processes of institutional change in welfare states in The Netherlands and in comparative perspective.

Karen Fisher is Professor at the Social Policy Research Centre, UNSW Australia. Her research interests are the organisation of social services in Australia and China, including disability and mental health services and community care; inclusive research and evaluation methodology; and social policy process.

Julien Forder is the Director of PSSRU at the University of Kent and a Principal Research Fellow at the London School of Economics. Julien was the Principal Investigator for the Department of Health-funded evaluation of the personal health budget pilot programme. The national evaluation began in 2009 and a final report was published in November 2012.

John Hudson is Professor of Social Policy and Co-Director of the Centre for Research in Comparative and Global Social Policy (CRCG) in the Department of Social Policy and Social Work at the University of York, UK. His recently completed projects include a cross-national comparison of inequality in child well-being (UNICEF) and an historical analysis of attitudes to welfare in the UK (Shelter).

Hannah Jobling is a Lecturer in Social Work at the University of York. Until fairly recently she worked as a practitioner in the youth justice field. Since joining academia she has researched and written on mental health policy and practice, social work with young people, the policy-practice relationship, ethics in everyday practice and critical realism.

Karen Jones is a Senior Research Fellow at Personal Social Services Research Unit (PSSRU) at the University of Kent. Karen has been involved in a number of evaluations that have explored the effectiveness and costs of personal budgets in both social and health care, which sit at the heart of the personalisation agenda in England. Karen managed the evaluation of the personal health budget pilot programme, which followed being a quantitative analyst during the social care evaluation that explored the effectiveness of individual budgets.

Philippa Locke is a research student in the School of Languages and Social Sciences at Aston University. Her research is situated in sociology and social policy. Drawing on narrative methods, she explores the ways in which the journey of care unfolds for older people. Starting from the first realisation that there is a need for care and the ways that care choices are negotiated with friends, family members and significant others, she goes on to explore the ways in which formal and informal care arrangements overlap as care needs increase.

Ariella Meltzer is a Research Associate at the Social Policy Research Centre and Centre for Social Impact, UNSW Australia. Ariella's research is about the relationships between different groups in society, including between people with and without disability, families and young people. She also works on research and evaluations about the social and economic participation of people with disability and of young people. She is experienced in using accessible methods to include people with disability in research.

Catherine Needham is a Reader in Public Policy and Public Management at the Health Services Management Centre at the University of Birmingham. She has written extensively on themes related to personalisation and co-production in public services, including an edited collection entitled *Debates in Personalisation* with Professor Jon Glasby (Policy Press, 2014).

Robert M. Page is currently Reader in Democratic Socialism and Social Policy at the University of Birmingham. He has written extensively about the welfare state in Britain since 1945. Recent publications include the monograph, *Clear Blue Water? The Conservative*

Party and the Welfare State in Britain since 1940 (Policy Press, 2015) and a chapter on the social policy record of the Wilson government in A.S. Clines and K. Hickson (eds) *Harold Wilson: The Unprincipled Prime Minister? Reappraising Harold Wilson* (Biteback, 2016: 149–64).

Ruth Patrick is a Postdoctoral Researcher in the School of Law and Social Justice at the University of Liverpool. Her most recent research explores the lived experiences of welfare reform, and she has a particular interest in social citizenship, welfare conditionality and qualitative longitudinal methodologies.

Martin Powell is Professor of Health and Social Policy at the Health Services Management Centre, University of Birmingham. He has published on the British National Health Service for 30 years, including *Evaluating the National Health Service* (Open University Press, 1997). His recent work includes co-editing works on the social policy and health policy of the coalition government, with Hugh Bochel, and Mark Exworthy and Russell Mannion, respectively (both published by Policy Press, 2016).

Christiane Purcal is a Research Associate at the Social Policy Research Centre, UNSW Australia. She is a researcher and project manager on evaluations that focus on disability and mental health policies, child and family services and informal carer policies. Recent projects include: Supported Accommodation Evaluation Framework (Ageing Disability and Home Care, NSW Government), Individual funding: building community capacity through action research (National Disability Research and Development Grant) and Families at the Centre, ARC Linkage Grant.

Mark Stephens is Professor of Public Policy at the Institute for Social Policy, Housing, Environment and Real Estate at Heriot-Watt University, Edinburgh. He has led major evaluations of housing policy for the Office of the Deputy Prime Minister and the European Commission, and led the Department of Communities and Local Government's Expert Panel on housing and surveys analysis. He recently joined the editorial team of the UK Housing Review, and is an editor of Urban Studies and Convenor of Scottish Property Tax Reform.

Adam Stephenson is a PhD candidate/researcher at the Institute for Social Policy, Housing, Environment and Real Estate at Heriot-

Watt University, Edinburgh. He has experience of the initiation and implementation of local welfare policy. His current research interests include localisation, sub-state welfare systems and the role of the market in the provision of housing welfare. He has experience of initiating and implementing local welfare policy.

Elizabeth Welch is a Research Officer at the Personal Social Services Research Unit at the University of Kent. She has over nine years' experience of health and social care academic research projects. Her work centres on the personalisation of health and social care. She worked on the Personal Health Budgets Evaluation, funded by the Department of Health, and continues to work on a research study examining the continued impact of Personal Health Budgets.

Karen West is a Senior Lecturer in Sociology and Policy in the School of Languages and Social Sciences at Aston University, where she lectures and publishes on critical policy analysis and ageing studies. Recent research projects have examined life in extra care retirement communities and, in particular, on the experiences of residents in transition from the third age to the fourth age, and the experiences of older workers in a number of European countries of staying in employment or getting back into employment.

Karen Windle is Reader in Health at the University of Lincoln. Karen's research activities are to explore well-being for older people, including early intervention, prevention, personalisation and service integration across the social and health care fields. She focuses particularly on different policy innovations and implementation involving older people. Karen has provided a range of evidence to support future decision making and policy development. Her evidence has supported policy provision and she has recently published on prevention and early intervention for the Government Office of Science.

Part One
Continuities and change in
UK social policy

Menno Fenger

Amid all the process of welfare reform, cutbacks, and austerity measures, we would almost forget that the British welfare state offers its citizens historically almost unprecedented protection against the risks of illness, old age, invalidity and unemployment, among other things. It was Sir William Beveridge who identified the five 'evil giants' of the society of his time: want, disease, ignorance, squalor and idleness. The welfare state was the solution he proposed to combat these giants. Since then, his ideas – and those of many other 'founding fathers' of the welfare state – have relieved the hardship for many Brits who suffer from unemployment, illness or other social risks. However, in our current time, the solutions that modern welfare states have offered increasingly are considered as part of the problem themselves. Therefore, traditionally, Part One of *Social policy review* focuses on the state of affairs in each of the pillars of the welfare state. It assesses to what extent the evil giants have been defeated, which new problems and unintended consequences have emerged and how this affects the policies. In this year's edition, we focus on four policy areas: pension policies, health care, income benefits and housing.

In Chapter One, Gordon Clark reassesses the behavioural assumptions underlying pension policies and its recent reforms. To guarantee the sustainability of the British pension system, defined benefit pension systems with a guaranteed benefit at retirement have been replaced by so-called defined contribution systems in which the benefit at retirement depends on external conditions and choices made by citizens themselves. This implies that people are becoming increasingly responsible for their own pensions. This presumes that people are capable of making decisions about their pensions. Clark argues that the behavioural paradigm that has recently became popular in many social-scientific disciplines challenges the ideas of individuals as rational decision makers. Therefore, he argues that it is not surprising that many of those participants tend to make decisions that, when considered over the long term, are not in their best interests. So, according to Clark, in addition to the neo-liberal paradigm that grounds the reforms of the British pension policies, a neo-paternalistic one is needed to correct the decision-making pitfalls of individuals.

The NHS is the British answer to the evil giant of 'disease'. However, according to many commentators, the NHS itself suffers from many bigger and smaller diseases. In Chapter Two, Martin Powell analyses the development of the NHS under the coalition government. While some argue that under the coalition government the UK approached the end of the NHS, Powell shows that the reforms that have been initiated by the coalition government have diverging directions and diverging ideological foundations. Whereas in the first part of the coalition government's rule, merely competition, privatisation and marketisation dominated the debate, the second part still carries the heritages of the neo-liberal paradigm but also introduces other measures to improve the performance of the NHS and guarantee its financial sustainability: prevention, integration and localisation. Powell questions if these initiatives are strong enough to guarantee a bright future for the NHS.

The third chapter in this part shows how the evil giant of 'idleness' has returned in the political debate, but with new features. In the current age, the welfare state is no longer considered as a solution for idleness, it is also assumed to cause idleness. In Chapter Three, Peter Dwyer shows how T.H. Marshall's notion of social citizenship in which largely unconditional, de-commodified social rights has been replaced by a system of behavioural conditions and sanctions in different domains of the welfare state. Dwyer specifically focuses on conditionality in social security benefits, housing and homelessness. The chapter shows an intriguing picture of how the 21st century welfare state is concerned with regulation of individual behaviour.

In the final chapter of this part, Mark Stephens and Adam Stephenson assess the state of the UK's responses to the evil giant of 'squalor'. Their assessment is sceptical of the current state of British housing policy. They observe a strong tendency to favour home ownership and worsening financial and regulative conditions for those who are not (yet) capable of buying a home. A variety of financial measures has increased the costs of housing for low incomes, whereas safety measures to protect these groups gradually have been abolished. Moreover, legal reforms with regard to tenure security for new tenants have even further worsened the position of low-income newcomers on the housing market. Stephens and Stephenson therefore conclude that British housing policy redistributes rights away from low-income groups in favour of other groups.

ONE

Behaviour, choice, and British pension policy

Gordon L. Clark

Introduction

Twenty years ago, the British pension system relied upon three separate but interrelated pillars – the Basic State Pension (BSP), occupational pensions, and personal saving and investment. If praised for its resilience, more recently the system is believed by many to be unable to deliver on its (collective) promise; some commentators believe the UK pension system is not fit for purpose. Rising real incomes, combined with higher levels of income inequality have, in effect, discounted the value of the Basic State Pension for lower income retirees. Private sector occupational pensions have withered and died, leaving legacy schemes teetering on bankruptcy (Clark, 2006). Replacement schemes are less lucrative, and shift the risks associated with pension saving and investment to participants. Notorious instances of 'mis-selling' by the financial services industry have further diminished public confidence in pension saving products that rely upon commercial providers (Thoresen Review, 2008).

The apparent fragility of the system is commonly interpreted through the lens of neo-liberalism (Langley, 2008). Invoked are a sequence of events or tendencies: the breakdown of the Bretton Woods agreement; the Thatcher years; financial market deregulation in the mid-1980s; and global economic and financial integration. Among the various narratives told about the rise of neo-liberalism are three key beliefs with regard to the stability of inherited institutions like pension systems. First, neo-liberalism has undercut social solidarity, replacing equitability between generations and social classes with deference to the individual (Preda, 2004). Second, the price of maintaining inherited institutions has been rendered transparent, and integrated into the 'value' attributed to the public and private organisations that sponsor these institutions. Third, the value of any institution is relative compared to other ways of organising society (at home, across Europe, and around the world) (Clark, 2003).

Lord Turner's Report (Pensions Commission, 2004; 2005) on the British pension crisis and the pathway to resolution was a comprehensive response to the problems apparent in each component of the British pension system. Maintaining and enhancing the value of the Basic State Pension (Pillar 1) was linked to the establishment of a state-sponsored workplace pension savings scheme (Pillar 2) and a commitment to better regulate the financial services industry, especially in relation to consumer savings products. The Report could also be read as a response to the constraints on solutions to the pensions' crisis imposed by neo-liberalism – increasing the value of the Basic State Pension within market expectations of British long-term economic growth and the government's capacity to fund the BSP. In a related vein, the new state-sponsored workplace pension saving model was a defined contribution (DC) rather than a defined benefit (DB) scheme. Nonetheless, the Report was a remarkable example of consensus building, which attracted bipartisan support (reinforced by the election of the coalition government between the Conservative Party and the Liberal Democrats in 2010).

Underwriting the Turner Report was a broad-based acceptance of the principles and implications of the behavioural revolution sweeping the behavioural sciences and economics (see Mitchell and Utkus, 2004). In a nutshell, this research programme has empirically demonstrated that individuals are not well-placed to make effective decisions as regards their long-term welfare, and are instead subject to status quo bias and prevarication in the face of changing circumstances (O'Donoghue and Rabin, 1999). Moreover, people discount the future, are risk-averse and loss-averse, and are preoccupied by the present (Kahneman and Tversky, 1972; 1979). In essence, behavioural research has undercut standard economic models of individual behaviour and decision making (Ainslee, 2001; Laibson, 2003). Recognising the intellectual foundations of the Turner Report, British political parties agreed a way forward which sought to protect the interests of the average 'participant' notwithstanding his or her responsibilities for their own welfare.

In this chapter I explain the significance of the behavioural revolution in relation to economic theory and situate its experimental protocols within the context of cognitive science and behavioural psychology (see Hertwig and Ortmann, 2003). It is shown that the behavioural revolution has significant implications for understanding patterns of pension saving and investment. However, it is also shown that understanding behaviour should be embedded in context as there are important societal factors that may amplify or dampen behavioural biases and anomalies (Clark, 2014). These themes are linked to British pension policy given that Lord Turner's reforms owe a great deal to behaviouralism. Looking ahead, however, one can discern the increasing importance of political claims for greater respect for individual autonomy and volition (Osborne, 2014). Whereas the behavioural revolution is founded upon an empirically-informed understanding of rationality, idealism could trump this research programme to the detriment of many UK residents.

Behaviour and rationality

One result of the ascendancy of the neoclassical paradigm in economics over the 50 years following the Second World War was the almost exclusive focus upon the rational economic agent. Each new generation of scholars was trained to respect the axioms of microeconomic theory and the presumption in favour of rationality (both as a norm and as a lived reality). Observed behaviour not consistent with those norms was either reinterpreted, so as to demonstrate its underlying rationality (Becker and Murphy, 1988), or dismissed as exceptional, and therefore unrelated to core principles. Early economic theorists like Keynes (1936) had suggested that aberrant behaviour could lock in markets into undesirable states. These ideas were sidelined until the stock market bubble of the early 2000s and the subsequent global financial crisis (see Shiller, 2005 and Stiglitz, 2014).

In any event, it was widely believed that 'exceptional' behaviour would be priced out of the market as informed traders took advantage of neophytes. Herbert Simon, a remarkably talented social scientist, equally at home with organisation theory, cognitive science, and artificial intelligence was one of the few economists to suggest that non-optimal behaviour could be systematic in the sense that people typically satisfy rather than optimise utility (Simon, 1982). Relying upon a rudimentary model of cognition, Simon argued for physiological limits to people's capacity to process information, retrieve from memory relevant past experience and compute the desirability or otherwise of possible options (see Harvey, 2012 for a recent review of the evidence in favour of these hypotheses). Simon coined the phrase 'boundedly rational', thereby introducing an idea that was to haunt economics for at least a generation. Perversely, this phrase and its underlying argument were later interpreted to mean that people are either less rational than they should be and/or that these limits or constraints could be overcome with effort and/or public policy.

While Simon relied upon direct observation and laboratory-based testing procedures, Kahneman and Tversky (1979) utilised the testing procedures of experimental psychology to alter the terms of the debate by demonstrating that people are systematically loss-averse. In fact, this research programme began with the premise that people are ipso facto rational (a human trait), but concluded that environments characterised by risk and uncertainty reveal human frailties in long-term decision making. This finding has had significant implications for the robustness of conventional economic theory (Shafir et al, 1997). Furthermore, as related research uncovered evidence that people heavily discount the future, overweight the present in relation to the past, and prevaricate rather than make commitments, it became clear that the axioms underpinning the rational economic agent could not withstand empirical scrutiny (Kahneman et al, 1997). In effect, Simon was vindicated and the Carnegie School sustained.

Other economists, experimental psychologists, and cognitive scientists have brought forth evidence of behavioural 'anomalies and biases' (Krueger and Funder, 2004). One reason for the success of Kahneman and Tversky and those that have followed in their wake was the utilisation of experimental findings to narrow the domain in which the standard version of rationality could be plausible, rather than focusing on the plausibility of rationality. Another was the testing of behavioural predispositions in environments characterised by risk and uncertainty. These types of environments are not unusual, as most people are required to take decisions and make plans for the future whether in developed, developing, or less-developed economies. Finally, Kahneman and Tversky's testing procedures and problems were aligned with the research traditions of behavioural psychology (Baron, 2008).

Equally significant, but oftentimes less discussed, is how people revise their expectations on the basis of past and current experience (Oaksford and Chater, 2007). The standard model is based upon Bayes' theorem in which past information is used to compose a model of the world by noting the range and frequency of possible outcomes (Jones and Love, 2011). As each new piece of data emerges, the model is re-estimated by incorporating new information with past data, with the result that people are better able to predict the likelihood of certain outcomes. However, experimental evidence suggests that most people, most of the time, are not Bayesian; they overweight the immediate past in relation to the distant past – in some cases, excluding altogether data that is deemed (by reference to current circumstances) irrelevant (see also Ungemach et al, 2009). The temptation is to assign too much significance to current events, viewing the immediate future as an extension of the present (see generally Tversky and Simonson, 1993). People can be taught to be Bayesian (Sedlmeier and Gigerenzer, 2001), but, intuitively, they prefer simpler and more cost-effective heuristics (Gigerenzer and Todd, 1999).

There are many reviews and critiques of the behavioural paradigm. Three specific issues should be noted in relation to pension policy and design. First, the unit of analysis in much of behavioural psychology, cognitive science, and psychological research is the individual, whatever their immediate circumstances. Second, it should also be acknowledged that the behavioural paradigm was developed in a quite distinctive milieu – namely the universities of advanced Western economies. Third, the strength of the behavioural paradigm lies in its capacity to interrogate the use of the rational economic agent as the representative of individuals in diverse settings or environments (Henrich et al, 2004). Whereas the rational economic agent was typically personified as a man not a woman, the behavioural paradigm has revealed significant differences in the behavioural predispositions between men and women in terms of their risk aversion and loss aversion (Clark et al, 2015).

A related issue concerns the laboratory testing procedures that underpin the results of the behavioural paradigm. Overwhelmingly, the subjects of the testing regime are university students – undergraduates and postgraduates. Students are confronted with synthetic problems, described in simple terms. Recognising the ever-present danger of 'framing' the interpretation of the problem (and therefore prompting a certain result), simple and synthetic problems – shared between research groups and tested on multiple occasions in different settings – are preferred over problems anchored in specific settings. It has proven challenging to integrate prior knowledge, experiential learning and social position into tests of decision making without confounding the overarching goal; that is, the search for, and identification of, human traits and behavioural predispositions (Clark et al, 2006).

Behaviour and pension design

Whether people are rational in either the neoclassical or the behavioural sense is not relevant if they rely upon government pensions and/ or defined benefit pensions. In these circumstances, institutions and organisations make decisions on their behalf and bear, when necessary, the risks associated with long-term commitments. Equally, whether people are effective decision makers in the context of risk and uncertainty is irrelevant if the financial decisions they must make in such environments have only a limited impact on their long-term wellbeing. By the early 1980s, in the United States and elsewhere, it had become apparent that an increasing proportion of the population were being required to make significant decisions about their long-term welfare. These types of decisions (including saving decisions) can have adverse consequences in the event of a systematic mismatch between the nature and scope of these determinations, and the skills and expertise required for effective decision making (Ainslie and Haslam, 1992; Lowenstein and Prelec, 1992).

At the time, US private sector unionization rates were in freefall, deindustrialisation was ravaging the US economy and, parallel to the decline of private sector well-paid jobs with defined benefit pensions, a new compensation model was being adopted in the service sectors (Jensen, 1993). It is, perhaps, no coincidence that academic interest in decision making under risk and uncertainty accelerated as increasing numbers of academics were enrolled into defined contribution pension plans. In 1988, Samuelson and Zeckhauser published a paper in the first issue of the *Journal of Risk and Uncertainty* showing that, once enrolled, the overwhelming majority of DC participants did not vary their initial asset allocations or, indeed, switch between investment products. The phrase 'status quo bias' was coined to describe the apparent inertia of most participants, a finding that was to have far-reaching consequences for the design and management of DC pension systems (Madrian and Shea, 2001).

Suppose pension plan participants are offered a choice of assets (for example, equities, government bonds and property), a choice of investment products representing those assets, and a choice as to whether to make a fixed-term commitment to a set of chosen options or allow those commitments to rollover time and again. Samuelson and Zeckhauser showed that the majority of participants made an initial 50-50 allocation to equities and bonds. Later, it was shown that adding property to the options, most participants would probably allocate assets as follows: 40-40-20. As for the choice of investment products within asset classes, most participants would choose those providers with recognised names and/or would probably allocate the available assets equally between providers (Benartzi and Thaler, 2001). It is no surprise that most participants would prefer commitments to rollover time and again rather than revisit the issue in the future. In any event, those that would indicate a preference to revisit their initial choices in the future tend not to take up the option unless compelled to do so (see generally, Choi et al, 2002).

Academic research has addressed each of these issues. It has been found that people prefer heuristics rather than tackling each issue on its merits. In addition, how a choice is framed can determine the manner by which people evaluate the options and then act (Benartzi and Thaler, 2005). Elsewhere, it has been demonstrated that many people are overwhelmed by the description or framing of issues, often failing to 'see through' issues to their underlying properties and shared characteristics (Clark et al, 2006). One implication is that if a choice is 'reframed' by changing its description, behaviour changes to match the frame rather than making the obvious connection between the previous and current form of the same issue. It has been found that notwithstanding the costs and consequences of failing to revisit an initial decision or set of decisions, many people are loath to return to the issue. When they do so, their 'solutions' are simplistic to a fault.

Two behavioural research programmes are particularly relevant to the issue of behaviour and pension design. Thaler and Sunstein's (2008) 'liberal paternalism' introduced into global policy circles the concept of 'nudge'. Thaler has been especially influential in bringing the results of behavioural research into the mainstream of economics. Sunstein, on the other hand, has been influential in jurisprudence and public policy, articulating a modern form of liberalism and government regulation. Together, they suggested that the results of the behavioural revolution were so significant that governments should design policy regimes that enable individuals to make decisions in their best interests while limiting the availability of options that, if chosen, would not be consistent with their long-term interests. This framework was conceived in relation to pension policy and design but has had wide appeal (UK Government, 2010). Indeed, the UK coalition government established an office in Downing Street to apply a 'nudge' across a range of policy areas where individual decision making was at a premium (Halpern, 2015).

Another research programme influenced by the behavioural paradigm is that associated with Lusardi and Mitchell's (2007) 'financial literacy'. To be effective in environments such as financial markets, and overcome the apparent behavioural biases and anomalies, which discount the effectiveness of decision making in these environments, it is believed that people should be better informed about the principles that govern performance in financial markets. Tests of financial literacy were established and validated via a global field-based testing regime. Underpinning this research is an assumption that financial skill and expertise is vital if people are to avoid the costs and consequences of behavioural biases and anomalies when saving for the future. Lusardi and Mitchell's research programme and policy prescription is optimistic in the sense that it is assumed that most people can improve their decision making in these situations. Many cognitive scientists and behavioural psychologists believe biases and anomalies to be 'hardwired' and resistant to mollifying strategies, even if people are self-conscious in their effects (compare Kahneman, 2011 with Doherty, 2003).

These were the building blocks for the reformed British occupational pension system. All UK employees are required to be auto-enrolled by their employer into an appropriate pension scheme (typically DC). After a certain time, employees can leave such a scheme for another or not contribute to an occupational pension. Should they do so, at a later stage the employer is required to auto-enrol them again. It is expected that once enrolled most participants won't leave a scheme and, should they do so, when they are re-enrolled by their employer they won't again choose to leave such a scheme. Typically, those auto-enrolled into an occupational scheme are allocated to the default pension savings product; otherwise, they must make conscious choices about asset allocation and investment products. Most participants do not switch from the default fund, which often contains a mix of asset types determined by the age of the participant. As they grow older, the mix of assets shifts towards bonds over equities. Participants are not required to make these decisions and typically would not do so if required.

Behaviour and society

This brief account of the relationship between advocates of the rational economic agent and cognitive scientists and behavioural psychologists, does not do justice to related, but less explored research concerning the relationship between behaviour and society. Henrich et al's (2004) report on a major interdisciplinary research programme, which sought to determine whether standard models of behaviour – as found in game theory and related models of individual behaviour – are applicable across different societies. In broad terms, the authors concluded that when using common tests of behaviour across 15 different small societies, the results were not consistent with 'the canonical model of purely self-interested actors'. An additional finding was that there were considerable variations between groups of people (within and between societies) in terms of their commitment, or otherwise, to the axioms of economic rationality.

To summarise, Henrich et al (2004) demonstrate that social preferences, commitments, and modes of cooperation structure behaviour in all societies, but in different ways. It is not obvious that the research programme on behaviour and society is particularly relevant to modelling individual savings behaviour within a society and/or within Anglo-American societies. Likewise, it could be argued that making the link between behaviour and society complicates an already involved story, rendering policy making more difficult and, paradoxically, strengthening the hand of those that promote the rational agent model because of its simplicity. Nonetheless, it is important to acknowledge the influence of culture and society on attitudes to risk taking and behaviour – across whole societies and within societies (see Douglas and Wildavsky, 1982 and Bröder, 2003).

To illustrate, consider the following:

Instance 1: household behaviour. Many people over the age of 30 years live together either in a formal arrangement underwritten by marriage or in less formal arrangements that embody long-term commitments. Whereas much of social science is focused upon individual behaviour, it is often meaningful to talk of household behaviour such that one person's actions are framed by others. This point is developed in Clark et al (2012) where it is demonstrated that households often pursue a collective risk and return retirement saving strategy, wherein one partner (often the higher income partner) takes on more risk in their investment portfolio than the other partner (often the lower income partner). Considering their separate rather than collective behaviour, it could be (mistakenly) concluded that lower income people are more risk averse than higher income people.

Instance 2: behaviour of older households. We have also shown that older, higher income individuals tend to have an extensive portfolio of retirement saving instruments compared to older, lower income individuals, and younger, higher income individuals (Clark et al, 2012). In effect, a successful professional, well situated in the labour market benefits from the continuity of employment. Their success over the long term is expressed in terms of higher overall economic welfare and a broader range of savings instruments than others not so well placed. Diversity in the range of savings' instruments means that these individuals, and those reliant upon their success, are able to self-insure the risks associated with taking investments that fall outside the instruments available to most people. Furthermore, diversity in the range of savings instruments can provide those involved with a premium on investment returns, which shifts their wellbeing far beyond that of the average pension plan participant. Hardly studied, but of considerable long-term importance to British social solidarity, is the increasing levels of income inequality among older-aged households.

Instance 3a: not taking risk. As indicated by behavioural researchers, many people are loss-averse (in the first instance) and risk-averse (in the second instance). Furthermore, in some sections of British society, social mores dampen the appetite of many for taking a risk in terms of their immediate and long-term welfare. There are two elements in this argument. First, a significant minority of the population are exposed to variable employment prospects, low earned incomes, and low rates of labour market participation at higher ages (Goos and Manning, 2007; McDowell et al, 2009). In these circumstances, it is not surprising that some people pursue a safety-first risk management strategy, limiting exposure to any risk (investment and saving or otherwise) (Roy, 1950). Second, in these circumstances, any loss is more significant in absolute terms than a possible long-term reward for taking risk. In a sense, this is myopic behaviour. But it is justified myopia.

Instance 3b: taking risk. Risk taking is integral to saving and investment. In some quarters, however, risk taking is believed to be synonymous with gambling. In some cases, this is entirely true (Clark et al, 2015). But a sophisticated investor not only calculates the odds of realising planned returns, he or she brings to bear knowledge and understanding of financial markets thereby informing the investment process in the light of experience (Sharpe, 2007). Sophisticated investors also seek ways of managing risk, in many cases trading off the rate of return against the variance in returns. Put slightly differently, a sophisticated investor takes advantage of compounding, eschewing higher than average returns at any point in time in favour of a steady stream of returns that, over time, can match expectations (Clark et al, 2012). To do so requires patience and a willingness to look beyond immediate circumstances to long-term well-being. In this respect, myopia is antithetical to being an effective investor. But who is so well-placed as to be a sophisticated investor?

Instance 4: Winners and losers. Defined contribution pension systems tend to reward patience and penalise myopia. These systems also benefit those that have continuity in employment and contributions which, in turn, increase commensurate with their earned incomes during their careers. Furthermore, these types of systems tend to reward those who can ride out financial market volatility while holding to investment strategies that appear, at any point in time, to be less aggressive than some, but have the virtue of being relatively insulated from market volatility. The losers tend to be those that have variable employment histories, interruptions in the flow of contributions, and earned incomes that don't keep pace with the growth in average incomes. In these ways, defined contribution pension schemes amplify labour market inequality and reinforce the advantages due to social position, education, gender and household status (Bajtelsmit, 2006). Long-term retirement income is less about the first ten to 15 years of work than it is about capitalising upon labour market position and family over the last 15 to 20 years of work (Clark et al, 2012).

Pension policy and politics

In the March 2014 Budget, under the heading 'Greater freedom and choice at retirement', the Chancellor announced changes in tax rules allowing people to gain access to their DC pension savings. In doing so, it was proposed that those eligible could draw down on their pension assets as income, purchase an annuity or extract all the pension savings in a lump sum. On this last option, rather than relying upon the sponsoring institution or a third party organisation, individuals would be entitled to manage their pension savings as they would see fit. This unheralded policy initiative was said to be 'the most fundamental change to the way people access their pension in almost a century' (HM Treasury, 2014a: Budget Report Sec. 1.154, 42). This initiative was, nonetheless, claimed to be consistent with the government's previously announced pension reforms and, specifically, the introduction of auto-enrolment (Sec. 1.156, 42).

In his 2014 ministerial statement, the Chancellor of the Exchequer, George Osborne, made a number of related comments, including recognition of the importance of saving for retirement and the fact that when retiring 'one of the biggest financial decisions' is how to manage accumulated savings. Most importantly, standing back from the government's previous commitment to promoting policies consistent with individuals' decision-making skills and expertise, the Chancellor went on to say that the change in policy was 'a radical departure', which gave 'choice back to individuals'. At the same time, he was mindful of the importance of ensuring that people are 'equipped and ready to make informed decisions'. And like other Western governments, he indicated that it was important to ensure that people would receive impartial guidance on the management of their pension assets free from conflicts of interest.

It is possible to read this initiative as an entirely reasonable response to a long-running but unresolved policy problem, aggravated by declining and extremely low interest rates and the sparsity of the UK annuities market: the requirement imposed on all retirees with DC benefits to convert those assets into an annuity by the age of 75. Interest rates have been declining for some years (Clark and Monk, 2013). The thinness of annuity markets has dampened competition and limited innovation in terms of the structure and value of annuity products. At the same time, it has been widely recognised in the UK and elsewhere that financial advisers, often tied to financial service companies, do not always honour the best interests of their clients. Indeed, the apparent opaqueness of the market for financial services and the inability of many people to assess whether those offering advice do so without regard to their commercial interest have been recognised by academics and practitioners as key factors that discount market efficiency and social welfare (Clark and Urwin, 2011).

It is also important to acknowledge that those affected by this policy, in fact, were a small proportion of UK retirees or intending retirees over the age of 55. In the UK, few employers have, until recently, offered DC pension schemes to employees. Those that have done so have provided benefits as either supplements to existing defined pension benefits or as benefits tied to specific types of jobs in the private sector. It was announced that the policy would not apply to defined benefits plans. Behavioural researchers have been mindful of the vulnerability of consumers to advisory services and the financial services industry. This issue is relevant to both ends of the income distribution, recognising the exploitive pricing policies of payday loan providers at the bottom end of the income distribution (Leyshon et al, 2004; 2006). It is telling that the government drew a distinction between 'advice' and 'guidance', referring throughout to the latter, but not the former. Once more, government has avoided the harder problem of regulating the financial advice industry, instead preferring to give life to the guidance process notwithstanding the obvious limits of guidance relative to advice.

It is arguable that the previous coalition government and the recently elected Conservative government have returned to the principles of liberalism. Without belabouring the obvious, liberalism presumes the sovereignty of the individual and defers to the individual's judgement as regards their own best interests. Liberalism also presumes that an individual's best interests will vary both between individuals and over time. In this respect, rather than deciding for an individual how best to accomplish certain goals and objectives – thereby running the risk of imposing on individuals what they desire and how it should be realised – it is assumed that the state is best placed to provide a well-regulated environment in which individuals can realise their objectives in their own way. So, for example, the state could underwrite the integrity of commercial contracts, thereby enhancing the effectiveness of individual planning for the future.

This sentiment idealises the individual, and takes no account of the findings of the behavioural revolution. Further, it ignores a related thread of research and policy analysis that draws its inspiration from the behavioural revolution: the use of field experiments to determine the effectiveness of policy instruments, incentives and sanctions with respect to intended goals and objectives (List, 2011). If we assume that people are sensitive to policy instruments, incentives and sanctions, and if we assume that their sensitivity will vary by cognitive predisposition and their place in society, then it would make sense to experiment with different types of policies and instruments so as to fine tune their effectiveness both with respect to policy goals and objectives and with respect to the responsiveness of those for whom the policy is intended to affect (Ludwig et al, 2011 in refs). If an obvious implication to be drawn from the behavioural revolution, it is not obvious that the government considered these issues when introducing the pension choice framework.

More broadly, the choice framework ignores studies of financial literacy both in the United Kingdom and elsewhere, and provides little in the way of a robust regulatory framework for the effective provision of untainted guidance (let alone advice). On guidance, it offers an idea that has no recognisable institutional form except for perhaps the Citizens Advice Bureau, and raises the prospect of yet another round of 'mis-selling' by the financial services industry. It empowers community organisations without substantiation. It shifts into the future and, given the small numbers of people involved, discounts the adverse consequences of such a policy for the current government. This is not to say, of course, that the government was mistaken in recognising the problems of requiring the purchase of an annuity, including the obvious failings of the annuities market. But, in the light of the findings of the behavioural revolution, the 'solution' seems little more than a rhetorical gesture in a contested political environment (Runciman, 2008).

Conclusions

Over the past 50 years, successive governments have sought to ensure the resilience of the British pension system, at times modifying or adapting its component parts and at other times seeking to formulate a comprehensive framework. The Turner Report was a moment in which a comprehensive 'solution' was offered and accepted by the major political parties. One of its key components was the proposal to establish a policy framework consistent with the shift in the private sector from defined benefit to defined contribution workplace pensions. Another element was utilisation of the lessons found in behavioural research so as to 'encourage' low and high income workers to participate in workplace pension schemes. Over the past five years, this policy framework has been implemented along with the establishment of the National Employment Savings Trust.

At the same time, the problems associated with DB pensions have, if anything, become more apparent. The long-term decline in interest rates – evident in the first half of the first decade of the 21st century – has accelerated through the global financial crisis and its aftermath. Furthermore, it seems obvious that any substantial recovery in interest rates could take some years and may not return to a level consistent with the solvency of these institutions or, for that matter, their sponsors. On this issue, no government appears to have an appetite for formulating a policy that would encourage the orderly exit of private sponsors from DB pension schemes. The financial crisis accelerated the closure of DB schemes, and the introduction of defined contribution (DC) schemes that shift the burden of responsibility in their administration and management from the employer to a third party. In many respects, occupational pensions in the private sector have been outsourced.

Defined contribution schemes shift responsibility for investment strategy and choices from the employer to the employee. If, as the behavioural research suggests, the average employee is unable to be an effective decision maker when it comes to managing their DC account, it is not surprising that he/she is prone to status quo bias. Likewise, it is not surprising that many of those participants who are active in this type of environment tend to make decisions that, when considered over the long term, are not in their best interests. Financial markets are demanding environments that require skill and expertise as well as a degree of judgement sufficient to balance the temptation to emphasise the short term over the long term. Recognising the costs and consequences of poor decision making, in some countries DC platforms have been introduced so as to 'automate' decision making; a case in point has been the introduction of target-date funds, which automatically rebalance an individual's investment portfolio as they age and as they approach their planned retirement date (Bodie and Treussard, 2007).

Inherent in auto-enrolment, target-date funds, contribution escalators and limited choices between screened and simplified investment options, is the empirically justified belief that the average participant should be guided, or channelled, through decision frameworks that dampen the costs and consequences of behavioural biases and anomalies. Thaler and Sunstein (2008) describe this type of decision framework as liberal paternalism. Other related formulations drop the reference to liberalism, and seek to protect the interests of the average participant. Notwithstanding the argument that DC pensions place a premium on individual decision making and the capacity to manage risk and uncertainty, structured choice frameworks are less a form of neo-liberalism and, more likely, a form of neo-paternalism.

Even so, considerable variations among participants, in terms of their background characteristics and levels of sophistication, exist. One response to this reality has been to shift to a regulatory and tax framework that allows for greater variety in saving instruments. This option was noted in the government's report on 'Freedom and choice in pensions: government response to the consultation', where it was stated that the government would introduce a regulatory framework for 'defined ambition pension schemes' among other types of arrangements (HM Treasury, 2014b: 8). In part, this proposal was justified by citing research from the National Association of Pension Funds (NAPF) to the effect that 'greater freedom and choice will lead to higher levels of savings and a greater number of people saving to support their retirement'. Whatever the basis of the NAPF's belief, one implication to be drawn from behavioural research is that this supposition is not supported by the evidence, if what is meant is that the 'average' participant is, in fact, just like the rational economic agent of yesteryear.

Acknowledgements
This paper was made possible by support for research on behaviour, financial markets and pension policy, provided by a number of institutions and organisations including Allianz Global Investors, the National Association of Pension Funds, MetallRente, Oxford University's Fell Fund, the Monash–CSIRO research programme on the Australian superannuation system, and Mercer (Australia and the UK). I am pleased to acknowledge the collaboration, help, and advice provided by many people including the late John C. Marshall and Emiko Caerlewy-Smith, Kendra Strauss and Janelle Knox Hayes, Csaba Burger, Heribert Karch and Dorothee Franzen, Christine Brown, Paul Gerrans, Carly Moulang, Dane Rook and Maria Strydom, Maurizio Faschetti, Peter Tufano and MichaelViehs, and Deborah Ralston. None of the above should be held accountable for the views and opinions expressed herein.

References

Ainslie, G. (2001) *Breakdown of will*, Cambridge: Cambridge University Press.

Ainslie, G. and Haslam, N. (1992) 'Self-control', in G. Lowenstein and J. Elster (eds) *Choice over time*, New York: Russell Sage Foundation, pp 177–209.

Bajtelsmit, V. (2006) 'Gender, the family, and economy', in G.L. Clark, A. Munnell and J.M. Orszag (eds) *The Oxford handbook of pensions and retirement income*, Oxford: Oxford University Press, pp 121–40.

Baron, J. (2008) *Thinking and deciding* (4th edn), Cambridge: Cambridge University Press.

Becker, G.S. and Murphy, K.M. (1988) 'A theory of rational addiction', *Journal of Political Economy*, 96(4):675–700.

Benartzi, S. and Thaler, R. (2001) 'Näive diversification strategies in defined contribution savings plans', *American Economic Review*, 91(1), 71–99.

Benartzi, S. and Thaler, R. (2005) 'Save more tomorrow: Using behavioral economics to increase employee savings', *Journal of Political Economy*, 112(1), 164–87.

Bodie, Z. and Treussard, J. (2007) 'Making investment choices as simple as possible, but not simpler', *Financial Analysts Journal*, 63(3), 42–47.

Bröder, A. (2003) 'Decision making with the 'adaptive toolbox': influence of environmental structure, intelligence, and working memory load', *Journal of Experimental Psychology: Learning, Memory and Cognition*, 29(4), 611–24.

Choi, J.J., Laibson, D., Madrian, B.C. and Metrick, A. (2002) 'Defined contribution pensions: Plan rules, participant decisions, and the path of least resistance', in J.M. Poterba (ed) *Tax policy and the economy, Vol. 16*, Cambridge, MA: MIT Press, pp 67–113.

Clark, G.L. (2003) *European pensions and global finance*, Oxford: Oxford University Press.

Clark, G.L. (2006) 'The UK occupational pension system in crisis', in H. Pemberton, P. Thane and N. Whiteside (eds) *Britain's pensions crisis: History and policy*, London: Oxford University Press for the British Academy, pp 145–68.

Clark, G.L. (2014) 'Roepke lecture in economic geography - financial literacy in context', *Economic Geography*, 90 (1): 1–23.

Clark, G.L. and Monk, A.H.B. (2013) 'Financial institutions, information, and investing-at-a-distance', *Environment and Planning A*, 45(6): 1318–36.

Clark, G.L. and Urwin, R. (2011) 'DC pension fund best-practice design and governance', *Benefits Quarterly* 27(4): 39–49.

Clark, G.L., Caerlewy-Smith, E. and Marshall, J.C. (2006) 'Pension fund trustee competence: decision making in problems relevant to investment practice', *Journal of Pension Economics and Finance* 5(1): 91–110.

Clark, G.L., Fischetti, M., Tufano, P. and Viehs, M. (2015) 'Compulsive gamblers: the frequency and timing of trades by UK DC plan participants', *Social Science Research Network*, http://ssrn.com/abstract=2643616

Clark, G.L., Strauss, K. and Knox-Hayes, J. (2012) *Saving for retirement: Intention, context, and behavior*, Oxford: Oxford University Press.

Doherty, M.E. (2003) 'Optimists, pessimists, and realists', in S.L. Schneider and J. Shanteau (eds) *Emerging perspectives on judgement and decision research*, Cambridge: Cambridge University Press, pp 643–79.

Douglas, M. and Wildavsky, A. (1982) *Risk and culture*, Berkeley: University of California Press.

Gigerenzer, G., Todd, P.M. and the ABC Research Group (1999) *Simple heuristics that make us smart*, New York: Oxford University Press.

Goos, M. and Manning, A. (2007) 'Lousy and lovely jobs: The rising polarization of work in Britain', *Review of Economics and Statistics*, 89(1): 118–33.

Halpern, D. (2015) *Inside the nudge unit: How small changes can make a big difference*, London: WH Allen.

Harvey, N. (2012) 'Learning judgement and decision making from feedback', in M.K. Dhami, A. Schlottmann and M.R. Waldmann (eds) *Judgement and decision making as a skill*, Cambridge: Cambridge University Press, pp 199–223.

Henrich, J., Boyd, R., Bowles, S., Camerer, C., Fehr, E. and Gintis, H. (eds) (2004) *Foundations of human sociality: Economic experiments and ethnographic evidence from fifteen small-scale societies*, Oxford: Oxford University Press.

Hertwig, R. and Ortmann, A. (2003) 'Economists' and psychologists' experimental practices: How they differ, why they differ, and how they could converge', in I. Brocas and J.D. Carrillo (eds) *The psychology of economic decisions, Volume 1: Rationality and well-being*, Oxford: Oxford University Press, pp 253–72.

HM Treasury (2014a) *Budget 2014*, HC 1104, London: The Stationery Office.

HM Treasury (2014b) *Freedom and Choice in Pensions: Government Response to the Consultation*, Cm 8901, London: The Stationery Office.

Jensen, M.J. (1993) 'The modern industrial revolution, exit, and the failure of internal control systems', *Journal of Finance*, 48(3): 831–80.

Jones, M. and Love, M.S. (2011) 'Bayesian fundamentalism or enlightenment? On the explanatory status and theoretical contributions of Bayesian models of cognition', *Behavioral and Brain Sciences*, 34(4): 169–87.

Kahneman, D. (2011) *Thinking fast and slow*, London: Allen Lane.

Kahneman, D. and Tversky, A. (1972) 'Subjective probability: a judgement of representativeness', *Cognitive Psychology*, 3: 430–54.

Kahneman, D. and Tversky, A. (1979) 'Prospect theory: an analysis of decision under risk', *Econometrica*, 47(2): 263–91.

Kahneman, D., Schwartz, A., Thaler, R. and Tversky, A. (1997) 'The effect of myopia and loss aversion on risk taking: an experimental test', *Quarterly Journal of Economics*, 112(2): 647–61.

Keynes, J.M. (1936) *The general theory of employment, interest and money*, London: Macmillan.

Krueger, J.I. and Funder, D.C. (2004) 'Towards a balanced social psychology: Causes, consequences, and cures for the problem-seeking approach to social behavior and cognition', *Behavioral and Brain Sciences*, 27(3): 313–28.

Laibson, D. (2003) 'Golden eggs and hyperbolic discounting', *Quarterly Journal of Economics*, 62: 443–77.

Langley, P. (2008) *The everyday life of global finance: Saving and borrowing in Anglo-America*, Oxford: Oxford University Press.

Leyshon, A., Burton, D., Knights, D., Alferoff, C. and Signoretta, P. (2004) 'Towards an ecology of retail financial services: understanding the persistence of door-to-door credit and insurance providers', *Environment and Planning A*, 36(4): 625–45.

Leyshon, A., Burton, D., Knights, D., Alferoff, C. and Signoretta, P. (2006) 'Walking with moneylenders: the ecology of the UK home-collected credit industry', *Urban Studies*, 43(1): 161–86.

List, J.A. (2011) 'Why economists should conduct field experiments and 14 tips for pulling one off', *Journal of Economic Perspectives*, 25(3): 3–16.

Lowenstein, G. and Prelec, J. (1992) 'Anomalies in inter-temporal choice: evidence and an interpretation', in G. Lowenstein and J. Elster (eds) *Choice over time*, New York, NY: Russell Sage Foundation, pp 119–46.

Ludwig, J., Kling, J.R. and Mullainathan, S. (2011) 'Mechanism experiments and policy evaluations', *Journal of Economic Perspectives*, 25(3): 17-38.

Lusardi, A. and Mitchell, O.S. (2007) 'Baby boomer retirement security: the roles of planning, financial literacy, and housing wealth', *Journal of Monetary Economics*, 54(1): 205–24.

Madrian, B. and Shea, D.F. (2001) 'The power of suggestion: inertia in 401 (K), participation and savings behaviour', *Quarterly Journal of Economics*, 116(4): 1149–87.

McDowell, L., Batnitzky, A. and Dyer, S. (2009) 'Precarious work and economic migration: emerging immigrant divisions of labour in Greater London's service sector', *International Journal of Urban and Regional Research*, 33(1): 3–25.

Mitchell, O.S. and Utkus, S.P. (2004) 'Lessons from behavioral finance for pension plan design', in O.S. Mitchell and S.P. Utkus (eds) *Pension design and structure: New lessons from behavioral finance*, Oxford: Oxford University Press, pp 3–42.

O'Donoghue, T. and Rabin, M. (1999) 'Doing it now or later', *American Economic Review*, 89(1): 103–24.

Oaksford, M. and Chater, N. (2007) *Bayesian rationality: The probabilistic approach to human reasoning*, Oxford: Oxford University Press.

Osborne, G. (2014) *Written ministerial statement: Pensions,* 21 July, London: HM Treasury.

Pensions Commission (2004) *Pensions: Challenges and choices: The first report of the Pensions Commission*, London: The Stationery Office.

Pensions Commission (2005) *A new pension settlement for the twenty-first century: The second report of the Pensions Commission*, London: The Stationery Office.

Preda, A. (2004) 'The investor as a cultural figure of global capitalism', in K. Cetina and A. Preda (eds) *The sociology of financial markets*, Oxford: Oxford University Press, pp 141–62.

Roy, A.D. (1952) 'Safety first and the holding of financial assets', *Econometrica*, 20(3): 431–49.

Runciman, D. (2008) *Political hypocrisy: The mask of power, from Hobbes to Orwell and beyond*, Princeton: Princeton University Press.

Samuelson, W.A. and Zeckhauser, R. (1988) 'Status quo bias in decision making', *Journal of Risk and Uncertainty*, 1(1): 7–59.

Sedlmeier, P. and Gigerenzer, G. (2001) 'Teaching Bayesian reasoning in less than two hours', *Journal of Experimental Psychology*, 130(3): 380–400.

Shafir, E., Diamond, P. and Tversky, A. (1997) 'Money illusion', *Quarterly Journal of Economics*, 112(2): 341–74.

Sharpe, W.F. (2007) *Investors and markets: Portfolio choices, asset prices and investment markets*, Princeton, NJ: Princeton University Press.

Shiller, R.J. (2005) *Irrational exuberance* (2nd edn), Princeton, NJ: Princeton University Press.

Simon, H.A. (1982) *Models of bounded rationality*, Cambridge, MA: MIT Press.

Stiglitz, J.E. (2014) 'The lessons of the north Atlantic crisis for economic theory and policy', in G. Akerlof, O. Blanchard, D. Romer and J.E. Stiglitz (eds) *What have we learned? Macroeconomic policy after the crisis*, Cambridge MA: MIT Press, 335–47.

Thaler, R. and Sunstein, C. (2008) *Nudge: Improving decisions about health, wealth and happiness*, New Haven, CT: Yale University Press.

Thoresen Review (2008) *Thoresen review of generic financial advice: Final report*, London: HM Treasury.

Tversky, A. and Simonson, I. (1993) 'Context-dependent preferences', *Management Science*, 39(10): 1179–89.

UK Government (2010) *Applying behavioural insight to health*, London: Cabinet Office.

Ungemach, C., Chater, N., and Stewart, N. (2009) 'Are probabilities overweighted or underweighted when rare outcomes are experienced (rarely)?', *Psychological Science*, 20(4): 473–79.

TWO

Coalition health policy: a game of two halves or the final whistle for the NHS?

Martin Powell

Introduction

The King's Fund audit of coalition health policy (Ham et al, 2015: 1) claims that the first half of the 2010–15 parliament was taken up with debate on the Health and Social Care Bill (HSCB), while the second half was devoted to limiting the damage caused by the Bill and subsequent Act and dealing with the effects of growing financial and service pressures in the NHS (see also, Seldon and Snowdon, 2015: 540). While previous *Social Policy Reviews* have focused on the first half (Ruane, 2010; 2012; Mays, 2011; Heins, 2013), there has been little coverage of the second half. However, was it a case of a game of two halves or did the coalition reforms bring about the final whistle, signalling the end of the NHS?

This chapter examines both halves of the coalition government's health policy (see, for example, Burchardt, 2015 and Glasby, 2016, on social care). After a brief 'extra time' exploring the early period of the Conservative government elected in May 2015, it provides a 'match report' of temporal, intrinsic and comparative evaluation templates. 'The final whistle?' explores the debate on the 'end of the NHS' in terms of the issues of privatisation and financial crisis/sustainability.

First half: the Health and Social Care Act

Many commentators regard the reorganisation of the White Paper, *Equity and Excellence: Liberating the NHS* (Department of Health, 2010a) and the subsequent Health and Social Care Act (HSCA) of 2012 as the biggest change in the history of the NHS (for example, Ruane, 2010; 2012; Mays, 2011; Heins, 2013). For example, according to Hunter (2013b), the changes ushered in by the HSCA are different in both scope and intent from anything to which the NHS has previously been subjected. According to Seldon and Snowdon (2015: 181), this 'NHS debacle' was 'the biggest cock-up of Cameron's premiership'. Widely regarded as a 'car crash' of both politics and policy making, it was, in the words of Sir David Nicholson, then NHS chief executive, 'the only change management system you can actually see from space' (quoted in Timmins, 2012).

Timmins (2012) relates the story that before the 2010 election, David Cameron promised 'no top-down reorganisations' of the NHS (see also, Seldon and Snowdon, 2015). The discussions leading to the coalition agreement attempted to form a synthesis of Conservative and Liberal Democrat manifesto promises on health, but this led to, in the words of Number 10 insiders, 'a cut and shut' job (where the good back half of a crashed car is welded to the good front half of another wreck to produce a vehicle that may look roadworthy but is in fact potentially lethal). The Coalition Agreement (Cabinet Office, 2010) 'repeated the pledge that had gone missing in the Tory manifesto': 'We will stop the top-down reorganisations of the NHS that have got in the way of patient care', which was 'a phrase to haunt the debate about the NHS reforms throughout their parliamentary life' (Timmins, 2012).

However, Secretary of State for Health, Andrew Lansley, was horrified by these proposals, and simply ignored them. *Equity and Excellence: Liberating the NHS* (Department of Health, 2010a), was produced far faster than any previous health White Paper, only some 60 days after the coalition government was formed. It announced that the entire existing commissioning structure of the NHS (strategic health authorities and 152 primary care trusts) was to be abolished, and replaced by consortia involving GPs, which would be overseen by a new national commissioning board. A new economic regulator was planned to oversee choice and competition, both of which were to be extended. 'Any willing provider' from the private and voluntary sectors was to be allowed to supply NHS care at agreed NHS prices. Much of the public health budget would be transferred to local authorities. Health and Wellbeing Boards were to be created in local government to join up the commissioning of NHS services, social care and prevention. Finally, a new patient's voice organisation, 'Healthwatch', was to be created (Timmins, 2012; Powell, 2014a; Carrier and Kendall, 2015; Ham et al, 2015; Baggott, 2016).

This formed the basis of the vast HSCB (Health and Social Care Bill) which, with more than 280 clauses and some 550 pages in all, was three times the size of the 1946 Act that founded the service. The opposition to the White Paper and subsequent Bill over the next 20 months forced the government onto the back foot. In an unprecedented 'pause' and 'listening' exercise, the government set up the independent 'Future Forum', described by Klein (2013) as a kind of instant royal commission that consulted widely and reported rapidly. The government accepted most of its recommendations, but critics argue that this did not change the fundamental direction of travel (Hunter, 2013a). Some 2,000 amendments had been made, although the overwhelming majority were technical, such as name changes. Timmins (2012: 118) notes that 50 days of debate in Parliament had produced a piece of legislation even longer, more complex, and in some areas appreciably less clear than the original huge edifice.

The HSCA passed into law on 27 March 2012, with the reorganised NHS scheduled to go live on 1 April 2013, which some have seen as the end of the NHS (for example, Hunter, 2013b; but see Le Grand, 2013; Powell, 2015). While the HSCA dominated the first half of coalition health policy, it is important not to forget that a public health White Paper (Department of Health, 2010b) promised a radical shift in the way of tackling public health challenges, and 'new era for public health' (see Baggott, 2016). It was stated that localism will be at the heart of this system, with local government and local communities at the heart of improving health and wellbeing for their populations and tackling inequalities. A dedicated new public health service, 'Public Health England', was set up, and public health funding was ring-fenced within the overall NHS budget. It is far from clear what impact this will have. The revived role of local authorities is potentially very significant, but a greater stress on localism broadly tends to increase inequalities between areas.

Second half: Mid Staffordshire and the 'Five Year Forward View'

In September 2012, Jeremy Hunt was appointed Secretary of State for Health, with a brief to keep the NHS from being a major political problem before the 2015 election. His main credential for the post appeared to be that he was not Andrew Lansley, but as Jarman and Greer (2015) point out, he was not the most obvious figure for the post, having co-authored two books calling for the NHS to be replaced with arrangements that transfer responsibility to individuals.

Mid Staffordshire

In March 2009, the Healthcare Commission, the hospital inspectorate that preceded the CQC, published a scathing report about the standards of care at Mid Staffordshire NHS Hospital Trust (Taylor, 2013), which largely corroborated the concerns of some local people that had been dismissed by the hospital, and local and national agencies (Bailey, 2012). The Labour government set up an independent inquiry (Francis, 2010), which concluded that the failings in care between 2005 and 2009 brought suffering to a large number of patients and may have been responsible for an unknown number of premature deaths. However, the report also flagged up failings that went beyond the trust, among the regulatory bodies, commissioners and wider management system. Hunt stated that, 'Almost the first thing I did when I was appointed as Health Secretary was to read Sir Robert Francis QC's initial report on the scandal at Mid Staffordshire NHS Foundation Trust' (Department of Health, 2015a). In June 2010, the incoming coalition government ordered a full public inquiry with a wider remit on the 'system', also chaired by Francis. As Taylor (2013: 205) put it, 'this is the NHS on trial'.

The 'Francis Report' of February 2013 contained 290 recommendations, with an 'executive summary' of 125 pages, while the full report is over 1,700 pages in length (Francis, 2013). It called for a 'fundamental culture change' across the health and social care system to put patients first at all times, with action across six core themes: culture, compassionate care, leadership, standards, information, and openness, transparency and candour.

The government's initial response, 'Patients First and Foremost' (Department of Health, 2013a) was followed by a more detailed response 'Hard Truths' (Department of Health, 2013b). The government commissioned six independent reviews to consider some of the key issues identified by the Inquiry: Quality of Care and Treatment Provided by 14 Hospital Trusts in England (Keogh); Healthcare Assistants and Support Workers (Cavendish); Improving the Safety of Patients in England (Berwick); NHS Hospitals Complaints System (Clwyd and Hart); Challenging Bureaucracy (NHS Confederation); and Children and Young People's Health Outcomes Forum (Lewis and Lenehan). Francis considered that 'all but a very few of the Public Inquiry's recommendations were accepted in full by the Department of Health, and all were in principle' (Thorlby et al, 2014). Yet another report, *Culture change in the NHS: Applying the lessons of the Francis Inquiries* (Department of Health, 2015a) set out progress, which included a new, rigorous CQC inspection regime for hospitals, GPs and adult social care, extra clinical staff working in the NHS and the special measures regime for failing trusts.

Taylor (2013: vii) writes that the name of Mid Staffordshire has been 'hung around the neck of the NHS as a badge of shame', which has led to a focus (once more) on the quality and safety agenda (Ham et al, 2015; Powell and Mannion, 2015). However, it is difficult to say whether it was one apple or the whole fruit bowl that was rotten (see Taylor, 2013), and to what extent the situation is improving. The NHS Medical Director, Bruce Keogh, identified 14 providers with higher-than-expected mortality rates, which led to 11 of them being placed in 'special measures' (Thorlby et al, 2014; Ham et al, 2015; Baggott, 2016). It seems that, like acne, as soon as one sore is treated, another appears. For example, there were other specific concerns about the abuse of vulnerable patients in hospitals and other care settings, raised for example, by reports on the Winterbourne View case (Department of Health, 2012). Following concerns over serious incidents in Furness General Hospital's maternity department covering January 2004 to June 2013, the report of the investigation into University Hospitals of Morecambe Bay NHS Foundation Trust (Morecambe Bay Investigation, 2015) concluded that the maternity unit was dysfunctional and that serious failures of clinical care led to avoidable and tragic deaths of mothers and babies.

Five Year Forward View

If one agenda was generated by quality, another was generated by finance. In 2014, Simon Stevens, a former NHS manager, Blair advisor and then Executive Vice President of the US private health company, UnitedHealth, was appointed as the new Chief Executive of NHS England. The 'NHS Five Year Forward View' (FYFV) is a joint vision by the Care Quality Commission, Health Education England, Monitor, NHS England, NHS Trust Development Authority and Public Health England (NHS England, 2014), although it is generally associated with Stevens.

Ham et al (2015) state that taking the longer-term view, the FYFV may well be seen by historians as one of the most important events in health policy under the coalition government. It set out a direction for the future of health and social care by describing the challenges facing the NHS and the care models needed to tackle these challenges. It identified 'a mismatch between resources and patient needs of nearly £30 billion a year by 2020/21', which requires 'transformational changes' in the way the NHS operates to close the gap. It argued that in order to sustain a comprehensive high-quality NHS, action is needed on three fronts: managing demand, improving efficiency and additional funding. It is a plan to bring about patient-centred, coordinated integrated care. It focuses on prevention, out-of-hospital care and the integration of primary, secondary and community care (also see Social Care, below). It argues for a 'radical upgrade on prevention and public health', which includes 'hard hitting national action on obesity, smoking, alcohol and other major health risks', and 'stronger public health-related powers for local government and elected mayors'; greater control of their own care by patients, and 'decisive steps to break down the barriers' in how care is provided between family doctors and hospitals, between physical and mental health, and between health and social care (NHS England, 2014, p 3). It recognises 'emerging models' but also outlines 'radical health care delivery options' such as 'new care models' of 'Multispecialty Community Providers', 'Primary and Acute Care Systems', 'urgent and emergency care networks', 'viable smaller hospitals', 'specialised care', 'modern maternity services', and 'enhanced health in care homes'.

The FYFV 'Time to Deliver' (NHS England, 2015b) outlined progress to date. It reported that 269 local areas came forward with their ideas on how to design new models of care. It provided a 'pilot programme map' of: 57 Prime Minister's Challenge Fund sites; 29 Vanguards; 25 Integration Pioneers; 9 Integrated Care Pioneer Pilots; 7 Diabetes Demonstrators; 3 'success regimes' (for the most challenged areas where conditions for transformation do not yet exist); and one, Devo Manc, where the £6 billion health and social care budget for Greater Manchester is to be taken over by the region's councils and health groups (but no sign of the partridge in a pear tree pilot).

Some commentators appear to view these initiatives with some optimism. For example, Ham et al (2015) write that the establishment of the Better Care Fund, involving almost £4 billion of pooled funds at a national level, helped move integrated care from the margins to the mainstream, and that early reports from the Integrated Care and Support Pioneers programme are promising, offering some hope of progress in reducing inappropriate use of hospitals and delivering more care in people's homes. However, others seem to suggest a NHS 'Groundhog Day' in that previous aspirations of integration, 'care closer to home' and prevention were largely dashed. For example, the Better Care Fund's evolution was heavily criticised by the National Audit Office (2014); and the key bet of 'FYFV' on integrated systems, a model that is heavily espoused by American health management thinkers but generally unimplemented by other health care systems, rests on a surprisingly thin evidence base (Jarman and Greer, 2015).

Extra time?

The Conservative government elected in May 2015 stated that it would 'secure the future of the NHS' by implementing the NHS's own FYFV, by increasing the health budget, integrating health care and social care; ensuring the NHS works on a seven-day basis; and by taking measures to increase access to general practitioners and to mental health care.

In July 2015, the Secretary of State set out the direction of reform for the future NHS (Hunt, 2015). He discussed a number of measures such as an 'international buddying scheme' (learning from the best), seven day working, and from 2016, becoming the first country in the world to publish avoidable deaths by hospital trust. He argued that in order to change from a bureaucratic to a patient-centric system, the NHS needs a profound transformation in its culture; an inquisitive, curious and hungry learning culture needs to be fostered. The world's fifth largest organisation needs to become the world's largest learning organisation. In the longer term, he pointed to a radical permanent shift in power towards patients. The FYFV sets the course for five years, but the transition to patient power will dominate healthcare for the next 25 years. 'If intelligent transparency is Patient Power 1.0, this is Patient Power 2.0. We have the chance to make NHS patients the most powerful patients in the world' (Hunt, 2015). Rather worryingly, given the sorry history of IT in the NHS, he predicted that new medical devices will mean an ambulance arrives to pick us up not after a heart attack but before it – as they receive a signal sent from a mobile phone.

Match report

There are a number of possible evaluation templates (see Powell, 1997; 2014a): temporal (is the NHS getting better over time?); intrinsic (is it delivering its aims, or being consistent with its principles?) and extrinsic/comparative (how does it compare to other health systems?).

The NHS generally scores well on temporal evaluation. Health has clearly increased over the past 60 years or so, although how much of that is due to changes in medical science such as new drugs and treatment, or environmental factors outside the NHS is difficult to say. Moreover, there are clearly new health challenges such as obesity, with the UK being the most obese nation in Western Europe (Department of Health, 2010b).

Intrinsic evaluation of the NHS is difficult due to the problems of defining performance, with some tensions between the different criteria of the 'balanced scorecard'. For example, Gregory et al (2012) focus on nine dimensions of care that makes an effective health care system, while Gardner (2015) examines nearly 300 indicators that can be used to monitor changes over time in the quality of services provided. There are many bodies that provide an 'official' view on NHS performance, with a large variety of different perspectives (for example, CQC, 2015; Monitor, 2015; NHS England, 2015a).

In the *NHS England Annual Report* (2015a), NHS Chief Executive, Simon Stevens, writes that 2014/15 was a year in which the Health Service responded – largely successfully – to wide-ranging operational pressures. The document claims that 'unprecedented numbers of patients were treated by the NHS last year' for both urgent and planned care. The NHS met its target that 92% of patients should be waiting no more than 18 weeks for planned care from referral by a GP, with the median wait for planned hospital care being 10 weeks. However, NHS hospitals missed their A&E target during the winter – that 95% of patients should be seen and treated, admitted or discharged within four hours – but the position improved in the spring. Overall, NHS A&E services continued to meet this standard for more than nine in 10 patients in England – the best performance measured by a major industrial country. The document claims that most associated with the goals of the 25 objectives of the Government's Mandate for 2014/15 'were met or were close to being met'. However, it is difficult to judge this claim from the material given (Appendix 1 of the document), and despite government claims that outcomes would be stressed (Department of Health, 2010a), many of the indicators relate to inputs and processes rather than outcomes. For example, Objective 1 (Improvement against the NHS Outcomes Framework) provides 48 metrics with data available from 2013 onwards. Of these, it is claimed that notable progress has been made against 40%, a further 40% have remained fairly static and deterioration shown in 20%.

The Department of Health (2015b) provides an annual assessment of NHS England's performance during 2014/15, based on evidence from NHS England's own annual report and accounts for 2014/15; available data; feedback from stakeholders; and the discussions that the Secretary of State and his departmental team have held with NHS England's team throughout the year. It agrees with the assessment of the annual report for 2014/15 (NHS England, 2015a) that NHS England has made good progress against the mandate. In a challenging year, NHS England has made progress on the majority of the mandate objectives, with the majority of the 68 indicators of the NHS outcomes framework, showing improvements in outcomes over the past year. However, there were some areas where more progress against the mandate is required. For example, over the second half of 2014/15, performance against the access standards set out in the NHS Constitution deteriorated, particularly during the winter period. This does not appear to be a particularly focused or rigorous assessment, similar to a rather vague school report card. Moreover, it is not clear who assesses the assessors, or what actions result if progress is unsatisfactory.

The Care Quality Commission (2015) reported the results of its 'new tougher approach' of inspection. It focused on higher risk acute trusts first: of the 38 acute trusts, nine were rated good, improvement was required at 24, and five were inadequate. Safety was the biggest concern: four out of every five safety ratings were inadequate or required improvement. It inspected GP practices for the first time in 2013/14, and found variations in the quality of care. The majority of the services were safe, effective, caring, responsive and well led. The quality of dental care was generally good, and continued to be lower risk than most other sectors. It found wide variation in care between trusts, between hospital sites, between hospital services and within each service – from outstanding to inadequate. It stated that this variation in the quality and safety of care in England is too wide and unacceptable. The public is being failed by the numerous hospitals, care homes and GP practices that are unable to meet the standards that their peers achieve and exceed. It concluded that CQC is calling time on the unacceptable lottery of poor care.

According to Monitor (2015), the financial performance of foundation trusts (FTs) 'revealed an exceptionally challenging year'. For the first time, they reported an overall deficit of £345 million, which was £479 million worse than 2013/14, with over 50% of FTs in deficit at the end of the year. Many FTs did not meet key operational performance standards. FTs missed the A&E target in every quarter in 2014/15, with annual performance of 93.5% significantly below the 95% target and the 95.4% achieved in 2013/14. FTs achieved the 92% standard for incomplete pathways (92.73%); achieved the elective waiting time standard for non-admitted pathways with a performance of 95.5%, but failed the standard for admitted pathways with a performance of 88.2%. The number of FTs breaching at least one of the three standards increased, when compared with the same period in 2013/14, from 24 to 53. The total number of reported Clostridium difficile (C. difficile) cases saw an increase in 2014/15 compared with 2013/14 (806 compared with 676).

The number of FTs achieving the 62-day standard for cancer treatment has been declining since 2013/14. By the end of March 2015, 29 FTs (or 19% of the total) were in breach of their licence and subject to regulatory action by Monitor. In the past 12 months, 10 more FTs were in breach of their licence, while eight FTs demonstrated sufficient improvements to be removed from formal action. Twelve FTs are in special measures or have been during last year, while three have exited special measures.

There are a number of 'unofficial' assessments. Ham et al (2015) consider that, 'Historians will not be kind in their assessment of the coalition government's record on NHS reform'. According to the King's Fund 'mid-term' assessment, it appears that the performance of the NHS is holding up despite financial pressures and the disruption of reforms, but cracks are now emerging (Gregory et al, 2012: 56). The overall verdict of the final assessment (Appleby et al, 2015) is that NHS performance held up well for the first three years of the parliament but has now slipped, with waiting times at their highest levels for many years and an unprecedented number of hospitals reporting deficits. Despite this, patient experience of the NHS generally remains positive and public confidence is close to an all-time high.

QualityWatch (2015) presents three main conclusions. First, care services are improving in many markers of quality. However, second, there are clear signals that performance in many areas is declining, and it seems that the NHS has been unable to reverse the trends of deteriorating access to hospital, mental health and social care services that were identified in their 2014 report. Third, given the relationship between engaged staff and good quality care, there is a substantial risk that the current staffing situation in both health and social care may be reducing the quality of care received by patients and service users, with worrying indications of stress, high vacancy rates and increases in instances of bullying.

Debates about the principles of the NHS are most problematic. There is often a tendency to 'over-read' changes. Among the first to 'cry wolf', predicting 'the end of the NHS' was its founder, Aneurin Bevan in about 1952, and yet over 60 years later it is still around (Powell, 2015). There is also a tendency to point to a perfect imagined past, forgetting scandals such as at some long-stay hospitals in the 1960s and 1970s. It may be unfair to judge the NHS on what it gets wrong rather than what it does right, but a series of scandals such as Ely, Bristol, Shipman, Alder Hey, Mid Staffordshire, Winterbourne View, and so on, show that every period of the NHS has experienced some serious deficiencies.

Finally, the NHS can be compared to other health systems. First, the English NHS can be compared with other systems within the UK. There is some evidence that England has demonstrated greater improvement on some indicators, particularly reducing waiting lists, than other countries, although some commentators have attributed this more to 'command and control' rather than market mechanisms (see for example, Mays et al, 2011: 131-2). Bevan et al (2014) state that there is little sign that one country is consistently moving ahead of the others.

Second, the English NHS can be compared to health systems outside the UK. There are many different studies (see Kossarova et al, 2015), but international comparisons are problematic (Appleby et al, 2015), with different studies at different times stressing that different measures have produced rather different results. The NHS has tended to do well in the annual Commonwealth Fund study, with the latest study (Davis et al, 2014) placing the UK among the best of 11 countries on overall rank and for nine of 11 criteria. However, Niemietz (2014) claims that this study is different from most others in two respects. It is mostly based on inputs and procedures as opposed to outcomes, and it is mostly based on doctors' and patients' survey responses as opposed to clinical data. Only one category is concerned with outcomes, and in that category, the UK comes out second to last. He cites the *Guardian*'s (presumably non-ironic) verdict that, 'The only serious black mark against the NHS was its poor record on keeping people alive'. Moreover, the data relates to 2011–13, and it is possible that a future ranking may show a sharp decline. The Economist Intelligence Unit (2014) produced a report measuring population outcomes and spending across 166 countries. The UK came 23rd, which was a fairly mediocre performance for a wealthy country. This was followed by a study of 30 countries with a wider range of measures based on data from around 2012 (Economist Intelligence Unit, 2015). The UK was ranked third on equity and access, 14th on disease outcomes, 16th on expenditure, 17th on healthcare costs, 19th on population health outcomes and 28th on healthcare resources. Kossarova et al (2015) use Organisation for Economic Co-operation and Development (OECD) data to explore care in four sectors – primary care, hospital care, cancer care and mental health – across 15 countries over the period 2000–2013. The UK does not consistently over perform or under perform when compared with the pool of the other 14 countries. Absolute and relative trends – that is, whether the UK is improving or deteriorating and how it is performing in relation to other countries – are also mixed. While it is encouraging that the UK is stable or improving on 25 out of 27 indicators, it is worrying that the UK performs worse than most countries on 14 out of 27 indicators and performance is deteriorating on two indicators.

The final whistle?

Some commentators have written of 'the end of the NHS' (see Powell, 2015). It is possible that the murder weapon is politics or ideology, or an 'insider job' of finance or economics, with demand outstripping financial supply.

Privatisation

Many commentators have regarded the coalition reforms as a continuation or acceleration of trends by New Labour on the basis of criteria such as marketisation, provider pluralism, choice and competition (Mays, 2011; Timmins, 2012; Ham et al, 2015). For example, Heins (2013) points to an accelerated move to a fully functioning market for health care in England, concluding that 'in the light of the ongoing marketization, the NHS risks becoming little more than a logo' (page 61). However, according to Jarman and Greer (2015), instead of seeing the coalition as a story about marketisation, it could be better be understood as a story about centralisation.

Some commentators claim that the NHS is being privatised (for example, Hunter, 2013a; b; Davis et al, 2015). However, Klein (2013) states that the NHS in England is being neither privatised nor destroyed. According to Ham et al (2015), the reforms have certainly resulted in greater marketisation in the NHS, but claims of mass privatisation were and are exaggerated. Powell and Miller (2013) argue that the term privatisation is multidimensional, and definitions and operationalisations of the term are often implicit, unclear, and conflicting, resulting in conflicting accounts of the occurrence, chronology and degree of privatisation in the NHS.

There appears to be no clear 'tipping point' of privatisation. Moreover, private firms may be drawing back from secondary care due to the difficulty of making money out of the NHS. This can be illustrated by the failure of the 'iconic case of privatisation', where Hinchingbrooke hospital was handed over to a firm called Circle in February 2012, but handed back in January 2015 after a negative CQC report, which resulted in the trust being put into special measures (Jarman and Greer, 2015). Ham et al (2015) state that further management franchises by private sector providers now seem unlikely. However, increased private provision may continue in the community sector (Davis et al, 2015).

Klein (2013) claims that the NHS is not moving towards the USA, but evolving toward the kind of health service that would most probably have emerged had Britain's previous coalition government not been replaced by Labour in 1945. The recent coalition government appeared to be following, albeit unwittingly, in the footsteps of its long-ago predecessor (see also, Jarman and Greer, 2015)

Financial crisis/sustainability

A number of commentators have discussed short- or longer-term financial crises and the financial sustainability of the NHS. After the financial crisis, feast turned to famine, initially under Labour and continued by the coalition. Although the NHS was relatively protected by the coalition government, with small real-terms increases in funding, this was much smaller than both the previous long-term and recent New Labour increases. According to Appleby (2013), net spending on the NHS grew by around 4.04% in real terms per annum over the period between 1950/51 and 2010/11, with increases of 3.48%in the 20th century and 6.56% in the 21st century. Lafond et al (2015) state that the financial performance of NHS providers in England deteriorated sharply since 2013, from a net surplus of £582 million in 2012/13 to a net deficit of £108 million in 2013/14. By the end of the third quarter of 2014/15 the deficit had grown to £789 million. Moreover, this is mirrored by declining productivity for acute and specialist hospital care, with crude productivity falling by almost 1% in both 2012/13 and 2013/14, after increasing in the first two years of the coalition government. This 'highlights the mountain the NHS must climb to square austerity with rising demand and expectations for the quality of care'. Similarly, according to Monitor (2015), there is no escaping the fact that there are huge challenges ahead as the NHS manages rising demand and flat budgets.

The long-term drivers for increased health spending are pressures from demography, medical advances and rising expectations (Appleby, 2013). By about 2060, it is estimated that public health spending as a percentage of GDP could vary from between 7.6 % to 14.9%. Appleby (2013) points out that if the next 50 years follow the trajectory of the past 50, then by 2062 the UK could be spending nearly one fifth of its entire wealth, or roughly half of all government revenue on the NHS. There is a debate on whether this is sustainable (for example, Taylor,

2013). The FYFV (NHS England, 2014) argues it is – provided the NHS changes, but some of these changes such as prevention and integration have been discussed for at least 40 years and have never appeared to deliver (Powell, 2014b).

Conclusions

Health policy under the coalition government does appear to be a game of two halves. The first half was dominated by the HSCA, but less stress appears to have been placed upon the terms 'competition' and 'market' in the second half. For example, the terms do not appear in the FYFV (NHS England, 2014; but see Davis et al, 2015: 276-8). However, it may be very difficult to put the market genie back in the bottle. 'Privatisation' in the form of publicly funded private providers has increased over the period of later New Labour and the coalition, and may increase further in particular areas such as community services (Davis et al, 2015). There are clear trends towards the NHS being a regulated market (for example, Mays, 2011; Heins, 2013), but it is less clear that this will mean 'privatisation' in the form of commodification. Similarly, it is possible to argue that the NHS is becoming more (continental) European rather than American.

It is possible that some commentators have taken their eye off the ball by talking up 'internal' dangers (for example, privatisation), but 'talking down' external dangers such as financial sustainability. A great deal of hope appears to be placed on 'Groundhog Day policies', such as prevention, integration and care closer to home that have largely failed to deliver in the past. It is possible that 'necessity is the mother of invention' and that NHS leaders are really serious about them this time but, to adapt the words of Aneurin Bevan, 'gazing in the crystal ball' may be more optimistic than 'reading the bloody book'.

Powell (2015) considers that many previous commentators have 'cried wolf', with accounts of the death of the NHS exaggerated. The NHS appears to be like the proverbial cat with nine lives, but the wolf may be now at the door. A DHSS document from the 1970s stated that, 'Much of the responsibility for ensuring his own good health lies with the individual', and that 'much ill-health in Britain today arises from over-indulgence and unwise behaviour'. In 2006, Tony Blair considered that, 'Our public health problems are not, strictly speaking, public health questions at all. They are questions of individual lifestyles' (in Powell 2014b). The future answer to the question of who killed the NHS may be Agatha Christie's least likely suspect ... us – for eating, drinking and smoking too much … and living too long! However, for now, adapting the words of one of the most famous football commentaries, 'they think it's all over … it isn't yet'.

References

Appleby, J. (2013) *Spending on health and social care over the next 50 years*, London: The King's Fund.

Appleby J., Baird B., Thompson J. and Jabbal J. (2015) *The NHS under the coalition government. Part two: NHS performance*, London: King's Fund.

Baggott, R. (2016) 'Health policy', in H. Bochel and M. Powell (eds) *The coalition government and social policy*, Bristol: Policy Press, forthcoming.

Bailey, J. (2012) *From ward to Whitehall. The disaster at Mid-Staffs*, Stafford: Cure the NHS.

Bevan, G., Karanikolos, M., Exley, J., Nolte, E., Connolly, S. and Mays, N. (2014) *The four health systems of the United Kingdom: How do they compare?* London: Health Foundation/Nuffield Trust.

Burchardt, T., Obolenskaya, P. and Vizard, P. (2015) 'The coalition's record on adult social care: Policy, spending and outcomes 2010–2015', *Social Policy in a Cold Climate Working Paper 17*, London: LSE.

Cabinet Office (2010) *The coalition. Our programme for government*, London: Cabinet Office.

Care Quality Commission (2015) *The state of health care and adult social xare in England 2013/14*, London: CQC.

Carrier, J. and Kendall, I. (2015) *Health and the National Health Service* (2nd edn), London: Routledge.

Davis, J., Lister, J. and Wrigley, D. (2015) *NHS for sale*, London: Merlin Press.

Davis K., Stremikis K., Squires D. and Schoen C. (2014) 'Mirror, Mirror on the Wall, How the performance of the US health care system compares internationally', *The Commonwealth Fund*, http://www.commonwealthfund.org/ publications/fund-reports/2014/jun/mirror-mirror

Department of Health (2010a) *Equity and excellence: Liberating the NHS*, Cm 7881, London: The Stationery Office.

Department of Health (2010b) *Healthy lives, healthy people*, Cm 7985, London: The Stationery Office.

Department of Health (2012) *Transforming care: A national response to Winterbourne View Hospital – Final Report*, London: Department of Health.

Department of Health (2013a) *Patients first and foremost: The initial government response to the report of the Mid Staffordshire NHS Foundation Trust public inquiry*, London: The Stationery Office.

Department of Health (2013b) *Hard truths: The journey to putting patients first*, London: The Stationery Office.

Department of Health (2015a) *Culture change in the NHS: Applying the lessons of the Francis Inquiries*, Cm 9009, London: The Stationery Office.

Department of Health (2015b) *Annual assessment of the NHS Commissioning Board (known as NHS England) 2014–15*, London: Department of Health.

Economist Intelligence Unit (2014) *Health outcomes and cost: A 166-country comparison*, London: EIU, www.eiu.com/healthcare

Economist Intelligence Unit (2015) *The NHS: How does it compare?* London: EIU, www.eiu.com/healthcare

Francis, R. (2010) *Independent inquiry into care provided by Mid Staffordshire NHS Foundation Trust January 2005 – March 2009 Volume I*, HC 375-I, London: The Stationery Office.

Francis, R. (2013) *The Mid Staffordshire NHS Foundation Trust Public Inquiry – Final Report* (Francis Report), HC 947, London: The Stationery Office.

Gardner, T. (2015) *Swimming against the tide? The quality of NHS services during the current parliament*, London: The Health Foundation.

Glasby, J. (2016) '"It ain't what you do, it's the way that you do it" : Adult social care under the Coalition', in H. Bochel and M. Powell (eds) *The coalition government and social policy*, Bristol: Policy Press, forthcoming.

Gregory, S., Dixon, A. and Ham, C. (eds) (2012) *Health policy under the coalition government. A mid-term assessment*, London: King's Fund.

Ham, C., Baird, B., Gregory, S., Jabbal, J. and Alderwick, H. (2015) *The NHS under the coalition government Part one: NHS reform*, London: King's Fund.

Heins, E. (2013) 'Doctors in the driving seat? Reforms in NHS primary care and commissioning', in G. Ramia, K. Farnsworth, and Z. Irving (eds) *Social Policy Review 25*, Bristol: Policy Press, pp 47–65.

Hunt, J. (2015) *Making healthcare more human-centred and not system-centred*, Speech, 16 July, London: Department of Health, https://www.gov.uk/government/speeches/making-healthcare-more-human-centred-and-not-system-centred

Hunter, D. (2013a) 'Point-counterpoint. A response to Rudolf Klein: a battle may have been won but perhaps not the war', *Journal of Health Politics, Policy and Law*, 38(4): 871–77.

Hunter, D. (2013b) 'Will 1 April mark the beginning of the end of England's NHS? Yes.' *British Medical Journal*, 346.

Jarman, H. and Greer, S. (2015) 'The big bang: health and social care reform under the coalition', in M. Beech and S. Lee (eds) *The Conservative-Liberal Coalition*, Basingstoke: Palgrave, pp 50–67.

Klein, R. (2013) 'The twenty-year war over England's National Health Service: a report from the battlefield', *Journal of Health Politics, Policy and Law*, 38(4): 849–69.

Kossarova, L., Blunt, I. and Bardsley, M. (2015) *Focus on: International comparisons of healthcare quality: What can the UK learn?* London: Health Foundation/Nuffield Trust.

Lafond, S., Charlesworth, A. and Roberts A. (2015) *Hospital finances and productivity: In a critical condition?* London: The Health Foundation.

Le Grand, J. (2013) 'Will 1 April mark the beginning of the end of England's NHS? No', *British Medical Journal*, 346.

Mays, N. (2011) 'The English NHS as a market: challenges for the Coalition government', in C. Holden, M. Kilkey and G. Ramia (eds) *Social Policy Review 23*, Bristol: Policy Press, pp 185–205.

Monitor (2015) *Annual report and accounts 1 April 2014 to 31 March 2015*, HC 237, London: Monitor.

Morecambe Bay Inquiry Investigation (2015) *Report* (the Kirkup Report), London: The Stationery Office.

National Audit Office (2014) *Planning for the Better Care Fund*, London: National Audit Office.

National Health Service England (2014) *Five year forward view*, London: NHS England.

National Health Service England (2015a) *Annual report and accounts 2014–15*, HC 109, London: NHS England.

National Health Service England (2015b) *Five year forward view. Time to deliver*, London: NHS England.

Niemietz, K. (2014) *Health check, IEA Discussion Paper No. 54*, London: Institute of Economic Affairs.

Powell, M. (1997) *Evaluating the National Health Service*, Buckingham: Open University Press.

Powell, M. (2014a) 'Health policy', in H. Bochel and G. Daly (eds) *Social policy*, London: Routledge, pp 349–70.

Powell, M. (2014b) 'Neo-republican citizenship and the British National Health Service since 1979', in F. Huisman and H. Oosterhuis (eds) *Health and citizenship: Political cultures in modern Europe*, London: Pickering and Chatto, pp 177–90.

Powell M. (2015) 'Who killed the English National Health Service?', *International Journal of Health Policy and Management*, 4(5): 267–69.

Powell, M. and Miller, R. (2013) 'Privatizing the English National Health Service: an irregular verb?', *Journal of Health Politics, Policy and Law*, 28(5): 1051–59.

Powell, M. and Mannion, R. (2015) 'England', in J. Braithwaite et al (eds) *Healthcare reform, quality and safety*, Farnham: Ashgate, pp 227–36.

QualityWatch (2015) *Closer to critical?*, London: Health Foundation/ Nuffield Trust.

Ruane, S. (2010) 'Health policy under New Labour: not what it seems?' in I. Greener, C. Holden and M. Kilkey (eds) *Social Policy Review 22*, Bristol: Policy Press, pp 51–70.

Ruane, S. (2012) 'Division and opposition: the Health and Social Care Bill 2011', in M. Kilkey, G. Ramia and K. Farnsworth (eds) *Social Policy Review 22*, Bristol: Policy Press, pp 97–114.

Seldon, A. and Snowdon, P. (2015) *Cameron at 10*, London: William Collins.

Taylor, R. (2013) *God bless the NHS*, London: Faber and Faber.

Thorlby, R., Smith, J., Williams, S. and Dayan, M. (2014) *The Francis Report: One year on*, London: Nuffield Trust.

Timmins, N. (2012) *Never again? The story of the Health and Social Care Act 2012*, London: The King's Fund and the Institute for Government.

THREE

Citizenship, conduct and conditionality: sanction and support in the 21st-century UK welfare state

Peter Dwyer

Introduction

The extent to which an individual's rights to social welfare should be linked to personal responsibility and behaviour is an enduring theme of social policy and welfare debates. In the post-Second World War period social democratic theorists such as Marshall (1950) and Titmuss (1958), who were influential in setting out the scope and vision of the welfare state, emphasised the fundamental importance of universal citizenship and entitlement to an extensive set of (largely unconditional) social rights, with individuals meeting their responsibilities through a shared sense of duty. Focusing on the substantive rights, rather than the attendant responsibilities, of citizenship, they wished to ensure that public welfare would lessen inequalities and foster a sense of social solidarity between citizens, and were largely dismissive of explanations of poverty based on personal failings or inappropriate individual behaviour (Deacon, 2002). Subsequently, such rights-based conceptualisations of social citizenship and their envisioning of unconditional, status-based entitlement to welfare, have been comprehensively challenged. New Right thinkers (for example, Murray, 1984; 1999; Mead, 1986; 1997), new communitarian commentators (Etzioni, 1997; 1998) and proponents of conservative, centre right 'Third Way' politics (Giddens, 1994; 1998; Blair, 1998; Etzioni, 2000) all share a common view that unconditional entitlement to social welfare benefits promotes passive welfare 'dependency'. In the UK this has led to a

> [...] broad and far reaching shift towards greater conditionality in
> welfare. The idea that those claiming welfare should be required

to fulfil conditions regarding their own behaviour and that of their children has been extended across a swathe of social policy: from welfare to work, to education, health, and of course housing. (Deacon, 2004: 911–12)

Today social citizenship has been reframed around a logic of individualised responsibility whereby the right to claim welfare is directly linked to distinct, specified and socially valorised prior contributions (Taylor-Gooby, 2009; Lister, 2011); an understanding that undermines the value and legitimacy of certain other social contributions (such as informal, familial care), while emphasising the validity of paid employment, as central to definitions of citizenship. Beyond the UK, welfare conditionality has been a vital component of much welfare reform within and beyond Europe (Cox, 1998; Dwyer, 1998; 2004; 2008; Lødemel and Trickey, 2001; Deacon, 2002; Dean et al, 2005; Wright, 2012) and is a fundamental element of the ongoing shift from the so called 'passive' welfare state of the past to the 'active' welfare state of today (Walters, 1997). The unequivocal rolling out of a principle of conditionality, which holds that eligibility to certain basic, publicly provided, welfare entitlements should be dependent on an individual first agreeing to meet particular compulsory duties or patterns of behaviour (Deacon, 1994), has been a key way in which governments have looked to rewrite 'the terms and conditions of the welfare contract' (Buck et al, 2006: 1). While eligibility conditions have long been integral to social provision, 'conditions of conduct', that is, 'behavioural requirements and constraints imposed on different kinds of benefit recipients' (Clasen and Clegg, 2007: 174) have become more prominent in many nations since the 1990s (for example, Commonwealth of Australia, 2007; Mulgan, 2010; Southerton et al, 2011; Gray et al, 2016). An intensification of conditionality has been a feature in many welfare states in recent decades, with enhanced use of sanctions and realigned relationships between entitlement, conduct and support within, and beyond, the UK (Handler, 2004; Betzelt and Bothfeld, 2011).

Different aspects of conditionality need to be recognised when considering this behavioural turn in social policy. Not least, that while sanctions are one aspect of conditional welfare interventions, additional support may also be on offer to those whose behaviour is deemed as irresponsible or problematic. Critics of conditionality routinely focus on the impacts of sanctions but may fail to recognise that 'coercive welfare', that is, support offered under threat of sanction may potentially have a positive impact on people's lives (Phoenix, 2008). When seeking to make access to social rights contingent on citizens' required behaviour, distinctions can also be made between vague requirements, such as behaving responsibly, and more concrete or tightly specified conditions such as applying for a specified number of jobs and/or accepting any job offer (Paz-Fuchs, 2008). In a similar vein, Flint highlights a difference between 'conditional' and 'earned' citizenship. The former refers to 'pre-existing entitlements being rescinded as a result of inappropriate conduct' (Flint, 2009: 89). For example, applying sanctions in response to 'irresponsible' negative behaviour, for example, removing or reducing unemployment benefits when claimants refuse to undertake a job search or training activities. Conversely, 'earned citizenship' rewards positive behaviour and links social rights to the proactive endeavour of citizens. Here rights are secured in the first instance through positive contribution and/or meeting communally defined requirements. For instance, linking citizenship and settlement rights among migrants to language or financial self-sufficiency requirements or making social housing tenancies dependent on acceptance of wider communal engagement through mechanisms such as a Mutual Aid Clauses (Young and Lemos, 1997) and Good Neighbour Agreements (Croucher et al, 2007).

Influenced by New Right and new communitarian critics, the UK Conservative administrations (1979–97) established and advanced conditionality in several key spheres. Throughout the 1980s receipt of unemployment benefit became subject to claimants meeting new obligations such as regular 'restart' interviews. The Jobseekers Act (1995) is seen by many as a watershed moment as this introduced the 'Jobseekers Agreement' and established new powers for advisers who could require claimants (under threat of benefit disqualification) to alter their behaviour or appearance if they felt that either was damaging to an individual's likelihood of securing paid work. Elsewhere, in an attempt to ensure absent fathers met the financial responsibilities for their children, the Child Support Agency (1993) was established. In order to ensure women would cooperate, a mother's right to benefit was made conditional on her first agreeing to name the father of her children so that he could be pursued for maintenance payments. The Housing Act (1996) also enabled local authorities to grant introductory (probationary) tenancies, for a period of up to one year, to new tenants. These tenancies, and potential future rights to social housing, could be revoked and tenants evicted if they engaged in irresponsible or antisocial behaviour (Dwyer, 2000; Watts et al, 2014).

Building on the approach of their Conservative predecessors, successive New Labour Governments (1997–2010) advanced welfare conditionality as a core element of their reform agenda, based on 'the principle that aspects of state support, usually financial or practical, are dependent on citizens meeting certain conditions which are invariably behavioural' (DWP, 2008: 1). This emphasis underpinned interventions in policy areas including social security, social housing, homelessness, antisocial behaviour, criminal justice and migration (Dwyer, 2004; 2008), with a common goal of 'personalised conditionality'. The UK coalition government (2010–15) further intensified this approach (Wright, 2011a, 2012) and in a continuing period of austerity it is now clear that extending and intensifying welfare conditionality, alongside delivering a further £12 billion reduction in the welfare budget, are central elements of the welfare reforms planned by the Conservative government elected in May, 2015 (Kennedy, 2015). More broadly, welfare conditionality is supported across the mainstream UK political parties and also, it seems, by large sections of the general public (Kellner, 2012).

Social welfare in the UK: towards comprehensive conditionality

In the UK, concerns about the conduct and 'irresponsibility' of recipients of social welfare benefits and services noted above have increased the application of conditionality within income, unemployment and disability/incapacity related welfare benefits as well as in the wider fields of housing, homelessness and migration policy. A variety of sanctions, support and behavioural interventions that combine penalties and incentives in diverse ways, for different groups of welfare recipients, are being applied across a range of policy fields (King, 2004; DWP, 2008; Gregg, 2008; Dwyer, 2010; 2016; Griggs and Evans, 2010; Johnsen and Fitzpatrick, 2010; Flint et al, 2011a; 2011b; HM Government, 2011; Patrick, 2012). Such developments create a new, more constrained and qualitatively different welfare state than that envisaged by its post-Second World War architects (Dwyer, 2008; Wright, 2011b). Against this backdrop the next section of the chapter sets out some of the key developments and debates in respect of welfare conditionality across a range of UK social policy domains.

Social security benefits: intensified, extended and personalised conditionality

Unemployment benefits have always been conditional on unemployment being involuntary, with an expectation of active job search, and also past contribution records in the case of National Insurance-based benefits. However, since the introduction of Jobseeker's Allowance (JSA) in 1995 there has been a standardisation of specific behavioural instruments, for example the Jobseeker's Agreement, back-to-work action plan and the Looking for Work diary, through which unemployed people are required to provide evidence of compliant job search behaviour. The support side of conditionality was also developed in a number of significant ways during the New Labour years, most notably through the establishment of the national minimum wage, various tax credit schemes and an enhanced and extended system of publicly funded childcare. Nevertheless, they also introduced a range of progressively more mandatory Welfare-to-Work schemes and Work Focused Interviews for the vast majority of out of work benefit claimants (Stewart and Wright, 2014).

In a period characterised by 'creeping conditionality' (Dwyer, 2004), welfare policy under New Labour shifted away from an initial emphasis on enabling and supporting disabled people (Dwyer, 2016) and lone parents (Johnsen, 2014) into paid employment, towards one in which compulsory job search/preparation and training were increasingly to the fore. The incorporation of these two groups of benefit recipients within an extended conditional welfare state was presaged by the Freud Report, which stated:

> The government has made a commitment to rights and responsibilities a central feature of policy… The report recommends maintaining the current regime for the unemployed, introducing stronger conditionality in line with the Jobseeker's Allowance for lone parents with progressively younger children and moving to deliver conditionality for other groups (including people already on incapacity benefits). (Freud, 2007: 9)

The subsequent introduction of Employment and Support Allowance (ESA) in October 2008 (which replaced Incapacity Benefit, Income Support paid on grounds of disability and Severe Disablement Allowance), marked a step change in the delivery of incapacity benefits in the UK. ESA clearly signalled that the majority of disabled people, with the exception of those with severe impairments placed in the unconditional 'support group', would be subject to conditionality. Following, a Work Capability Assessment, which attempts to measure the level of individuals' impairments, others are either declared 'fit for work' and disqualified from ESA and transferred onto the JSA regime with its stricter conditionality rules and lower benefit level, or placed in the 'Work Related Activity Group (WRAG).

Those in the WRAG receive an enhanced rate of benefit compared to JSA but are also required to engage in work-related activity such as job search, attending interviews with personal advisers or participation in work experience schemes (Patrick, 2012; Dwyer et al, 2014).

Similarly, a comparatively 'light touch' that originally typified welfare conditionality for lone parents has been supplanted by a regime that increasingly ties their rights to benefit to compulsory job preparation requirements. The introduction of Work Focused Interviews (WFIs) in 2001 and the launch of Lone Parent Obligations (2008), which required lone parents in receipt of income support with children over the age of 12 to be available for, and actively seeking paid work, on broadly the same terms as JSA claimants, were significant. The ongoing reduction in the age thresholds at which eligibility to benefit becomes conditional on active job search activities also further signals the extent to which lone parents are no longer exempt from behavioural requirements (Johnsen, 2014).

The Conservative/Liberal Democrat coalition government further enhanced and extended conditionality within social security in several important policy initiatives. First, June 2011 saw the national roll out of the Work Programme, which replaced New Labour's flexible New Deals and attendant welfare to work schemes. The Work Programme offers back to work and job sustainment support for the longer-term recipients of JSA, ESA and Universal Credit. It is delivered by a range of private and third sector organisations who, under the so called 'black box' approach, are allowed a large degree of discretion in the mix of personalised sanction and support that they use to get individual clients to connect with the paid labour market. Failure to engage with any specified requirements leads to individuals being sanctioned (Newton et al, 2012; Stewart and Wright, 2014). Second, the introduction of Mandatory Work Activity, which is 'intended to help claimants move closer to the labour market, enabling them to establish the discipline and habits of working life, such as attending on time regularly, carrying out specific tasks and working under supervision while delivering a contribution to the community' (DWP, 2015: 6).

This empowers advisers to instruct individual claimants, who they believe will benefit from the imposition of workplace discipline, to attend up to 30 hours per week unpaid compulsory work placements for a maximum of four weeks; again sanctions apply for non-compliance. Third, the Welfare Reform Act (2012) also heralded Universal Credit

(UC). Initiated in 2013 for new claimants, the ongoing roll out of UC is expected to be completed in 2017.

UC replaces six means-tested benefits and tax credits, Income Support (IS), Jobseeker's Allowance (JSA) Employment and Support Allowance (ESA), Housing Benefit, Working Tax Credits (WTC), Child Tax Credits (CTC) , with a single monthly benefit payment that varies depending on an individual's earnings from paid work each month. The aim of UC is to reduce barriers to employment and incentivise people on benefits to start paid work or increase their hours (Pennycook and Whittaker, 2012). The coalition stated that UC would simplify and make the social security benefits fairer and more affordable, while simultaneously reducing poverty, worklessness and welfare dependency and levels of fraud and error. However, while the government's own impact assessment estimated that approximately 3.1 million households would be better off under UC in the longer term, their evaluation also indicated that approximately 2.8 million households faced an 'average reduction in entitlement' of £137 per month (DWP, 2012a). Significantly, UC extends behavioural conditionality and sanctions to low-paid workers (and their partners), who are in receipt of in-work benefits for the first time (Bennett, 2012). Those UC recipients who are in low-paid or part-time employment and whose wages fall below the 'conditionality threshold' can be instructed to seek better paid or more hours of employment up to a 35-hour per week combined work/work search threshold. UC thus enables 'a bolstered system of "personalised conditionality" – directed mandatory activity to prepare for and obtain work and tough sanctions for non-compliance' (Pennycook and Whittaker, 2012: 5). The intensity of welfare conditionality applied varies (dependent on people's circumstances), along a spectrum ranging from no conditionality for people with severe impairments, to keeping in touch with the labour market/work preparation requirements for less severely impaired people and lone parents of young children, to the default option of full conditionality, which applies the full work search requirements and sanctions of JSA to the majority of UC recipients and their partners. Central to UC is the Claimant Commitment, which sets out specific required job search and work preparation/training requirements for each recipient as agreed between the claimant and their 'job coach' (Dwyer and Wright, 2014).

Furthermore, the Welfare Reform and Work Bill (2015) contains proposals to further reduce the current children's age thresholds at which lone parents are to be subject to conditionality and sanctions; from three to two years old for work preparation, and from five to three years for full work-related requirements. Additionally, the Bill outlines the Conservative government's plans to abolish the enhanced payment of £29.05 per week, which is currently paid to those in the ESA Work Related Activity Group and align it with standard JSA rates from April 2017 (Kennedy, 2015). Additionally, in August 2015 the government announced that mandatory Intensive Activity Programmes, that combine 'intensive support in a "boot camp" environment', will be rolled out nationally for 18- to 21-year-old benefit claimants in 2017. Young people will be required to attend 71 hours of training over a three week period at the start of a claim or lose their benefit (Mason and Perraudin, 2015). Within the contemporary UK social benefit system the majority of claimants are now routinely required to engage in and prove specified high levels of job search activities in frequent interviews with advisers and/or engage in schemes such as the Work Programme and in some cases undertake mandatory 'workfare' type job placements (Stewart and Wright, 2014).

For some specific groups, particular additional requirements are also set out. For example, in a concerted attempt to help offenders into work, the active welfare state has been extended into the criminal justice system with the coalition government outlining specific requirements for offenders. Recognising that many prison leavers continue to experience significant barriers to work and that early intervention is crucial in preventing recidivism, all prison leavers who claim JSA are required to enter the Work Programme on 'day one' of their release. In addition, any offender claiming JSA within 13 weeks of leaving custody is mandated to attend the Work Programme (Fletcher, 2014). Such requirements are, however, not without potential pitfalls. Policy makers and practitioners have expressed concerns that offenders and those with 'chaotic lifestyles' may not fully understand the attendant sanctioning regimes at the heart of such schemes and may therefore (unintentionally) fall foul of its requirements (Fletcher et al. 2012). There is thus a risk that welfare reform may serve to strengthen the traditional hostility of offenders towards forms of authority and propel increasing numbers further away from the formal labour market and mainstream welfare institutions (Fletcher, 2008).

Welfare conditionality has significance for international migrants in two linked ways. First, in a broad sense related to the ways in which UK immigration and welfare policies intersect to establish and structure the diverse rights and responsibilities of different migrant groups living in the UK. Second, and more narrowly, in respect of how migrants may experience behavioural conditionality in their interactions with welfare agencies that implement interventions, which combine elements of sanction and support. Certainly in recent decades, UK immigration and asylum legislation has consolidated the long established link between specific immigration status and migrants' rights to residence, work and welfare. For many migrants, the concept of 'earned citizenship' has increasingly come to the fore, including the introduction of a probationary period during which mainstream benefits or social housing may not be accessed. In effect, permanent residence and access to full welfare rights are increasingly conditional on migrants proving economic self-sufficiency over a number of years, and conditionality may also encompass cultural elements, for example requirements to develop English language skills (Dwyer and Scullion, 2014).

With the Prime Minister pledging to make entry rules for non-European Economic Area (EEA) entrants to the UK (with exception of very wealthy and/or highly skilled migrants) the toughest in Europe (Cameron, 2013), and the ongoing development of an 'activationist-plus' regime (O'Brien, 2013) designed to curtail EEA migrants' entitlements to JSA, Housing Benefit and additional allowances available under Universal Credit rules, exclusive policy sets the broader context in which behavioural conditionality is applied to migrants who remain able to access social benefits and services in the UK. A tendency towards 'welfare chauvinism' whereby 'harsher policies have been introduced and implemented more eagerly when the target group for activation reforms has been immigrants' (Breidahl 2012: 119) is evident in both Scandinavian countries and the USA (Monnat, 2010). In a similar vein, in both England and Scotland, a more punitive approach to the application of benefit sanctions for both refugees and young people from black and minority ethnic communities has been noted (Hudson et al, 2006; Scottish Refugee Council, 2013). Additionally, there is some evidence of migrants being inappropriately sanctioned because of misunderstandings caused by their lack of English language capabilities (Dwyer, 2009); a situation that is unlikely to be improved by the removal of routine access to interpreters for new JSA claimants from 2014 (HMT et al, 2014). Research by Shutes (2011) has also noted 'creaming' and 'parking' strategies among welfare to work providers working with refugees.

The extension and intensification of welfare conditionality to cover all economically inactive benefit recipients including lone parents, many people with impairments, the partners of benefit claimants and those people with complex needs due to 'chaotic lifestyles', appears unlikely to abate in the near future. However, welfare conditionality is also increasingly a feature of policy and practice in other areas of welfare provision. Relevant developments and debates are considered in the next section.

Conditionality, housing, homelessness and antisocial behaviour

As Fitzpatrick, Watts and Johnsen note, welfare conditionality has become an important mechanism of governance 'for regulating the conduct of low income populations' (2014: 1) in the closely related fields of housing, homelessness and antisocial behaviour. Within social housing, successive New Labour governments utilised enhanced conditional tenancies and housing-related benefits to influence behaviour (Flint and Nixon, 2006) and introduced a range of starter, introductory and family intervention tenancies that curtailed tenants' rights to social housing if they engaged in antisocial behaviour or accrued rent arrears. Subsequently, in an attempt to try to ensure that scarce social housing resources are available on a time-limited basis to those most in need (Fitzpatrick and Pawson, 2014), the Coalition's Localism Act (2011) further allowed social landlords in England to offer fixed-term (minimum, two-year, renewable), tenancies to new social tenants. When renewing social tenancies, landlords also now have flexibility to take into account issues such as income level, employment status, past behaviour and/or contribution to the local community.

> Ending security of tenure for new social tenants is ostensibly aimed at ensuring the efficient allocation of scarce housing to those most in need but at the same time social landlords are being encouraged to give longer tenancies to employed people or those who contribute positively to their neighbourhoods. (Fitzpatrick et al, 2014: 3-4).

In a further development, that may yet prove to be significant, the current government is considering whether or not to scrap lifetime tenancies in England altogether (Fitzpatrick and Watts, 2015).

Behavioural conditionality has progressively become an element of policy in the related area of homelessness support, with many services demanding more from their clients in return for the opportunities and support they deliver, and homeless peoples' conduct being identified, by some, as a factor in their ongoing exclusion (see Whiteford, 2008). This has been accompanied by increasing use of 'conditional, enforcement and/or interventionist' tools, such as antisocial behaviour orders (ASBOs), when responding to begging and other behaviours (for example, street drinking) associated with the homeless population. Debate about the effectiveness of these assertive methods continues. Some research indicates that beneficial outcomes may ensue for some individuals when appropriate support is provided alongside enforcement measures (Johnsen and Fitzpatrick, 2007; 2010; Fitzpatrick and Johnsen, 2009). However, conditionality can in certain instances lead to the most excluded homeless people avoiding services that make access to support conditional on specific behavioural requirements (Bowpitt et al, 2014). Increasing interest in 'Housing First' approaches (Johnsen, 2013) and the use of flexible individualised budgets (Brown, 2013), both on terms negotiated with service users, are indicative of less coercive policies finding favour with some service providers within the homelessness sector (see Johnsen et al, 2014 for details).

The emergence of antisocial behaviour legislation that utilised behavioural conditionality in an attempt to curb the irresponsible behaviour of 'problematic' populations was a significant aspect of New Labour's policy agenda (Flint, 2006; 2014). For example, section 31 of the Welfare Reform Act (2007) allowed for the reduction or loss of right to Housing Benefit if an individual has been evicted on grounds of antisocial or criminal behaviour (CPAG, 2007). New Labour's message was clear: where individual's contact with services was 'driven by problematic behaviour resulting from their chaotic lives – such as anti-social behaviour, criminality and poor parenting', the government was prepared to apply tough 'sanctions such as prison, loss of tenancy and possible removal of children' (SETF, 2007 :74).

Further policy development occurred under the coalition government, most notably in the Anti-social Behaviour, Crime and Policing Act (2014). This Act replaced the 19 previously existing powers introduced by New Labour to tackle antisocial behaviour, including antisocial behaviour orders, with six new ones. The definition of antisocial behaviour was also broadened (under section 2(1)(a)-(c) of the Act) to include:

(a) conduct that has caused, or is likely to cause, harassment, alarm or distress to any person;

(b) conduct capable of causing nuisance or annoyance to a person in relation to that person's occupation of residential premises;

(c) conduct capable of causing housing-related nuisance or annoyance to any person.

In moves that echo the localism favoured by the current government, a 'community trigger' that requires the authorities to take action when multiple complaints about a particular issue or household are received has also been written into the legislation. Similarly, the new 'community remedy' requirement obliges the Police and Local Crime Commissioners to consult with local communities about the range of appropriate sanctions to be used in tackling antisocial behaviour (see Flint, 2014; Home Office, 2014 for details).

In an allied area of policy, the coalition's Troubled Families Programme required every local authority in England to identify its most troubled families, by reference to four key criteria, that is, involvement in antisocial behaviour, non-attendance at school by children, an adult family member in receipt of out of work benefit and families generating a high cost to the public purse (DCLG, 2012). Interestingly, the last two were not previously used as indicators of a 'troubled family' by the coalition's predecessors. This perhaps suggests that the coalition and the current Conservative government endorse the view that labour market inactivity is, for a minority at least, due in large part to personal failings and poor individual choices rather than structural factors such as fluctuations in the numbers of jobs available in the wider economy. While successive governments of different political persuasions have been keen to engage in rhetoric that emphasises the differences in their particular approach to policy in this area, as Flint notes, all commonly endorse 'early intervention, intensive whole family projects, sanctions and a belief in non-negotiable, coercive welfare' (2013: 2) as the most appropriate mechanisms to reduce the irresponsible behaviour of 'troubled families'.

Conclusions: a conditional, sanctioning welfare state

Since the introduction of an enhanced sanctions regime in October 2012, tough penalties for non-compliance are now routinely applied to all who fail to punctually attend WFIs or who do not meet their personalised work preparation or job search requirements specified by their advisers. Sanctions range from a loss of benefit for four weeks, for an initial low level transgression (for example, non-attendance at a specified interview with an adviser), to up to three years loss of entitlement for a repeat third, high level offence such as failure to apply for a job (DWP, 2012b). In his ongoing critical analysis of the DWP's published statistics, Webster (2015) cites a range of facts and figures that illustrate the extent to which sanctions have become a routine component of the social benefit system in the UK.

He notes that benefit sanctions have doubled since 2010, that one fifth of all JSA claimants have been sanctioned and that of those sanctioned in 2013/14, almost a third have been sanctioned more than once at a combined cost to JSA and ESA claimants of nearly £333 million in lost benefits. Aggregate data on the application of sanctions in other policy areas is more difficult to gather. However, unpublished analysis by Watkins et al (2014) reports the following. Figures provided by large private registered providers in England (for example, generally Housing Associations with over 1,000 social housing units/bed spaces) to the Homes and Communities Agency, suggest that antisocial behaviour was a factor in approximately 15-16% of evictions, that is 11,206 cases over the period 2005/06 to 2012/13. The available figures in Scotland for registered social landlords suggest that antisocial behaviour is a factor in around 10% of evictions annually. Additionally, a total of 23,078 ASBOs were issued in England and Wales during the period 1999–2012.

This shift towards a more overtly conditional and sanctioning welfare state represents a significant reformulation of the rights and responsibilities of social citizenship in the UK and is occurring against a backdrop of major budget cuts and unprecedented 'root and branch restructuring' of the welfare state (Taylor-Gooby, 2012), which has seen the support services available to many vulnerable people wither or disappear entirely. The social rights of citizens highlighted by T.H. Marshall in 1950 have been relegated to secondary importance by policy makers convinced by the need to reinvigorate individual responsibility in an era of 'ubiquitous conditionality' (Dwyer and Wright, 2014). A common criticism of the argument that citizenship has been reconfigured in recent decades is that individual citizens' responsibilities and duties have long been recognised as an integral part of citizenship and that any ensuing re-emphasis of such responsibilities is merely part and parcel of the contestation of values that T.H. Marshall himself recognised as an essential element of the processes of democratic citizenship. Indeed, some have pointed to a 'growing ambivalence about the proliferation and assertion of rights' (Rees, 1995: 357), and a heightened concern about the moral hazards of passive entitlement and its propensity to inculcate welfare dependency and worklessness in T.H. Marshall's later works (Rees, 1995; Powell, 2002). However, it is clear that in *Citizenship and social class* (1950) Marshall envisaged a notion of social citizenship in which largely unconditional, de-commodified social rights, 'granted on the basis of citizenship rather than performance' (Esping-Anderson, 1990: 21) would be available to citizens in times of need. This is a very different state of affairs to today where the rolling out, general acceptance and unproblematic use of 'behavioural conditionality' as a key element of a 'new politics of the welfare ... intent on converting the welfare benefits system into a lever for changing behaviour' (Rodger, 2008: 87), prevails.

Acknowledgement

The support of the Economic and Social Research Council (ESRC) under grant number ES/K002163/2 is gratefully acknowledged.

References

Bennett, F. (2012) 'Universal credit: overview and gender implications', in M. Kilkey, G. Ramia and K. Farnsworth (eds) *Social policy review 24: Analysis and debate in social policy 2012*, Bristol: Policy Press, pp 15–34.

Betzelt, S. and Bothfeld, S. (eds) (2011) *Activation and labour market reforms in Europe: Challenges to social citizenship*, Basingstoke: Palgrave.

Blair, T. (1998) 'The third way; new politics for a new century', *Pamphlet 588*, London: Fabian Society.

Bowpitt, G., Dwyer, P., Sundin, E. and Weinstein, M. (2014) 'Places of sanctuary for "the undeserving"? Homeless people's day centres and the problem of conditionality', *British Journal of Social Work*, 44(5): 1251–67.

Breidahl, K.N. (2012) 'Immigrant-targeted activation policies: a comparison of the approaches of Scandinavian welfare states', in M. Kilkey, G. Ramia and K. Farnsworth (eds) *Social policy review 24*, Bristol: Policy Press/Social Policy Association.

Brown, P. (2013) *Right time, right place? An evaluation of the Individual Budget approach to tackling rough sleeping in Wales*, Cardiff: Welsh Government/ University of Salford.

Buck, R., Phillips, C.J., Main, C.J., Barnes, M.C., Aylward, M. and Waddell, G. (2006) *Conditionality in context: Incapacity benefit and social deprivation in Merthyr Tydfil*, Discussion Paper, http://opus.bath. ac.uk/15119/1/Conditionality_in_Context.pdf

Cameron, D. (2013) 'Immigration speech by the Prime Minister', https://www.gov.uk/government/news/immigration-speech-by-the-prime-minister

Clasen, J. and Clegg, D. (2007) 'Levels and levers of conditionality: measuring change within welfare states', in J. Clasen and N.A. Siegel (eds) *Investigating welfare state change the 'dependent variable problem' in comparative analysis*, Cheltenham: Edward Elgar, pp 166–97.

Commonwealth of Australia (2007) *Changing behaviour: A public policy perspective*, Barton: Australian Government/Australian Public Services Commission.

Cox, R.H. (1998) 'The consequences of welfare reform: how conceptions of social rights are changing', *Journal of Social Policy*, 27(1): 1–16.

CPAG (2007) 'The Welfare Reform Act 2007', *Welfare Rights Bulletin 198*, London: Child Poverty Action Group.

Croucher, C., Jones, A. and Wallace, A. (2007) *Good neighbour agreements and the promotion of positive behaviour in communities, Report to Communities and Local Government and Home Office*, York: University of York.

DCLG (2012) *The Troubled Families programme: Financial framework for the Troubled Families programme's payment-by-results scheme for local authorities*, London: Department for Communities and Local Government.

Deacon, A. (2004) 'Justifying conditionality: the case of anti-social tenants', *Housing Studies*, 19(6): 911–26.

Deacon, A. (2002) *Perspectives on welfare: Ideas, ideologies and policy debates*, Buckingham: Open University Press.

Deacon, A. (1994) 'Justifying workfare: the historical context of the workfare debates', in M. White (ed) *Unemployment and public policy in a changing labour market*, London: PSI.

Dean, H., Bonvin, J., Vielle, P. and Faraque, N. (2005) 'Developing capabilities and rights in welfare-to-work policies', *European Societies*, 7(1): 3–26.

DWP (2008) *No one written off: Reforming welfare to reward responsibility*, London: Department for Work and Pensions.

DWP (2012a) *Impact assessment about Universal Credit introduced under the Welfare Reform Act 2012*, London: Department for Work and Pensions, www.gov.uk/government/uploads/system/uploads/attachment_data/file/220177/universal-credit-wr2011-ia.pdf

DWP (2012b) *Changes to Jobseeker's Allowance sanctions from 22 October 2012*, London: Department for Work and Pensions, http://webarchive.nationalarchives.gov.uk/20130627060116/http:/www.dwp.gov.uk/adviser/updates/jsa-sanction-changes/

DWP (2015) *Mandatory Work Activity provider guidance – incorporating Universal Credit (UC) guidance (April 2015)*, London: Department for Work and Pensions, https://www.gov.uk/government/uploads/system/uploads/attachment_data/file/420990/mandatory-work-activity-april-15.pdf

Dwyer, P. (2016, in press) 'Rewriting the contract? Conditionality, welfare reform and the rights and responsibilities of disabled people', in D. Horsfall and J. Hudson (eds), *Social policy in an era of global competition: Comparative, international and local perspectives*, Bristol, Policy Press.

Dwyer, P. (2010) *Understanding social citizenship: Issues for policy and practice* (2nd edn), Bristol: Policy Press.

Dwyer, P. (2009) *Integration? The perceptions and experiences of refugees in Yorkshire and the Humber*, Leeds: Yorkshire and Humber Regional Migration Partnership.

Dwyer, P. (2008) 'The conditional welfare state', in M. Powell (ed) *Modernising the welfare state: The Blair legacy*, Bristol: Policy Press, pp 203–21

Dwyer, P. (2004) 'Creeping conditionality in the UK: from welfare rights to conditional entitlements', *Canadian Journal of Sociology*, 29(2): 265–87.

Dwyer, P. (2000) *Welfare rights and responsibilities: Contesting social citizenship*, Bristol: Policy Press.

Dwyer, P. (1998) 'Conditional citizens? Welfare rights and responsibilities in the late 1990s', *Critical Social Policy* 18(4): 519–43.

Dwyer, P., McNeill, J. and Scullion, L. (2014) 'Conditionality briefing: disability', http://www.welfareconditionality.ac.uk/wp-content/uploads/2014/09/Briefing_Disability_14.09.10_FINAL.pdf

Dwyer, P. and Scullion, L. (2014) 'Conditionality briefing: migrants', http://www.welfareconditionality.ac.uk/wp-content/uploads/2014/09/Briefing_Migrants_14.09.10_FINAL.pdf

Dwyer, P. and Wright, S. (2014) 'Universal credit, ubiquitous conditionality and its implications for social citizenship', *Journal of Poverty and Social Justice*, 22(1): 27–36.

Esping-Andersen, G. (1990) *The three worlds of welfare capitalism*, Cambridge: Polity Press.

Marshall, T. (1950) *Citizenship and social class and other essays*, Cambridge: Cambridge University Press.

Etzioni, A. (2000) *The third way to a good society*, London: Demos.

Etzioni, A. (ed) (1998) *The essential communitarian reader*, Oxford: Rowman and Littlefield.

Etzioni, A. (1997) *The new golden rule*, London: Profile Books.

Fitzpatrick, S. and Watts, B. (2015) 'Fixing terms', *Inside Housing*, 18th November, http://www.insidehousing.co.uk/fixing-terms/7012754.article

Fitzpatrick, S. and Pawson, H. (2014) 'Ending security of tenure for social renters: transitioning to 'ambulance service' social housing?', *Housing Studies*, 29(5): 597–615.

Fitzpatrick, S., Watts, B. and Johnsen, S. (2014) 'Conditionality briefing: social housing', http://www.welfareconditionality.ac.uk/wp-content/uploads/2014/09/Briefing_SocialHousing_14.09.10_FINAL.pdf

Fitzpatrick, S. and Johnsen, S. (2009) 'The use of enforcement to combat 'street culture' in England: an ethical approach?' *Ethics and Social Welfare*, 3(3): 284–302.

Fletcher, D.R. (2014) 'Conditionality briefing: offenders', http://www. welfareconditionality.ac.uk/wp-content/uploads/2014/09/Briefing_ Offenders_14.09.10_FINAL.pdf

Fletcher, D.R. (2008) 'Offenders in the post-industrial labour market: from the underclass to the undercaste?' *Policy and Politics* 26(2): 283–97.

Fletcher, D.R., Flint, J., Gore, T., Powell, R., Batty, E. and Crisp, R. (2012) *Qualitative study of offender employment review, Research Report No 784*, London: Department for Work and Pensions.

Flint, J. (2014) 'Conditionality briefing: anti-social behaviour', http:// www.welfareconditionality.ac.uk/wp-content/uploads/2014/09/ Briefing_ASB_14.09.10_FINAL.pdf

Flint, J. (2013) 'Anti-social behaviour and troubled families scoping paper, for the Sanctions and Support Welfare project', Unpublished report, York: University of York.

Flint, J. (2009) 'Subversive subjects and conditional, earned and denied citizenship', in M. Barnes and D. Prior (eds) *Subversive citizens: Power, agency and resistance in public services*, Bristol: Policy Press, pp 83–98.

Flint, J. (ed) (2006) *Housing, urban governance and anti-social behaviour: Perspectives, policies and practice*, Bristol: Policy Press.

Flint, J., Jones, A. and Parr, S. (2011) *An evaluation of the sanction of Housing Benefit. Research Report No 728*, London: Department for Work and Pensions.

Flint, J., Batty, E., Parr, S., Platts-Fowler, D., Nixon, J. and Sanderson, D. (2011) *Evaluation of intensive intervention projects*, London: Department for Education.

Flint, J. and Nixon, J. (2006) 'Governing neighbours: anti-social behaviour orders and new forms of regulating conduct in the UK', *Urban Studies*, 43(6): 939–55.

Freud, D. (2007) *Reducing dependency, increasing opportunity: Options for the future of welfare to work. An independent report to the Department for Work and Pensions*, London: Department for Work and Pensions.

Gray, M. et al. (2016) 'New conditionality in Australian social security policy', *Australian Journal of Social Issues*, forthcoming.

Giddens, A. (1994) *Beyond left and right: The future of radical politics*, Cambridge: Polity Press.

Giddens, A. (1998) *The third way: The renewal of social democracy*, Cambridge: Polity Press.

Gregg, D. (2008) *Realising potential: A vision for personalised conditionality and support – An independent report to the Department for Work and Pensions*, London: Department for Work and Pensions.

Griggs, J. and Evans, M. (2010) *Sanctions within conditional benefit systems: A review of the evidence*, York: Joseph Rowntree Foundation.

Handler, J. (2004) *Social citizenship and workfare in the United States and Western Europe: The paradox of inclusion*, Cambridge: Cambridge University Press.

HM Government (2011) *Laying the foundations: A housing strategy for England*, London: HM Government.

HMT/DWP/HMRC (2014) 'Further curbs to migrant access to benefits announced', Press Release, 8 April, London: HM Treasury, Department for Work and Pensions, HM Customs and Excise.

Home Office (2014) *Anti-social Behaviour, Crime and Policing Act 2014: Reform of anti-social behaviour powers: Statutory guidance for frontline professionals*, London: The Home Office, https://www.gov.uk/government/uploads/system/uploads/attachment_data/file/352562/ASB_Guidance_v8_July2014_final__2_.pdf

Hudson, M., Barnes, H., Ray, K. and Phillips, J. (2006) *Ethnic minority perceptions and experiences of Jobcentre Plus, Research Report No 349*, London: Department for Work and Pensions.

Johnsen, S. (2013) *Turning Point Scotland's Housing First Pilot Evaluation: Final Report*, Edinburgh: Heriot-Watt University.

Johnsen, S. (2014) 'Conditionality briefing: lone parents', http://www.welfareconditionality.ac.uk/wp-content/uploads/2014/09/Briefing_LoneParents_14.09.10_FINAL.pdf

Johnsen, S., Fitzpatrick, S. and Watts, B. (2014) 'Conditionality briefing: homelessness and "street culture"', http://www.welfareconditionality.ac.uk/wp-content/uploads/2014/09/Briefing_Homelessness_14.09.10_FINAL.pdf

Johnsen, S. and Fitzpatrick, S. (2010) 'Revanchist sanitisation or coercive care? The use of enforcement to combat begging, street drinking and rough sleeping in England', *Urban Studies*, 47(8): 1703–23.

Johnsen, S. and Fitzpatrick, S. (2007) *The impact of enforcement on street users in England*, Bristol: Policy Press.

Kellner, P. (2012) 'A quiet revolution', *Prospect*, March, p 30–34.

Kennedy, S. (2015) 'Welfare Reform and Work Bill [Bill 51 of 2015-16]', *Briefing Paper, number 07252*, London: House of Commons Library.

King, P. (2004) 'What do we mean by responsibility? The case of UK housing benefit reform', *Journal of Housing and the Built Environment*, 21(2): 111–25.

Lister, R. (2011) 'The age of responsibility: social policy and citizenship in the early 21st century', in C. Holden, M. Kilkey and G. Ramia (eds) *Social Policy Review 23*, Bristol: Policy Press/SPA.

Lødemel, I. and Trickey, H. (eds) (2001) *'An offer you can't refuse': Workfare in international perspective*, Bristol: Policy Press.

Marshall, T. (1950) *Citizenship and social class and other essays*, Cambridge: Cambridge University Press.

Mason, R. and Perraudin, F. (2015) 'Unemployed young people will be sent to work boot camp, says minister', *The Guardian online*, 17 August, http://www.theguardian.com/society/2015/aug/17/unemployed-young-people-work-boot-camp-tory-minister

Mead, L.M. (1986) *Beyond entitlement*, New York, NY: Free Press.

Mead, L.M. (1997) 'Citizenship and social policy: T.H. Marshall and poverty', *Social Philosophy and Social Policy*, 14(2): 197–230.

Monnat, S.M. (2010) 'The color of welfare sanctioning: exploring the individual and contextual roles of race on TANF case closures and benefit reduction', *The Sociological Quarterly*, 51(4): 678–707.

Mulgan, G. (2010) *Influencing behaviour to improve health and wellbeing, an independent report. Department of Health*, London: The Stationery Office.

Murray, C. (1999) *The underclass revisited*, Washington: American Institute for Public Policy Research, http://www.aei.org/publication/the-underclass-revisited-2/

Murray, C. (1984) *Losing ground*, New York, NY: Basic Books.

Newton, B., Meager, N., Bertram, C., Corden, A., George, A., Lalani, M., Metcalf, H., Rolfe, H., Sainsbury, R. and Weston, K. (2012) *Work programme evaluation: Findings from the first phase of qualitative research on programme delivery*, Research Report No 821, London: Department for Work and Pensions.

O'Brien, C. (2013) 'From safety nets and carrots to trampolines and sticks: national use of the EU as both menace and model to help neoliberalize welfare policy', in D. Schiek (ed) *The EU Economic and Social Model in the Global Crisis*, Farnham: Ashgate, pp 93–116.

Patrick, R. (2012) 'All in it together? Disabled people the coalition and welfare to work', *Journal of Poverty and Social Justice*, 20(3): 307–22.

Paz-Fuchs, A. (2008) *Welfare to work: Conditional rights in social policy*, Oxford: Oxford University Press.

Pennycook, M. and Whittaker, M. (2012) *Conditions uncertain: Assessing the implications of Universal Credit in-work conditionality*, London: Resolution Foundation

Phoenix, J. (2008) 'ASBOS and working women: a new revolving door?' in P. Squires (ed) *ASBO nation: The criminalisation of nuisance*, Bristol: Policy Press, pp 289–303.

Powell, M. (2002) 'The hidden history of social citizenship', *Citizenship Studies*, 6(3): 229–24.

Rees, A.M. (1995) 'The other T.H. Marshall', *Journal of Social Policy*, 24(3): 341–62.

Rodger, J. (2008) *Criminalising social policy: Anti-social behaviour and welfare in a de-civilised society*, Cullompton: Willan Publishing.

Scottish Refugee Council (2013) *Inquiry into Jobcentre Plus: Evidence submitted by the Scottish Refugee Council*, Glasgow: Scottish Refugee Council.

SETF (Social Exclusion Task Force) (2007) *Reaching out: An action plan on social exclusion, The Social Exclusion Task Force*, London: The Cabinet Office.

Shutes, I. (2011) 'Welfare to work and the responsiveness of employment providers to the needs of refugees', *Journal of Social Policy*, 40(3): 557–74.

Southerton, D., McMeekin, A. and Evans, A. (2011) *International review of behaviour change initiatives*, Edinburgh: Scottish Government.

Stewart, A.B.R. and Wright, S. (2014) 'Conditionality briefing: unemployed people', http://www.welfareconditionality.ac.uk/wp-content/uploads/2014/09/Briefing_Unemployment_14.09.10_FINAL.pdf

Taylor-Gooby, P. (2012) 'Root and branch restructuring to achieve major cuts: the social policy programme of the 2010 UK Coalition government', *Social Policy and Administration*, 46(1): 61–82.

Taylor-Gooby, P. (2009) *Reframing social citizenship*, Oxford: Oxford University Press.

Titmuss, R.M. (1958) *Essays on the welfare state*, London: Allen and Unwin.

Walters, W. (1997) 'The active society: new designs for social policy', *Policy and Politics* 25(3): 221–34.

Watts, B., Fitzpatrick, S., Bramley, G. and Watkins, D. (2014) 'Welfare sanctions and conditionality in the UK', *Research round-up*, York: Joseph Rowntree Foundation, http://www.jrf.org.uk/sites/files/jrf/Welfare-conditionality-UK-Summary.pdf

Watkins, D., Bramley, G., Fitzpatrick, S., Watts, B. and Blenkinsopp, J. (2014) 'Welfare conditionality: sanctions, support and behaviour change review and analysis of existing secondary datasets', Unpublished internal report for the welfare conditionality project Edinburgh, IHURER, Heriot-Watt.

Webster, D. (2015) 'Briefing: the DWP's JSA/ESA sanctions statistics release', 18 February, http://www.cpag.org.uk/david-webster

Whiteford, M. (2008) 'Street homelessness and the architecture of citizenship', *People, Place and Policy Online*, 2(2): 88–100.

Wright, S. (2011a) 'Steering with sticks, rowing for rewards: the new governance of activation in the UK', in R. Van Berkel, W. de Graaf and T. Sirovátka (eds) *The governance of active welfare states in Europe*, Basingstoke: Palgrave, pp 85–109.

Wright, S. (2011b) 'Relinquishing rights? The impact of activation on citizenship for lone parents in the UK', in S. Betzelt and S. Bothfeld (eds) *Activation and labour market reforms in Europe*, Basingtoke: Palgrave Macmillan, pp 59–78.

Wright, S. (2012) 'Welfare to work, agency and personal responsibility', *Journal of Social Policy*, 41(2): 309–28.

Young, M. and Lemos, G. (1997) *The communities we have lost and can regain*, London: Lemos and Crane.

FOUR

Housing policy in the austerity age and beyond

Mark Stephens and Adam Stephenson

Introduction

This chapter charts the radical reorientation of housing policy in the UK that was set in motion by the coalition government elected in 2010 and accelerated by the majority Conservative government elected in 2015.

Before 2010, two very broad phases in housing policy can be identified. In the period from 1945 up to 1980, successive governments used social rented housing to improve general housing conditions, meet housing shortages and to house a wide cross section of the population. Simultaneously, home ownership was encouraged through favourable tax treatment, while the private rented sector was allowed to decline to residual status under the pressure of regulation and lack of subsidy.

From 1980 to 2010, home ownership was broadened through the Right to Buy and mortgage market deregulation. The social rented sector was allowed to decline, and now provided a safety net for a large number of households on low incomes, including statutorily homeless people. Subsidies were shifted emphatically from the supply side towards the demand side Housing Benefit, which became the largest financial subsidy to housing, especially after the phasing out of mortgage interest relief for home owners. The private rented sector was revived through deregulation, new mortgage products and indirect subsidy from Housing Benefit. By the end of this period, home ownership was in decline, and private renting is about to overtake social renting.

This chapter details the emergence of a third phase of housing policy since 2010 in which the safety net function of social rented housing and the wider housing system is being undermined, as security of tenure is weakened in the social sector, homelessness legislation weakened by allowing local authorities to meet their duties by allocating private in place of social tenancies, and Housing Benefit cuts. Home ownership is receiving increasing state support through state guarantees, state equity stakes, and now through the Starter Homes scheme and the extension of the Right to Buy scheme to housing association tenants.

However, the 'British' housing system is beginning to fragment, as different parts of the UK pursue their own priorities. This is seen most clearly in Scotland.

Context for policy change

The Conservative–Liberal Democrat coalition government of 2010-15 was formed in the aftermath of the global financial crisis. Over the weekend that followed the election in May 2010, the unfolding Greek economic crisis persuaded the Liberal Democrats to accept the Conservatives' case for prioritising budget deficit reduction or face the wrath of the international money markets. Consequently, the government's programme was driven by a deficit reduction strategy (which became known as 'austerity') unveiled in an 'emergency budget' in June 2010, which was used to justify radical changes to a range of social policies.

Although the Chancellor slowed the pace of deficit reduction during the course of the 2010–15 parliament, the majority Conservative government, which returned in May 2015 is committed to introducing £37 billion of 'consolidation' measures, including £12 billion arising from 'welfare reform' (HM Treasury, 2015). Some £17 billion of these reductions were announced in the summer budget and a further £20 billion of savings were announced in the autumn's comprehensive spending review (CSR).

Alongside deficit reduction, the Bank of England pursued a policy of ultra-low interest rates. The bank rate remained at the historically record low level of 0.5% throughout the lifetime of the parliament, and was supplemented by the continuation of the programme of quantitative easing begun in 2009. By 2012, the Bank of England had purchased £375 billion worth of government bonds from private investors in order to stimulate the economy (Bank of England, no date). Although there have been no further purchases, this balance has been maintained (Bank of England, no date).

Although fiscal consolidation and an expansionary monetary policy have therefore been the principal drivers of housing policy since 2010, it is clear that there has been a strong ideological underpinning in policy. This is reflected in the way in which policy has increasingly favoured home ownership (in order to reverse its decline), while undermining the levels of social protection afforded by social rented housing and Housing Benefit.

A housing strategy?

In recent decades it has been uncommon for governments to have a discernible housing strategy – a clear notion of how to deploy the variety of policy instruments available to meet sector-wide objectives. The lack of strategy arises in part from the division of responsibilities for housing-related policies between several departments: notional responsibility for housing policy lies with the Department of Communities and Local Government (DCLG), but responsibility for, by far, the largest financial subsidy to housing (Housing Benefit) lies with the Department of Work and Pensions. Meanwhile, taxation is controlled by the Treasury, monetary policy by the Bank of England, and the regulation of the mortgage market lies with the Financial Conduct Authority. Devolution to the governments and administrations in Scotland, Wales and Northern Ireland, has introduced further fragmentation into policy.

Apart from a brief period around 2003, when the Treasury possessed a strategic overview of the housing sector, as the unstable housing market emerged as a key impediment to British membership of the Euro, and reviews of housing supply and mortgage finance were put in place, the UK government has operated what amounts to an ad hoc tenure policy.

While such ad hoc tenancy-focused measures are leading to a fundamental change in the housing system, it is notable that the key strategic issue – the growing shortage of housing – has not been tackled. The last Labour government began to address the issue during its second term, but the uplift in private housebuilding was derailed by the economic crisis, while it allowed social housebuilding to fall to record lows. Housebuilding in England was under 100,000 units in 2010/11 and recovered to almost 125,000 in 2014/15 (DCLG, Live Table 208). However, these figures are well below the levels required to meet housing needs. The Future Homes Commission (2012) estimated that 300,000 new homes are needed each year in the UK. Holmans (2013) suggested that between 240,000 and 245,000 are needed. The UK government suggests that the figure lies between 200,000 and 300,000 units (House of Commons, 2015). The spending review in November 2015 placed much emphasis on tackling housing shortages, by increasing output to 200,000 units per year, partly through the Starter Homes programme discussed below.

Home ownership

Home ownership has been in decline for more than a decade, as would-be first time buyers have been priced out of the market. The government is now attempting to reverse this trend.

Promoting home ownership has been an objective of governments of all parties since at least the 1970s, and the 20th century saw the tenure grow from housing around one in 10 households before the First World War to a peak of some 70% in the early years of the 21st century. As Table 4.1 shows, since then, home ownership has declined from 69% (in 2003/04) to 64% (in 2013/14). While this 'headline' figure may not seem dramatic, the differences between age cohorts suggest a stronger underlying decline. Home ownership continued to rise among over 65s, but in every other age band it fell. The most dramatic falls have been among younger households, but they have now spread up the working age range. So home ownership fell by more than 20 percentage points among 25-34 year olds, by nine percentage points among 35-44s and five percentage points among 55-64s. There are now more outright owners than those with a mortgage – a clear sign of a maturing market.

What has caused home ownership to fall? One could point to societal changes since the early 1990s, such as the expansion of higher education and the postponement of entry into the labour market, the formation of households and starting families. Looking to the future we can anticipate that working lifetimes will more commonly stretch into people's 70s, so giving them longer to purchase a house.

Table 4.1: Tenure change 2003/04–2013/14

2003/04	Owned out-right	Buying with a mort-gage	Social rent-ed	Pri-vate rent-ed	2013/14	Owned out-right	Buying with a mort-gage	Social rent-ed	Pri-vate rent-ed
16-24	2	22	29	47		2	7	23	67
25-34	3	56	18	23		2	36	17	44
35-44	7	64	18	11		7	53	17	23
45-54	22	56	15	7		20	50	17	13
55-64	49	31	16	5		48	27	16	9
65+	65	4	26	5		71	4	19	5
All	30	39	20	11		33	31	18	19

Source: DWP (2015a), Table 2c

The tightening of the mortgage market as a result of the credit crunch and global financial crisis, reinforced by the Mortgage Market Review (MMR) (FSA, 2009), clearly means that mortgages are less readily available than at any time since the market was deregulated in the 1980s. The MMR introduced an obligation on lenders to assess potential borrower's ability to repay a mortgage on the basis of affordability criteria relating to their incomes, expenditure commitments, rather than on the traditional rules of thumb. While interest only mortgages are still permitted, they no longer offer a shortcut to improving affordability because the affordability calculation must be made on the assumption of a repayment mortgage.

However, home ownership was in decline before the credit crunch when 100% mortgages were still available. The problem was that as house prices rose, fewer potential purchasers could afford to service a 100% mortgage. They were becoming priced out of the market. One might have expected the market to have 'corrected' after the crisis, but, in contrast to the 1990s crash, the correction was limited. By April 2014, average UK house prices were 6.5% higher than the pre-crisis peak in 2007/08. This masks regional variations, so prices in London, South East and East regions were higher than before the crisis, but still lower elsewhere in Great Britain. Indeed London, with prices more than 30% above pre-crisis levels and approaching £500,000, increasingly appeared distinct from the rest of the country. Only in Northern Ireland – living with the repercussions of the Republic of Ireland's boom and bust – where prices in April 2014 were still almost 50% below the 2007 figure, had a large correction taken place (ONS, 2014).

The coalition government's response to the pricing out of young (and not so young) households from home ownership was to restate its commitment to it:

> For too long, millions have been locked out of home ownership. We want to build an economy that works for everyone, one in which people who work hard and play by the rules can expect to own a decent home of their own. This goes right to the heart of what this Government is about. (HM Government, 2011: v)

Help to Buy

Consequently, a scheme of equity loans for first time buyers and movers, labelled 'Help to Buy', was launched in 2013. Under the English version of this scheme, eligibility is limited to new properties priced under

£600,000 (more than twice the average house price). The government lends 20% of the property value, which is provided without fees for the first five years. The purchaser puts down a 5% deposit and a private lender provides a 75% mortgage to cover the remainder of the value. By June 2015 some 102,500 properties had been purchased under this scheme with loans worth £4.3 billion (DCLG, 2015a). Around 45% of the equity loans (by number and value) supported first time buyers. Separate schemes were introduced in Scotland and Wales. In the Comprehensive Spending Review, the government announced that this scheme will continue to 2021 and that the maximum government loan will be doubled to 40% of the property value in London.

Another scheme, whereby the government guarantees the top 20% of a 95% mortgage, was introduced (also under the 'Help to Buy' banner) for first time purchasers of both new and existing properties. Some 46,877 properties were purchased across the UK under this scheme between October 2013 and March 2015. More than 40% of properties were priced under £125,000 and more than 50% under £150,000 (HM Treasury, 2015). Some economists suggested that the scheme was causing another house price boom. However, in a letter to the Chancellor, the Governor of the Bank of England wrote, 'The scheme does not appear to be a material driver of [house price] growth – for example, take-up of the scheme has been weak in London where house price growth has been strongest.' (Carney, 2014)

Table 4.2 suggests that first time buyer's share of mortgage lending is higher now than before the crisis, and in absolute terms has recovered from 39% of pre-crisis levels (in 2009) to 86% (in 2015). However, this does not necessarily fully reflect the position of first time buyers in the market because of purchases made without mortgages. Nonetheless, Wilcox et al (2015) estimate that at least one third of first time buyers received state assistance in 2014.

Starter Homes

Following a manifesto pledge to promote some 200,000 'Starter Homes' for first time buyers, the newly-elected Conservative government addressed this issue in its Housing and Planning Bill. 'Starter homes' are defined as being homes sold to first time buyers aged under 40 at prices at least 20% below market value and at no more than £250,000 outside London and £450,000 within it. The details of the scheme are not stated definitively in the Bill, but it is anticipated that planning authorities will use Section 106 of the 1990 Town and Country Planning Act to require

Table 4.2: Lending to first time buyers 2007–15

Year (all Q2)	Percentage by value to FTBs	Total lent (£bn)	Total lent to FTBs (£bn)
2007	15.2	81.9	12.4
2008	11.9	61.0	7.3
2009	15.4	30.9	4.8
2010	18.5	33.4	6.2
2011	18.2	32.8	6.0
2012	18.9	32.4	6.1
2013	22.0	36.0	7.9
2014	25.9	43.8	11.3
2015	25.0	42.9	10.7

Source: Bank of England/Financial Conduct Authority (2015)

developers to include a certain proportion of starter homes within a development. (House of Commons, 2015). This will divert important resources away from conventional affordable housing. In 2013/14 Section 106 facilitated the completion of 16,193 affordable homes in England (37% of the total) and supported even higher numbers before the recession – 32,000 in 2006/07 (65% of the total).

Social renting

Social rented housing provides a vital safety net for households that cannot access home ownership. It is characterised by below market rents and security of tenure. However, these pillars are now being undermined as the government seeks to alter the nature of the tenure, and to make it more like the highly residualised systems operating in the USA and Australia.

The size of the social rented sector has been much more stable than the market tenures. The proportion of households renting from local authorities or housing associations has declined slightly over the past 10 years, so now slightly fewer than one fifth of households are living in this tenure (Table 4.1). There have been declines of six and seven percentage points respectively in the proportions of 16-24 and over 65 year olds who are social tenants, but otherwise, the proportions have been stable or have even increased.

However, this stability disguises the impact of qualitative changes in the tenure, which are having the effect of changing its character, as well as the likelihood of considerable loss of stock in England as the right to buy is extended to housing association tenants. The principal changes relate to allocations, tenancies and the very notion of a 'social' rent, which are discussed in turn.

Waiting lists and allocations

The coalition objected to the policy of 'open' waiting lists introduced by the previous Labour government, arguing that it raises 'false expectations and [are] likely to fuel the belief that the allocation system is unfair' (DCLG, 2010: 33). Instead the coalition favoured giving local authorities 'greater freedom to set their own policies about who should qualify to go on the waiting list for social housing in their area.' (DCLG, 2011: 15).

The Localism Act 2011 permits local authorities in England to prescribe by class, people who will be entitled to be allocated social rented housing. Wilson (2015) reports a survey of local authorities in 2014 that identified that 126 had used these powers to limit access to waiting lists. The most common requirement is for local authorities to require potential tenants to have a 'local connection' with the authority. As an example, the London Borough of Ealing has set a residency requirement of five years. Local authorities are also free to exclude people by virtue of unacceptable behaviour, with authorities now able to extend this beyond 'antisocial' behaviour. Another survey reported a fall in the number of local authority and housing association allocations to black and minority ethnic (BME) applicants, although the government has disputed the methodology (Wilson, 2015). Examples have also been found of local authorities rewarding contributions to the community in their allocations policies (Wilson, 2015). However, what is not beyond dispute is that following the Localism Act the pool of people on local authority housing waiting lists has declined by a quarter since 2012 to 1.4 million in 2014 (DCLG, Live Table 600).

Affordable Rent programme

The Affordable Homes programme was a major casualty of the coalition government's austerity programme, and capital funding was cut by 60%. However, in an attempt to maintain output, a new form of social rented housing was devised – 'Affordable Rent'. This programme offers housing associations a lower grant than previously, but rents are permitted to rise up to 80% of market levels. The higher rents increase the tenanted market value of the property, so enabling the housing association to lever in more private loan finance to support construction. Further financing is obtained by the conversion of some re-lets into lets at Affordable Rents, and the sale of vacant dwellings. Providers bid for the funds. Outputs were back-end loaded to the end of the programme in March 2015, by which time 90,528 Affordable Rent homes had been started and 64,728 completed (DCLG, Live Table 1012). The target had been 80,000 completions by March 2015. Meanwhile, outputs of traditional social rented housing fell. In the three years to 2011/12 an average of 34,000 such dwellings had been completed annually (Wilcox et al, 2015), but 2014/15 it was 6,192 (DCLG, Live Table 1021). Wilcox et al suggest that 'for every home built under the AHP when it ended in March [2015] at least one existing social rented home was re-let at higher rents or was sold'. (2015: 12). The successor programme is proceeding with even lower levels of per unit subsidy. For the year 2014/15, mean average 'affordable rents' for new general needs lettings were 46% higher than social rents for general needs across England. In London, the differential was 60% (DCLG, 2015c).

Rents: up for some, down for others

After the election, the new majority Conservative government unveiled policies to enforce rent reductions of 1% per year for four years from 2016/17 under the Welfare Reform and Work Bill (published in July 2015). The measure applies to both local authority and housing associations, and is motivated by a wish to reduce the pressure on Housing Benefit (HM Treasury (2015) predicts savings of £1.445 billion in 2020/21). The measure will reduce housing associations' ability to borrow to support the building of new social rented housing. At least one housing association (Genesis) announced its abandonment of new social rented housing, and others have considered doing the same (Slawson, 2015).

Meanwhile, the government's Housing and Planning Bill empowers it to require local authorities and housing associations to raise rents for 'high income social tenants', although the requirement for housing associations is now 'voluntary'. Technically, the measure applies to England and Wales, but in practice it is likely to be applied only to England. The Chancellor suggested that the threshold would be £30,000 outside London and £40,000 inside the capital (House of Commons, 2015). The Bill anticipates giving social landlords the right to require tenants to reveal their incomes, and for these to be verified by the HMRC. The additional revenue, estimated at £365 million in 2017/18 (HM Treasury, 2015: Table 2.1) will be passed on to the government. The legislation does not specify how high the rents would be, but it is expected that they will be close to market levels.

Security of tenure

Social rented housing has traditionally been a secure form of accommodation for its tenants – and legally so since council tenants were granted security of tenure in 1980. Provision was made for housing association affordable rent tenancies to be fixed term and the coalition government extended this to local authorities arguing:

> Under the previous system social landlords were normally only able to grant lifetime tenancies. Sometimes this meant that people acquire a social home at a moment of crisis in their life, and continue to live there long after their need for it has passed. Meanwhile there are people waiting for a social home who face much more difficult circumstances. This was unfair, and represented a poor use of valuable public resources. (DCLG, 2011: 15)

Under the Localism Act 2011 local authorities are able to offer fixed-term tenancies as short as two years. Of the fixed-term tenancies issued in 2014/15, most were for a period of three to five years (61% social rent and 69% affordable rent) (DCLG, 2015a, Table 2b). In England, the proportion of fixed tenancies issued increased from 9% in 2013/14 to 13% in 2014/15 (DCLG, 2015c). However, in November 2015, the government added amendments to the Housing and Planning Bill that will make 2–5 year fixed-term tenancies compulsory for all new tenants.

Right to Buy scheme

The Right to Buy scheme had appeared to be a policy that had run its course. The last Labour government introduced maximum discounts, which had the effect of greatly reducing sales. Measures introduced by the devolved administrations in Wales and Scotland had a similar effect. However, the coalition sought to revive the scheme in England by once again increasing the discounts available in 2012 (to a maximum of £75,000). Sales (for both local authorities and housing associations whose tenants had 'preserved' their right to buy when their houses were transferred from local authority to housing association ownership) fell from 58,648 in 2004/05 to just 3,179 in the last year of the Labour government in 2009/10 (calculated from DCLG, Live Table 682). Over this period, average discounts fell from an average of 34% to 27 of market value. Once the discounts were increased, sales revived to 15,682, with discounts averaging 48% (DCLG, Live Table 682). These numbers were, of course, small beer compared to the heyday of the Right to Buy scheme when well over 100,000 sales were completed in some years (Stephens, 2013). Sensitive to the loss of affordable housing, the government gave assurances that dwellings sold would be replaced with 'affordable' rent homes on a one-for-one basis. However, a survey by Shelter in September 2015 suggested that few councils had achieved this (BBC, 2015a).

The Conservative Party manifesto contained a commitment to extend the Right to Buy scheme to housing association tenants. This policy is more controversial than the original right to buy, because housing associations are legally independent of government, and mostly charitable in status. The housing associations warned that compulsion might lead them to becoming classified as being in the public sector with the consequence that their borrowing would now fall within the public sector. Ironically, one of the key motivations behind the Conservative government in the 1980s switching to housing associations as the main providers of new social rented housing was that, in contrast to local authorities, their borrowing would not affect the public finances directly. A similar motivation lay behind Labour's promotion of large scale voluntary transfers of local authority stock to housing associations (Stephens, 2013).

In the event, the government has accepted a proposition from the National Housing Federation, supported by its members in a hastily arranged ballot, for a voluntary scheme, and this appears in the Housing and Planning Bill published in October. This enables the government to compensate the housing associations for the discount granted on the sale of each dwelling, which is intended to allow the housing associations to replace properties sold on a one-for-one basis. However, the Bill also enables the government to require local authorities to make payments to it 'by reference to the market value of the high value vacant housing owned by the authority' (House of Commons, 2015: 28). The Bill requires local authorities to 'consider' selling such housing (House of Commons, 2015: 28). The revenue from such sales is intended to be used to compensate housing associations for the discounted sales of their properties.

The de facto extension of the right to buy will open up the possibility of ownership to some 1.8 million housing association tenants. Savills estimates that around one in five will be able to afford to buy and expects some 24,000 tenants to exercise this right annually. The scale of anticipated subsidy involved is very high indeed: some £95,500 per dwelling in London and £63,000 in the rest of the capital (Savills, 2015).

In marked contrast to the policy in England, the SNP Scottish government has legislated to end the Right to Buy scheme altogether in 2016, having removed the right from new tenants in 2010. The Labour administration in Wales, where sales are very low, halved the maximum discount (to £8,000) in 2015 and published a White Paper committing it to legislate to abolish the scheme (Twinch, 2015). The scheme continues in Northern Ireland.

Homelessness

The 'right to housing' for unintentionally homeless households in priority need, implied by the homelessness legislation, has been a distinctive feature of the British housing system for more than 35 years. (The legislation was extended to Northern Ireland in 1988; Fitzpatrick et al, 2009.) The practice has been for local authorities to house statutorily homeless people in priority need in temporary accommodation until a suitable social tenancy has become available. The Labour government pursued a policy of prevention, which was intended to identify solutions where possible without relying on the statutory system. Consequently, acceptances in England halved from almost 95,000 in 2005/06 to just over 40,000 in 2009/10 (DCLG, Live Table 770; DCLG, 2015b). Current trends demonstrate that assistance via the statutory homelessness system in England represents 'a small and declining proportion of all local authority homeless work' (Fitzpatrick et al, 2015a: 50; see also Figure 4.1).

The coalition government introduced a policy (applied to new cases from November 2012) under the Localism Act (2011) that allowed local authorities to discharge their legal duty to a homeless person in priority need via compulsory Private Rented Sector Offers (PRSOs). Prior to the reform, statutory homeless households could refuse qualifying offers of privately rented housing. This policy is intended to break the link between homelessness and qualification for social housing, the government having argued that the previous arrangements 'encourage[d] some households to apply as homeless in order to secure

Figure 4.1: Total local authority assistance provided to homeless (and potentially homeless) households, England 2010/11–2014/15

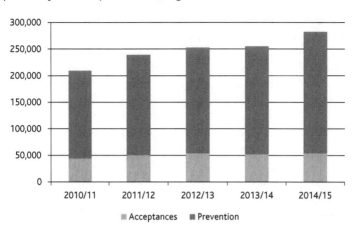

Source: DCLG Live Tables 770 and 787

reasonable preference and an effective guarantee of being offered social housing' (DCLG, 2010: 41). A second motivation behind the reform was to reduce the costs of temporary accommodation because 'homeless [households] were able to refuse offers of accommodation in the private sector, and insist that they should be housed in expensive temporary accommodation until a long-term social home becomes available' (DCLG, 2011: 16).

The overall impact of the new power is hard to gauge. Since 2013/14, when the new powers first began to affect the statistics, the number of PRSOs (including offers both accepted and refused by people experiencing homelessness) has increased from 1,581 cases to 2,671 cases in 2014/15 (DCLG, Live Tables 777; 778; DCLG, 2015b). However, the total number of private rental discharges (qualifying offers and PRSOs) is only marginally greater (3,730) than the total number of qualifying offers at their 2009/10 peak (3,440). Moreover, total private rental discharges almost halved (1,650) following the introduction of a new power in September 2012 (DCLG, Live Tables 777; 778; DCLG, 2015b). The increase in PRSOs has been almost entirely at the expense of qualifying offers. Although a survey of local authorities found that by the summer of 2014 most (55%) of them had adopted policies to allow them to use the private rented sector to discharge their duties, and this was expected to rise to almost three quarters, very few respondents believed that PRSOs would become the 'primary' means of discharge within the next two years (Fitzpatrick et al, 2015a).

However, another important amendment has been the relaxation of the 'suitability of accommodation' regulations that make it easier for local authorities to place families outside the area of the local authority. This is already a common practice when placing homeless people in temporary accommodation. Some 12,000 families were housed in temporary accommodation outside the local authorities' boundaries in 2013 and 2014 in London alone (Douglas, 2015).

While the Scottish government also adopted a policy of 'prevention', at the end of 2012 it implemented the law that extends the right to settled accommodation to all unintentionally homeless people. The measure was phased in by setting local authorities targets for reducing the proportion of cases which were not treated as being in priority need. Unsurprisingly, the extension of the priority need category has led to rising proportions of social housing lets being allocated to homeless people, and this was a factor in prompting the Scottish government to emphasise prevention alongside it. In contrast to England, statutory homelessness has fallen in Scotland (Scottish Government, 2015a). A study of homelessness in Scotland suggested that, 'This downward trend is wholly the result of the introduction of the 'Housing Options' model of homelessness prevention from 2010 onwards' (Fitzpatrick et al, 2015b: vii).

The Welsh government has shifted focus onto the prevention and relief of homelessness regardless of priority need (Fitzpatrick et al, 2015c). The Welsh legislation also permits local authorities to fulfil their obligations to homeless people through the private rented sector.

Housing Benefit

Housing Benefit plays a vital 'income support' role in the housing system by preventing households' incomes falling below socially acceptable subsistence levels because of rental costs. This function, already weakened by the 2010-15 government, is being undermined further by a new raft of restrictions.

Housing Benefit (HB) is the largest financial subsidy to housing. In 2009 it cost around £17 billion and by 2015 this had risen to around £24 billion (figures estimated from DWP, 2015b). The upward pressure on costs arose primarily from a rise in the numbers receiving the benefit. In December 2008 3.1 million social tenants and 1.1 million private tenants received Housing Benefit. In May 2015, around 3.3 million social tenants and 1.6 million private tenants received Housing Benefit

(DWP, 2015b). By the time the coalition came to office, Housing Benefit expenditure represented around 10% of spending on social protection and 3% of total government spending (Stephens and Whitehead, 2014). Overall costs rose by more than half in the private rented sector and just under one third in the social sector. However, average payments per claim rose by more than one fifth in the social rented sector, but only 5% in the private sector.

The latter statistic reflects the reforms introduced by the coalition in an attempt to contain the rising cost of Housing Benefit. The maximum rent on which Housing Benefit is calculated was reduced from the median local rent to the 30th per centile in April 2011. Thereafter, it was increased only by the CPI. Other reforms to Housing Benefit included a cap on the number of bedrooms on which the eligible rent would be based (a separate measure from the 'spare room subsidy'), a progressive increase in non-dependant deductions (in effect the contribution to rent that is assumed to be paid by adult relatives living in the same house as the claimant), and the extension of the 'shared accommodation rate' to single private tenants between the ages of 25 and 35. Meanwhile, an overall limit on benefits (to £26,000) affected mostly large families living in London.

The most controversial reform was the introduction in a reduction in the 'spare room subsidy': social tenants who had more than one spare room would have their HB cut by 14% and by 25% if they had two spare rooms. This 'bedroom tax' was perceived to be unfair by many tenants because the shortage of smaller properties meant that they were unable to trade down to avoid the penalty. Introduced in April 2013, this measure affects some 457,000 households and leads to an average reduction in their benefit of some £15.24 per week (DWP, 2015b).

Further cuts in Housing Benefit were announced in the post-election budget of 2015. The maximum rate of Housing Benefit for private tenants will be frozen for four years as part of the policy of a wider freeze on working age benefits. The family premium will be removed from Housing Benefit (along with family elements in tax credits) from April 2016, and the overall benefits cap (which is implemented by reducing HB) is being reduced to £20,000 (£23,000 in London). The government has also indicated that it will end the 'automatic entitlement' to Housing Benefit for out-of-work 18–21-year-olds (see Stephens and Blenkinsopp, 2015).

In the Comprehensive Spending Review, the government announced that the rent restrictions that apply to Housing Benefit in the private rented sector will be extended to social tenants. Thus, eligible rents will be set in relation to median market rents, which may affect tenants in lower value areas where social rents may fall outside these limits. More significant is the extension of the Shared Accommodation Rate to single social tenants aged under 35. The people affected by this are likely to include single homeless people in Scotland who are currently protected by the statutory homelessness system (see above).

While reforms have been mitigated to some extent by the use of Discretionary Housing Payments, it is not clear how long such protection will be offered. By basing fewer claims on actual rents, these reforms severely undermine the 'safety net' function that was an integral part of the design of the current Housing Benefit system when it was introduced in 1988. Since mainstream social security benefits make no allowance for housing costs, Housing Benefit allowed for the payment of all of the rent to prevent post-rent incomes falling below basic benefit rates. The same principle underpinned the function whereby if rents rose by £1, then so did Housing Benefit (and vice versa).

It is notable that the cuts to Housing Benefit do not apply to pensioners. Some deviation from the general policies has been apparent in Northern Ireland and Scotland. Social security is legally separate in Northern Ireland, although the practice has been to copy the system applied to the rest of Great Britain under the 'parity principle'. However, the coalition's welfare reforms were first delayed by two years and then voted down by the Northern Ireland Assembly, with the result that the Executive is effectively being 'fined' by the Treasury (Young and McHugh, 2015). The UK government indicated that it would legislate directly if the Northern Ireland parties were unable to agree to introduce the reforms (BBC, 2015b).

In Scotland, the government has fully mitigated the 'bedroom tax.' Moreover, it will be in a position to provide further protection as a result of the Scotland Bill. This was introduced following commitments given during the closing weeks of the referendum on Scottish independence. After the vote to remain in the union, the UK government established a cross-party ('Smith') commission to agree which additional powers should be devolved to Scotland. The subsequent Bill suggests that the Scottish government would be able to vary the eligible rent in the housing cost element within Universal Credit, which will gradually replace Housing Benefit for the working-age population. This would permit the definitive abolition of the bedroom tax, and indeed allow most of the reforms introduced in the 2010–15 parliament to be reversed. However, it would not allow any variation in tapers. In many ways the proposals 'appear reactive and backward looking. They would not permit further redesign of Housing Benefit, even within the constraints of the wider social security system' (Stephens et al, 2015: 21).

Private renting

Private renting increasingly plays a mainstream role in the UK housing system, particularly as more people have been priced out of home ownership. It is regarded by many as being unsatisfactory as it is insecure and rents are not controlled.

The growth in the private rented sector, principally at the cost of home ownership, represents a dramatic change. There are now more private renters than social renters, as the tenure has grown in every age group other than the over 65s (Table 4.1). The revival of private renting dates back to its deregulation in 1989, when new tenancies became subject to market rents and landlords could use short-term 'assured shorthold' tenancies, lasting a minimum of six months. Once a tenancy ends, landlords are able to gain possession of their properties without needing to give a reason – so-called 'no fault' evictions. These insecure tenancies have attracted more attention as private renting has grown and diversified, so that many more people with children live in it. Figure 4.2 shows that there has been a modest rise in possession claims from private landlords since the late 1990s. However, the true picture is difficult to assess because there has been a marked rise in 'accelerated' claims, which are used when tenancies are nearing their end. The statistics for these claims do not distinguish between social and private landlords.

There is a widespread perception that rents have risen rapidly. Certainly in London, nominal rents in June 2015 were nearly 18% higher than in January 2011, but the figures for England outside London (6.6%), Wales (3.3%) and Scotland (7%) are more modest (ONS, 2015a), and indeed below the rate of consumer price index, which grew by 9.2% over the same period (ONS, 2015b: Table 22a).

However, with more people being exposed to market rents and insecure tenancies, the consensus in favour of the current regime is weakening. The Labour Party, which had been happy to leave it unchanged during its long period in office, pledged in its 2015 manifesto to 'create a fairer private rented sector, so that in future, renting is a more secure long term option for families and individuals who cannot or prefer not to buy. We will legislate for rights to longer term lets, with predictable rents, to provide affordability, stability and security' (Labour Party, 2015: 33).

Figure 4.2: Landlord possession claims (England and Wales, 1999–2014)

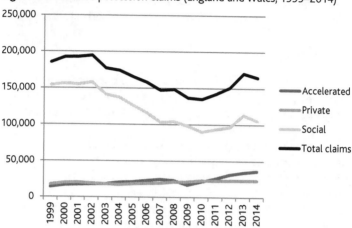

Source: Ministry of Justice (2015), Table 5

There seems little prospect of an early change in England given the outcome of the election, with the possible exception of London where price pressures are strongest and there exists electoral competition over the post of Mayor. In marked contrast, the Scottish government published, after a lengthy period of consultation, a new bill in October 2015 to introduce 'a new private residential tenancy for the private rented sector which will improve security of tenure for tenants and provide appropriate safeguards for landlords, lenders and investors' (Scottish Government, 2015b: 2).

In principle, the legislation will end 'no fault' evictions, but there remain grounds for possession, which include an intent to refurbish or sell the property. It also gives Ministers powers to impose caps on rent increases in 'rent pressure zones' bringing with it the prospect of the selective use of so-called 'second generation' rent controls.

Meanwhile, the Chancellor announced in his post-election budget that the tax relief that private landlords can claim against their mortgage interest payments will be reduced to the basic rate of tax over four years from 2017, arguing:

> The current tax system supports landlords over and above ordinary homeowners. Landlords can deduct costs they incur when calculating the tax they pay on their rental income. A large portion of those costs are interest payments on the mortgage. Mortgage Interest Relief was withdrawn from homeowners 15 years ago.

However, landlords still receive the relief. The ability to deduct these costs puts investing in a rental property at an advantage. (HM Treasury, 2015: para. 1.190).

However, as the Director of the Institute for Fiscal Studies observed, 'This line of argument is plain wrong. Rental property is taxed more heavily than owner occupied property' (Johnson, 2015: 4). While it is true that owner-occupiers no longer receive tax relief on mortgage interest payments, they pay no tax on imputed rental income. Moreover, they do not pay tax on capital gains, whereas landlords do. Landlords do, nonetheless, enjoy an advantage over (would-be) home-owners in the regulation of the mortgage market: unlike homeowners, landlords are not subject to an affordability assessment based on a repayment mortgage. If the Chancellor is concerned about a level playing field, an alternative approach would be to remove this anomaly, rather than creating another one.

Conclusion

The cumulative effect of five years of Coalition policies are changing the nature of the housing system, and these changes will be reinforced by the policies being introduced by the new majority Conservative government.

The social rented sector has been undermined by the Affordable Rents model, the shift in subsidy to Starter Homes, the extension of Right to Buy, and by the new proposals to end security of tenure for new tenants.

The statutory homelessness system in England has already been undermined by allowing local authorities to discharge their obligations by rehousing people in private rented accommodation. The extension of the Shared Accommodation Rate to the social sector is likely to undermine the more generous homelessness system in Scotland, which extends full protection to all non-intentionally homeless single people.

Cuts to Housing Benefit have already undermined the ability of the system to prevent rents taking people into deep poverty.

While social protection has been much reduced for low income households, policy now unashamedly favours home ownership. While tenants have their Housing Benefit limited, and new social tenants face losing security of tenure, better-off housing association tenants are being offered very substantial subsidies to buy their houses. What income limits that applied to some of the home ownership schemes (such as shared ownership) have been removed. The government will now advance an equity loan for 40% of the cost of buying a home in London, but low income tenants aged up to 35 are expected to live in a bedsit or shared house.

These examples illustrate that the UK government's housing policy has moved beyond austerity, to one that distributes away from people on low incomes.

References

Bank of England (n.d.) 'Quantitative Easing Frequently Asked Questions', http://www.bankofengland.co.uk/monetarypolicy/Documents/print/qe-faqs.pdf

Bank of England/Financial Conduct Authority (2015) 'Mortgage Lenders and Administrators Statistics (MLAS)', September, http://www.bankofengland.co.uk/pra/Pages/regulatorydata/mlar/2015/jun.aspx

BBC (2015a) 'One in three councils "not replacing Right to Buy homes"', 20 September, http://www.bbc.co.uk/news/uk-34305969

BBC (2015b) 'Welfare reform: Westminster may legislate directly as last resort', 5 September, http://www.bbc.co.uk/news/uk-northern-ireland-34164806

Carney, M. (2014) 'Letter from Mark Carney (Governor of the Bank of England) to the Rt Hon George Osborne MP (Chancellor of the Exchequer)', 2 October, http://www.bankofengland.co.uk/financialstability/Documents/fpc/letters/governorletter141002.pdf

DCLG Live Tables, https://www.gov.uk/government/organisations/department-for-communities-and-local-government/about/statistics

DCLG (2010) 'Local decisions: a fairer future for social housing, Consultation', London: DCLG, https://www.gov.uk/government/uploads/system/uploads/attachment_data/file/8512/1775577.pdf

DCLG (2011) 'A plain English guide to the Localism Act', London: DCLG, https://www.gov.uk/government/uploads/system/uploads/attachment_data/file/5959/1896534.pdf

DCLG (2015a) 'CORE summary tables: 2014 to 2015', London: DCLG, https://www.gov.uk/government/uploads/system/uploads/attachment_data/file/465819/CORE_Summary_Tables_2014-15.xlsx

DCLG (2015b) 'Homelessness statistics', London: DCLG, https://www.gov.uk/government/statistical-data-sets/live-tables-on-homelessness

DCLG (2015c) 'Social housing lettings April 2014 to March 2015, England', London: DCLG, https://www.gov.uk/government/uploads/system/uploads/attachment_data/file/465815/Social_housing_lettings_in_England_2014-15.pdf

DWP (2015a) 'Family resources survey 2013/14', London: DWP, https://www.gov.uk/government/uploads/system/uploads/attachment_data/file/437481/family-resources-survey-2013-14.pdf

DWP (2015b) 'Housing benefit caseload statistics: data to May 2015', London: DWP, https://www.gov.uk/government/statistics/housing-benefit-caseload-statistics

Douglas, D. (2015) 'Councils out-of-area placements breaking the law', *Inside Housing*, 23 April, http://m.insidehousing.co.uk/councils-out-of-area-placements-breaking-the-law/7009398.article

Financial Services Authority (2009) 'Mortgage market review: responsible lending', London: FSA, http://www.fsa.gov.uk/pubs/cp/cp10_16.pdf

Fitzpatrick, S., Bramley, G., Pawson, H., Wilcox, S. and Watts, B. (2015a) 'The homeless monitor: England 2015', London: Crisis, http://www.crisis.org.uk/data/files/publications/Homelessness_Monitor_England_2015_final_web.pdf

Fitzpatrick, S., Bramley, G., Pawson, H., Wilcox, S. and Watts, B. (2015b) 'The homeless monitor: Scotland 2015', London: Crisis, http://www.crisis.org.uk/data/files/publications/HomelessnessMonitorScotland_FINAL.pdf

Fitzpatrick, S., Bramley, G., Pawson, H., Wilcox, S. and Watts, B. (2015c) 'The homeless monitor: Wales 2015', London: Crisis, http://www.crisis.org.uk/data/files/publications/HomelessnessMonitorWales2015_final.pdf

Fitzpatrick, S., Quilgars, D. and Pleace, N. (eds) (2009) 'Homelessness in the UK: problems and solutions', Coventry: Chartered Institute of Housing.

Future Homes Commission (2012) 'Building the homes and communities Britain needs', London: Royal Institute of British Architects, https://www.architecture.com/Files/RIBATrust/FutureHomesCommissionLowRes.pdf

HM Government (2011) 'Laying the foundations. A housing strategy for England', London: DCLG, https://www.gov.uk/government/uploads/system/uploads/attachment_data/file/7532/2033676.pdf

HM Treasury (2015) 'Summer Budget 2015', HC 264, London: HMSO, https://www.gov.uk/government/uploads/system/uploads/attachment_data/file/443232/50325_Summer_Budget_15_Web_Accessible.pdf

Holmans, A. (2013) 'New estimates of housing demand and need in England, 2011 to 2031: Town and Country Planning: Tomorrow Series Paper 16', London: Town and Country Planning Association, http://www.cchpr.landecon.cam.ac.uk/Downloads/HousingDemandNeed_TCPA2013.pdf

House of Commons (2015) 'Housing and Planning Bill Explanatory Notes', London: TSO, http://www.publications.parliament.uk/pa/bills/cbill/2015-2016/0075/en/16075en.pdf

Johnson, P. (2015) 'Paul Johnson's opening remarks, Institute for Fiscal Studies Summer Post Budget Briefing 2105 [sic]', http://www.ifs.org.uk/uploads/publications/budgets/Budgets%202015/Summer/opening_remarks.pdf

Labour Party (2015) 'Changing Britain Together', http://action.labour.org.uk/page/-/Changing_Britain_Together.pdf

Ministry of Justice (2015) 'Mortgage and Landlord Statistical Tables April-June 2015', London: MoJ, https://www.gov.uk/government/statistics/mortgage-and-landlord-possession-statistics-april-to-june-2015

ONS (2014) 'Comparison of regional house price indices before and after the financial crisis', July, http://www.ons.gov.uk/ons/rel/hpi/house-price-index/april-2014/info-hpi-comparison.html

ONS (2015a) 'Index of Private Rental Housing Prices, Reference Tables', June, http://www.ons.gov.uk/ons/publications/re-reference-tables.html?edition=tcm%3A77-397831

ONS (2015b) 'Consumer price inflation reference tables', September, http://www.ons.gov.uk/ons/publications/re-reference-tables.html?edition=tcm%3A77-323657

Savills (2015) 'The potential impact of Government housing policy – Right to Buy', Local Government Association, unpublished.

Scottish Government (2015a) 'Operation of the Homeless Person Legislation, 2014-15', Edinburgh: Scottish Government, http://www.gov.scot/Resource/0048/00480524.pdf

Scottish Government (2015b) 'Private Housing (Tenancies) (Scotland) Bill. Policy Memorandum', Edinburgh: Scottish Government, http://www.scottish.parliament.uk/parliamentarybusiness/Bills/92310.aspx

Slawson, N. (2015) 'Profit or purpose? The fight over the future of social housing in Britain', 14 August, http://www.theguardian.com/housing-network/2015/aug/14/social-housing-britain-future-profit-purpose-genesis

Stephens, M. (2013) 'Social housing in the United Kingdom', in J. Chen, M. Stephens and Y. Man (eds) *The future of public housing: Ongoing trends in the east and the west*, Heidelberg: Springer, pp 199–213.

Stephens, M. and Blenkinsopp, J. (2015) 'Young people and social security: an international review', York: Joseph Rowntree Foundation, https://www.jrf.org.uk/report/young-people-and-social-security-international-review

Stephens, M., Gibb, K. and Blenkinsopp, J. (2015) 'The devolution of housing benefit and social security: rebalancing housing subsidies in Scotland', Edinburgh: Shelter Scotland, http://scotland.shelter.org.uk/__data/assets/pdf_file/0004/1096645/The_Devolution_of_Housing_Benefit_and_Social_Security_-_March_2015.pdf

Stephens, M. and Whitehead, C. (2014) 'Rental housing policy in England: post crisis adjustment or long term trend?', *Journal of Housing and the Built Environment*, 29(2): 201–20.

Twinch, E. (2015) 'Welsh Government slashes right to buy discount', *Inside Housing*, 3 June, http://www.insidehousing.co.uk/welsh-government-slashes-right-to-buy-discount/7010065.article

Wilcox, S., Perry, J. and Williams, P. (2015) 'UK housing review 2015 briefing paper', Coventry: Chartered Institute of Housing.

Wilson, W. (2015) 'Allocating social housing (England)', House of Commons Library Standard Note SN/SP/63, http://researchbriefings.files.parliament.uk/documents/SN06397/SN06397.pdf

Young, D. and McHugh, M. (2015) 'Stormont votes down welfare reform bill', *Belfast Telegraph*, 26 May, http://www.belfasttelegraph.co.uk/news/northern-ireland/stormont-votes-down-welfare-reform-bill-31253937.html

Part Two
Contributions from the Social Policy Association Conference 2015

John Hudson

Traditionally, Part Two of *Social policy review* draws together a selection of papers from the Social Policy Association's Annual Conference. The 2015 conference, hosted by the University of Ulster, addressed a wide range of issues under its umbrella theme 'Social Policy in the Spotlight: Change, Continuity and Challenge'.

Capturing the mood of the conference is a challenging task to the say least. But, as the conference organisers observed in their programme notes, the social policy implications of the outcome of the 2015 UK General Election was a major issue facing delegates. Indeed, the final day of the conference coincided with the new government's first budget, during which details of the £12 billion of 'welfare' cuts promised during the election campaign were outlined. The four chapters in Section Two offer insights into what this agenda might hold and how scholars might best interrogate it.

In Chapter Five, Robert Page explores the development of a 'progressive neo-liberal conservative' narrative under David Cameron's leadership. As he shows, in shifting the Conservative Party's narrative to embrace key social justice agendas from a non-egalitarian and more individualist perspective, Cameron has not only allowed the Conservatives to present themselves as being sympathetic to progressive ends but also to move the terms of debate to the efficacy of Labour's (more statist) means.

Ruth Patrick picks up many of these themes in Chapter Six. Her interviews with out-of-work benefit claimants found many were angered by the impacts of Cameron's welfare reforms on their own lives but nonetheless were supportive of the government's broad agenda. She suggests that this underlines the depth of a 'new moral consensus on welfare' that problematises out-of-work benefits and those who claim them. In such an environment, 'it is very difficult for individual claimants to make a positive case for "welfare" in general terms', which, in turn, helps further embed the Conservatives' welfare reform narrative.

In Chapter Seven, Stephen Crossley analyses the Troubled Families Programme. He shows the reality of the programme is rather different from the runaway success story presented by government, positive outcomes often owing 'much to local officers' negotiation and subversion of the programme'. Discretion built into the programme has allowed subversion and resistance to occur, but, as Crossley notes, 'these transgressions […] occur under the radar and do little to trouble the national narrative of an assertive central government policy working successfully with troublesome families'. This is significant given it is seen by the Conservatives as a key example of how a smaller, smarter state might function.

Resistance and transgression are also key themes in Chapter Eight, in which Hannah Jobling examines Community Treatment Orders (CTOs). She argues that 'individuals' conceptions of self in relation to disciplinary policy interventions can lead to complex, ambiguous and perhaps unexpected responses to compulsion, which are not easily categorised into binary forms of compliance and resistance'. Indeed, as she suggests, her analysis of CTOs underlines the value of a governmentality perspective that eschews simple linear understandings of how 'target' groups will respond to policy interventions.

FIVE

'Progressive' neo-liberal conservatism and the welfare state: incremental reform or long-term destruction?

Robert M. Page

Grandma's footsteps is a traditional children's game in which one player, acting as the main protagonist, faces the wall at one end of a room while fellow participants line up behind, a short distance away. The aim of the game is to displace Grandma by creeping up on her unseen and tapping her on the back. Grandma is, however, permitted to turn around at any time and if she spots a participant moving she can point at them and order them to return to their original starting position. Since the mid-1970s the Conservative Party could be said to have been engaged in a long-running game of Grandma's footsteps with the 'classic' welfare state (see Lowe, 2005). Instead of attacking 'Nanny' with a swift blow to the neck, a remedy favoured by many on the neo-liberal right of the party, a step-by-step 'reform' strategy has been pursued. It remains an open question as to whether the aim of these reforms has been to bring about the gradual demise of the welfare state or whether the underlying purpose has been simply to create a leaner, more effective institution.

This chapter will explore the approach of the modern Conservatives towards the welfare state since David Cameron became party leader in 2005. Are these contemporary Conservatives engaged in what they describe as a much-needed modernisation of the welfare state or might they be pursuing a longer-term dismantling strategy?

During the 'path breaking' Thatcher (1979–90) and 'consolidating' Major (1990–96) eras, the Conservative Party abandoned its apparent rapprochement with the 'social democratic' post-war welfare state. This change of approach was deemed necessary to bring the escalating cost of the welfare state under control and to provide citizens with an escape route from what were seen as 'stifling' forms of state dependency. Despite calls for the rapid demolition of the welfare state from some diehard elements within the party, a more measured incremental reform programme was undertaken by both these administrations, not least because of growing public anxiety about the pace and scale of change. Although the infrastructure of the welfare state was not dismantled by the time the Conservatives left office in 1997, there were signs that a cultural 'revolution' was starting to take hold whereby public attachment to this institution was increasingly based on individualistic and consumerist considerations rather than egalitarian or solidaristic sentiments (see Park et al, 2012; 2014).

The Conservatives and the Welfare State: the progressive turn from Hague to Cameron

Following the Conservatives' heavy defeat in the 1997 general election, the new leader, William Hague (June 1997–September 2001), recognised that the party needed to address the toxic 'social' legacies of both the Thatcher and Major eras. To overcome this problem, Hague embraced the compassionate Conservatism agenda, which was being pursued by the Republican Party in the United States (see Olasky, 2000; Montgomerie, 2004). This was not intended to demonstrate the party's acceptance of the statist 'social democratic' agenda, which had been influential for much of the post-1945 period in the UK. Instead, the aim was to acknowledge that there was a legitimate role for state action albeit of a different kind. The task of the state would now be to channel public funds to non-state private and third sector providers, who were considered to be best placed to develop the independence building skills which would help disadvantaged citizens avoid lengthy periods of state dependency. By the time of the 2001 general election, though, Hague had abandoned his flirtation with this strand of Conservative thinking and had reverted to a more conventional neo-liberal economic and social agenda. The party's general election manifesto, *Time for Common Sense* (Conservative Party, 2001), promised, for example, lower taxes for 'hardworking families', more economic deregulation and tighter control of public spending. In the case of social policy, there was a renewed focus on individual responsibility and further curbs on benefit dependency. More stringent rules were proposed for working age claimants. Benefits were to be withdrawn from unemployed claimants who refused to work under a so-called 'can work, must work guarantee' (Conservative Party, 2001: 34). Although Hague had hoped to restore his party's fortunes by the time of the 2001 general election, his ambitions were thwarted. On a historically low turnout (59.4%), New Labour returned to government for a second term. The Conservatives 'gained' just one seat and secured a minor increase in their share of the popular vote (31.7%).

Hague's successor, Iain Duncan Smith (September 2001–November 2003), sought to revive the compassionate Conservative agenda that his predecessor had initially embraced. Duncan Smith was adamant that the party needed to adopt a more sympathetic and supportive approach towards disadvantaged groups in society. While acknowledging that the Thatcher governments had been successful in delivering economic prosperity, Duncan Smith believed that social regeneration was now the pressing task for contemporary Conservatism, not least because of New Labour's failure to tackle what he deemed to be the five contemporary 'giants' that threatened British society – rising crime, inadequate healthcare, failing schools, child poverty and growing state dependency. Although Duncan Smith was instrumental in persuading the public to recognise that the modern Conservatives were interested in issues other than Europe, immigration and low taxation, his compassionate Conservative message lacked resonance not least because of his own perceived lack of charisma. After failing to improve the party's political standing the 'quiet man's' tenure as Conservative leader ended after just two years (see Hayton, 2012).

In 'selecting' Michael Howard, another deep blue neo-liberal Conservative, to succeed Duncan Smith, it seemed unlikely that the party would press ahead with the compassionate agenda that some MPs, and influential think tanks such as Policy Exchange, deemed necessary if the party's electoral fortunes were to be restored. Contrary to expectations, though, Howard sought to develop a more 'moderate' line on social and moral issues, by permitting, for instance, free votes on New Labour's Civil Partnership legislation and on the Gender Recognition Bill, which granted transsexuals enhanced legal protection. While this strategy proved controversial within party circles, it did help to convey the impression that the Conservatives were intent on challenging the assumption that they were simply a party of 'reaction'.

In terms of the welfare state, though, Howard showed little inclination to move away from neo-liberal Conservative orthodoxies. He rejected the need for more egalitarian social measures, confining himself to a focus on removing opportunity barriers and targeting assistance on those deemed to be in genuine need. His so-called 'British Dream' was one in which all citizens would be able to succeed through hard work and innate talent and where greater individual choice could be exercised in areas such as healthcare and schooling. Howard was insistent, though, that the Conservatives should be seen as a party that was committed to reforming, not dismantling the welfare state. Indeed, the party's prospective parliamentary candidate for Sedgefield, Danny Kruger, was forced to stand down after suggesting that that the Conservatives were intent on presiding over the 'creative destruction' of the welfare state (see Snowden, 2010).

The policies contained in the Conservatives' 2005 general election manifesto – *Are you thinking what we're thinking? It's time for action* (Conservative Party, 2005) – in relation to the welfare state were of a similar ilk to those proposed by Hague and Duncan Smith, in which the aim was to improve its performance rather than weaken its influence. To this end, the party pledged to match Labour's spending on services such as the NHS and schools, while simultaneously eliminating waste. In terms of education reform, school heads and governors were promised greater powers over admissions and expulsions. The National Curriculum was to be slimmed down and university tuition fees were to be abolished. In the case of the NHS, the reform agenda involved paring back Primary Care Trusts and assorted 'quangos, inspectorates and commissions' and the abolition of Strategic Health Authorities. Despite growing voter antipathy towards New Labour over issues such as the Iraq war and tuition fees, Howard proved unable to prevent a third consecutive electoral defeat for the Conservative Party (see Bale, 2010).

The emergence of progressive neo-liberal conservatism (PNLC)

The election of David Cameron as leader of the Conservative Party in October 2005 represented the decisive turn in the party's modernising approach. Taking a leaf out of the New Labour playbook, Cameron sought to jettison some of the damaging ideological 'baggage' associated with the Thatcher and Major eras. By adopting a progressive neo-liberal Conservative (PNLC) narrative, which stressed the positive virtues of change, Cameron sought to persuade the electorate that his party was now firmly committed to modern, forward looking economic and social policies. The embrace of this 'distinctive' stream of Conservative thought was not seen as necessitating any major overhaul of the party's long-standing commitment to the neo-liberal economic agenda, which had been pursued during both the Thatcher (1979–90) and Major (1990–97) eras. Cameron and his fellow PNLC acolytes such as Osborne and Gove remained supportive of the neo-liberal rationales for free market activity and light economic regulation (Cameron, 2009). Their continued commitment to neo-liberal economic thinking contained few political risks not least because of New Labour's conversion to this doctrine under both Blair and Brown (see Hay, 1999; Faucher-King and Le Gales, 2010; Steadman-Jones, 2012).

It was in the broad area of social policy that the PNLCs sought to mark out a territory that differed from the tenets of both neo-liberal and the overly 'statist' One-nation Conservative tradition of the 1950s and 1960s (see Seawright, 2005; Page 2015; Williams, 2015). Cameron believed that there were inherent flaws with the traditional neo-liberal Conservative approach to social issues, which had resulted in the public viewing the party as holding old-fashioned views about minority groups (see McManus, 2010; Brooke, 2011) and a barely concealed hostility towards those experiencing poverty and disadvantage. The intensity of the party's anti-state rhetoric had also resulted in key sections of the electorate harbouring fears that cherished institutions such as the NHS were no longer safe in Conservative hands.

After a lengthy gestation period, the 'distinguishing' features of Cameron's PNLC approach to social issues have become clear. First, there is a firm commitment to social liberalism, which involves the adoption of less judgemental attitudes towards those who choose alternative, albeit 'stable', lifestyles such as lone mothers or gay couples. Second, PNLCs have modified their party's approach to the state, social justice and poverty (see Hickson, 2008; Williams, 2015; Page, 2015). In terms of the state, this involves a reversion to support for the judicious forms of collective interventionism, favoured by former leaders such as Disraeli and Baldwin, which are designed to enhance the common good. Unlike luminaries such as Hayek (1944) and Powell (1969), PNLCs also believe that the pursuit of a non-egalitarian form of social justice is a legitimate aim for those on the progressive right, particularly if the painful social consequences of the 'regenerative' neo-liberal economic reforms of the Thatcher era are to be addressed (see Bercow, 2002; D'Ancona, 2012). While the removal of opportunity barriers and the promotion of social mobility are seen as an integral part of this process, it is not deemed necessary to narrow the gap between the rich and the poor nor to adhere to the 'bounded' form of equality favoured by One-nation Conservatives (see Dorey, 2011). With regard to poverty, PNLCs accept that this phenomenon should be regarded as a relative rather than absolute concept (see Hickson, 2008). However, this is not seen as necessitating the embrace of New Labour's 'outmoded' approach to poverty, which was seen as narrow and mechanistic with an undue focus on halving the number of children living in households below

60% of median incomes. Instead, a more holistic anti-poverty strategy
was to be devised based on non-financial as well as financial factors.

Third, as with all strands of conservatism, PNLCs emphasise the
importance of individual responsibility. As Cameron made clear in a
speech at the Sandwell Christian Centre in Oldbury in December 2011,
'my mission in politics – the thing I am really passionate about – is
fixing the responsibility deficit. That means building a stronger society,
in which more people understand their obligations, and [take] more
control over their own lives and actions'. The emphasis given to the
creation of a participative 'Big Society' was intended to distinguish the
PNLC vision of conservatism from the highly individualistic form of
neo-liberalism that had characterised the Thatcher years (see Cameron,
2009; Blond, 2010; Norman, 2010). It was envisaged that citizens would
take on greater responsibility for tackling pressing issues in their local
community rather than relying on the state. Government would lend its
support to such endeavour by liberalising obstructive planning laws and
providing information and guidance to local communities who were
seeking, for example, to take over the running of parks, libraries and other
valued amenities (see Ishkanian and Szreter, 2012). Fourth, and linked
to the notion of individual responsibility, PNLCs acknowledge that the
state will continue to have a role to play in contemporary society but
that this should be restricted where possible to an enabling and funding,
rather than provider, function (Letwin, 2002).

The long-term aim of the PNLCs is to create a society that is
characterised by social stability and an absence of opportunity barriers.
Although significant material inequalities will persist, reflecting variations
in both talent and endeavour, these differential rewards will, it is believed,
be seen by the majority of the public as legitimate and fair. A PNLC
society will also be one in which citizens act responsibly and with
consideration towards others and accept their obligations to pay fair
taxes and participate fully in their local community.

The PNLCs are keen to ensure that their desire to refashion the role
of the state is not equated with a doctrinaire anti-collectivist mindset.
This was reflected in their self-stated 'unashamedly progressive' election
manifesto of 2010 (Conservative Party, 2010: p ix). While accepting that
state action had resulted in many positive outcomes in the immediate
post-1945 era, it was contended that government intervention had
'reached a point where it is now inhibiting, not advancing, the progressive
aims of reducing poverty, fighting inequality, and increasing general wellbeing' (Conservative Party, 2010: 37). To counter this 'negative' trend,
citizens were invited to 'join the government of Britain'. By so doing

they could help build a nation 'with much higher levels of personal, professional, civic and corporate responsibility; a society where people come together to solve problems and improve life for themselves and their communities; a society where the leading force for progress is social responsibility, not state control.' (Conservative Party, 2010: 37).

What 'progressive' reforms of the welfare state were outlined in the manifesto? In education the expressed aim was to give many more children the kind of education that is currently 'only available to the well off' (Conservative Party, 2010: 51).This was to be achieved by enhancing the status of teaching, more rigorous exams, a challenging curriculum, well-targeted inspections, an increased number of autonomous academy and free schools and additional resources (a pupil premium) for schools which were able to recruit students from disadvantaged backgrounds. In the case of healthcare, the Conservatives declared themselves to be 'the party of the NHS' (Conservative Party, 2010: 45), who 'will never change the idea at its heart – that healthcare in this country is free at the point of use and available to everyone based on need, not ability to pay' (Conservative Party, 2010: 51). Real terms increases in health spending were promised as well as a range of reforms, which would enhance patient choice (including more non-NHS providers) and greater autonomy for clinicians in relation to decision making and commissioning.

In the field of social security, the 'progressive' manifesto promised to protect pensioner benefits and 're-link the basic pension state pension to earnings' (Conservative Party, 2010: 42), maintain tax credits for families and reduce 'welfare' dependency. As part of a 'firm but fair' approach to working age adult claimants, a work programme, delivered by private and voluntary sector providers, was to be introduced which would also embrace recipients of Incapacity Benefit. In housing, the long-term Conservative aim of 'creating a property-owning democracy' (see Torrance, 2010) was to be pursued by reductions in stamp duty for first-time buyers and part-ownership schemes for 'social tenants'.

The 2010 party manifesto also confirmed the shift in Conservative economic thinking following the economic crisis of 2008.The pre-crash commitment to match the then government's expenditure plans was withdrawn on the grounds that profligate spending by New Labour was now considered to be the prime cause of the economic downturn (Dorey, 2009). It was concluded that the key task for any incoming government was to eliminate 'the bulk of the structural current budget deficit' over the course of the next parliament (Conservative Party, 2010: 7).

Progressive neo-liberal conservatism and the welfare state in practice 2010–15

The formation of the Conservative-led coalition government following the inconclusive general election of 1 May 2010 raised questions as to whether the PNLCs would be able to implement their progressive policy agenda. Might there be significant ideological and policy differences between the two governing parties? The fact that the two coalition leaders (Cameron and Clegg) 'had spent the period before the 2010 election trying to cajole their parties towards ideological positions which, if not identical, were at least closely compatible' (Dorey et al, 2011: 185) made this unlikely. As a consequence, the governing agreement did not require the Conservatives to jettison any of the key elements of their social agenda (see Dorey et al, 2011: 185). With a shared 'conviction that the days of big government are over; that centralisation and top-down control have proved a failure' (Cabinet Office, 2010: 7), the coalition partners agreed to 'a sweeping reform of welfare, taxes, schooling and a breaking open of the state monopoly' (Cabinet Office, 2010: 7).

Key aspects of the PNLC reform of the welfare state contained in their 2010 manifesto were implemented following the establishment of the Conservative-led coalition government. In education, the new Secretary of State, Michael Gove (May 2010–July 2014), pressed ahead with the creation of a more challenging state-funded school system, which would enhance educational standards and increase social mobility in an effort to overturn what he regarded as Labour's long-standing, anti-aspirational, uniform approach to education (see Gove, 2013). Appealing to the supposedly consumerist mindset of contemporary parents, Gove oversaw an increase in the number of Academy and Free Schools. Pupils were encouraged to study 'traditional' subjects and be subjected to more exacting forms of assessment. The schools inspection system was also strengthened to counter the possibility of a 'coasting' mindset taking hold among educational providers. To underline the progressive nature of the reform agenda, Pupil Premiums, which had been highlighted in the manifesto, were introduced in the hope that high-performing state-funded schools would offer places to students from low-income families, thereby bolstering the possibility of enhanced forms of social mobility.

In social security, the progressive reform agenda outlined in the manifesto was implemented. Existing pensioner benefits such as free TV licences and winter fuel payments were protected and a simplified single-tier retirement pension was to be introduced from 2016, based on a 'triple lock' uprating mechanism designed to ensure that the benefits would be uprated by no less than 2.5% per annum. For working-age claimants, the introduction of a fairer, more demanding, income support system was deemed necessary if long-term benefit dependency was to be avoided. On grounds of 'fairness', this claimant group were expected to make a proportionate contribution to the government's 'austerity' programme. A benefit cap of £500 per week for all claimant couples was introduced in April 2013, while the annual uprating of non-pensioner benefits was restricted to 1% per annum for the following three years. In addition, claimants deemed to be living in 'under-occupied' accommodation were required to make higher contributions towards their housing costs (the so-called 'bedroom' tax). The passage of the Welfare Reform Act in 2012 paved the way for the phased introduction of Universal Credit, which was designed to smooth the transition from welfare to work by phasing out benefits such as Income Support, income-based Jobseeker's Allowance, income-related Employment and Support Allowance, Housing Benefit, Child Tax Credits and Working Tax Credits (DWP, 2010).

In a concerted effort to demonstrate the equitable nature of their social security strategy, the coalition withdrew Child Benefit from families with one higher-rate taxpayer in 2013 and froze the level of these payments for a further three years with effect from 2014. Child Tax Credits were also withdrawn from families whose annual incomes exceeded £26,000 a year.

PNLC support for the NHS did not dissuade them from putting forward plans to improve its effectiveness and responsiveness. Although the coalition agreement appeared to have ruled out further 'top-down reorganisations of the NHS that have got in the way of patient care' (Cabinet Office, 2010: 24), a transformative White Paper, *Equity and excellence: Liberating the NHS*, was introduced by the new Health Secretary, Andrew Lansley, just two months after the formation of the coalition government. It aimed to move away from New Labour's 'remote', target-driven, centralised control of the service. Primary Care Trusts and Strategic Health Authorities were to be abolished, GP groups were to be given budgetary responsibilities to commission health services and the remit of Monitor (the independent regulator of Foundation Trusts) was extended to include economic oversight of 'access, competition and price-setting in the NHS' (Cabinet Office, 2010: 25). One of the key features of this modernising agenda was to increase competition within the NHS by allowing independent contractors to provide an increasing range of services. In practice, however, this only fuelled the suspicion that the Conservatives were intent on dismantling rather than modernising the NHS. Indeed, widespread disquiet about this measure led to some

2,000 amendments being tabled in both Houses of Parliament during the passage of Lansley's legislation (see Timmins, 2012).

Significantly, growing criticisms of some of the adverse impacts of coalition social policy, such as increased levels of dependency on food banks and indications that the costs of austerity were bearing down most heavily on the poorest groups in society, did not derail the modernising reform narrative of the PNLCs (see Cooper et al, 2014). This was confirmed in the party's 2015 general election manifesto (Conservative Party, 2015) in which core PNLC themes such as social liberalism, social justice, the Big Society, personal responsibility and welfare state reform were once again highlighted. In the case of social liberalism, for example, the manifesto promised to build on the 'historic' decision to introduce gay marriage by ensuring greater 'equality for Lesbian, Gay, Bisexual and Transgender people' (Conservative Party, 2015: 46). In terms of welfare state reform, a guaranteed right to 'mutualise within the public sector' (Conservative Party, 2015: 49) was promised as a way of freeing up the 'entrepreneurial spirit of public servants' thereby giving rise to 'better value for money for taxpayers' (Conservative Party, 2015: 49). In addition, payment-by-results initiatives were to be scaled up to encompass 'youth unemployment, mental health and homelessness' (Conservative Party, 2015: 46). The manifesto also promised to eliminate the deep-rooted causes of child poverty and to maintain support for working-age adults outside the labour market provided that they made a concerted effort to become self-sufficient and participated in training and work schemes. Significantly, though, as part of the party's continuing deficit reduction strategy, a further £12bn of 'welfare savings' was promised by 2020 (Conservative Party, 2015: 8).

Under pressure? Second term progressive neo-liberal conservatism and the welfare state

In his first post-election budget following the party's pollster-defying, outright electoral victory in June 2015, George Osborne fleshed out some of the measures the new government would introduce in furtherance of their progressive brand of Conservatism. These included the introduction of what was termed the National 'Living' Wage (which would see the minimum wage rise from £7.20 an hour in 2016 to £9 an hour by 2020), the abolition of permanent 'non-domiciled' tax status from 2017, a reduction in tax relief for buy-to-let landlords and higher earners' pension contributions as well as further measures to tackle tax evasion and aggressive forms of avoidance.

While it proved relatively easy for the Chancellor to defend some of his spending plans, such as a proposed real terms increase in NHS spending by 2020, on progressive grounds, some of his other initiatives proved more controversial, suggesting that a more 'destructive' approach towards the welfare state was being formulated. These included the freezing of working-age benefits for a further four years, the restriction of tax and Universal Credit payments to families with no more than two dependent children with effect from 2017 and the reduction in the benefit cap from £26,000 a year to £20,000 a year for those households living outside London (see Bartholomew, 2015). Other controversial measures of this kind included the withdrawal of maintenance grants from poorer university students and curbing the entitlements of newly eligible claimants of 'work related' Employment and Support Allowance so that they matched those claiming Jobseeker's Allowance.

The decision to reduce the entitlements of existing tax credit claimants by up to £1,000 per year (see Elming et al, 2015) proved particularly controversial. While Osborne had always been keen to limit the scope of these benefits, his apparent willingness to betray the 'strivers', whom he had previously championed for their willingness to work for modest rewards, led to a concerted public backlash. Following a successful opposition motion in the House of Lords calling on the government to provide transitional protection for existing tax credit recipients, the Chancellor agreed to reconsider this matter as part of his Autumn Statement in November 2015. He remained adamant, though, that he would not be swayed from his long-term aim of reducing public spending, arguing that it was no longer feasible for a nation which is 'home to 1 per cent of the world's population', and which generates '4 per cent of the world's income' to continue to pay out '7 per cent of the world's welfare spending'. As he maintained, 'the real welfare of the people' could only be secured by moving from 'a low wage, high tax, high welfare society to a higher wage, lower tax, lower welfare economy' (Osborne, 2015a. See also Osborne, 2015b and Osborne and Duncan Smith, 2015).

In the 2015 Autumn Statement, Osborne reiterated his party's 'progressive' credentials and its continued commitment to delivering social justice and the building of a fairer society. Buoyed by Office for Budget Responsibility forecasts of higher than anticipated tax revenues, Osborne was able, for example, to withdraw his £4.4bn tax credits cuts (though cuts accompanying the introduction of Universal Credit would still take effect at a later date) and protect the police service from anticipated spending reductions. He also announced the frontloading of

£3.8 billion of a prospective £8 billion increase in NHS spending by 2020, as well as an extra £600 million for mental health services. Local authorities would also be permitted to levy a 2% 'precept' on council tax payers to help meet the escalating costs of adult social care.

Incremental reform or incremental destruction?

How then are we to assess the progressive neo-liberal Conservative approach to the welfare state? Are we witnessing further moves towards the dismantling of the welfare state or might we, instead, be observing a concerted attempt by the modern Conservatives to forge a new progressive 'settlement' in which the welfare activities of the state are scaled back rather than abandoned? Providing a definitive answer to this question is notoriously difficult given the historic reluctance of Conservatives to map out their long-term vision for the welfare state or indeed for British society more broadly (see Dorey, 2011; Page, 2015). Traditional Conservatives have long maintained that they do not subscribe to a pre-ordained ideological position, preferring to respond in pragmatic non-doctrinal ways to prevailing economic and social events, having due regard to the need to preserve long-standing institutions and social conventions (see Scruton, 2001; 2014; Gray, 2009; Ball, 2013). This 'common sense' approach to government is seen as superior to the 'ideological' doctrines of liberalism and socialism, which are regarded as nothing less than 'grand schemes of social engineering' (Eccleshall et al, 1984: 80). Non-ideological, pragmatic Conservatives regard it as futile for their political opponents to search for 'non-existent' masterplans or schemes. In contrast, those who are persuaded that Conservative economic and social policy has an underlying ideological rationale (see Green, 2002) point, for example, to the cumulative impact of the initiatives of both the Thatcher and Major governments, which were 'designed' to reverse what were deemed to be the damaging effects of the post-1945 'social democratic' welfare settlement. From this perspective, modern Conservative governments should be viewed as goal orientated. Certainly, the PNLCs could be said to have a discernible road map. In terms of social policy, the PNLC could be said at present to resemble 'regenerative' tree surgeons rather than forest-felling lumberjacks. They are seeking to fashion a leaner welfare state in which government spending will fall to 36% of GDP by 2020, thereby matching the historic post-war lows of 35.8% (1957–58) and 36% (1999–2000 – see Office for Budget Responsibility, 2014). This level of spending involves a significant shift away from Beveridge's notion of a 'cradle to grave' welfare state. Social spending will be increasingly focused on core service areas such as education, health and pensions. Local government's 'welfare' functions will continue to be hacked back with the result that their 'welfare' activities will largely be limited to the provision of basic levels of adult social care and child protection. The quality of such services will depend increasingly on locally generated resources with poorer authorities facing the prospect of being able only to provide rudimentary services. Progressive neo-liberal Conservatives will defend this retreat to 'core' functions as part of a much-needed modernisation of the welfare state rather than a further step on the path to demolition. Time will tell, however, whether the paring back of the welfare state will prove acceptable to the public over the longer term. Much will depend on whether persuasive counter narratives emerge and whether the quality and availability of key services such as healthcare and education can be maintained.

It might transpire that the election of the 'undiluted socialist', Jeremy Corbyn, as Labour leader will signal a revival of public support for the classic welfare state, thereby undermining the 'hegemony' of the PNLCs narrative. Certainly, there seems a willingness on the part of the members and supporters of the Corbyn-led Labour Party to press for the revival of the movement's long-standing support for the welfare state, which had been abandoned by New Labour on grounds that a 'modern' policy agenda should be guided by 'pragmatism' and non-ideological 'evidence'. Under Corbyn, Labour now seems prepared to move beyond Ed Miliband's conditional support for the welfare state. Although Miliband succeeded in breaking free from some of the more negative aspects of New Labour's social policy agenda, he proved unable to set out a more inspiring and positive vision because of fears that doing so would result in Labour being portrayed as an unelectable, anti-aspirational 'welfare' party. It is unclear at present, though, whether Corbyn's pro-welfare state sympathies will lead to the development of a more radical and popular social policy agenda, which can challenge the 'established' PNLC narrative.

It remains difficult to come to any definitive conclusions about whether the policy agenda of the progressive neo-liberal Conservative governments led by David Cameron are part of a concerted attempt to reform rather than destroy the welfare state. Unquestionably, there has been no let-up in attempts to pare back the protection afforded to working-age citizens in areas such as social security and social housing, where lifetime council tenancies are now under threat, since the party's election victory in 2015. Such moves continue to be presented as much needed progressive reforms to malfunctioning parts of an ageing welfare state rather than as part of a concerted strategy to dismantle it. Continued commitments to a free NHS, state-funded schooling and improved retirement pensions have been cited by Ministers as evidence that Conservative support for the welfare state remains solid. However, a further challenge to these core areas of the welfare state cannot be ruled out. The emergence of a resurgent 'Thatcherite' neo-liberal grouping within Conservative ranks (see Kwarteng et al, 2011; 2012) in a post-Cameron era might, for example, result in a further round of radical 'reforms' that will leave the welfare state struggling for survival. Finally, it remains to be seen whether the Cameron-led governments from 2010 to 2020 will come to be remembered as champions of progressive Conservative welfare 'reform' or whether they will be seen as having prepared the ground for a decisive final round of Grandma's footsteps in which the welfare state vanishes from view.

References

Bale, T. (2010) *The Conservative Party from Thatcher to Cameron*, Cambridge: Polity.

Ball, S. (2013) *Portrait of a party. The Conservative Party in Britain 1918–1945*, Oxford: Oxford University Press.

Bartholomew, J. (2015) 'Benefits Street will become a dead end', *The Daily Telegraph*, 9 July, p 19.

Bercow, J. (2002) 'Tories for social justice', *The Guardian*, 13 December, p 18.

Blond, P. (2010) *Red Tory*, London: Faber and Faber.

Brooke, S. (2011) *Sexual Politics*, Oxford: Oxford University Press.

Cabinet Office (2010) *The Coalition: Our Programme for Government*, London: The Stationary Office.

Cameron, D. (2009) 'The Big Society', *Hugo Young Memorial Lecture*, London, 10 November.

Conservative Party (2001) 'Time for Common Sense', *Conservative Party General Election Manifesto*, London: Conservative Party.

Conservative Party (2005) 'Are You Thinking what We're Thinking?' *Conservative Party General Election Manifesto*, London: Conservative Party.

Conservative Party (2010) 'Invitation to join the Government of Britain', *Conservative Party General Election Manifesto*, London: Conservative Party.

Conservative Party (2015) *The Conservative Party Manifesto 2015*, London: Conservative Party.

Cooper, N., Purcell, S. and Jackson, R. (2014) *Below the Breadline: The Relentless Rise of Food Poverty in Britain*, Oxford: Church Action on Poverty/The Trussell Trust and Oxfam.

D'Ancona, M. (2012) 'Cameron won't let the socialists have fairness all to themselves', *The Sunday Telegraph*, 8 January, p 22.

Department for Work and Pensions (2010) *Universal Credit: Welfare That Works*, Cm 7957, London: Stationery Office.

Dorey, P. (2009) "Sharing the proceeds of growth': Conservative economic policy under David Cameron,' *The Political Quarterly*, 80(2): 259–69.

Dorey, P. (2011) *British Conservatism. The Politics and Philosophy of Inequality*, London: I.B. Tauris.

Dorey, P., Garnett, M. and Denham, A. (2011), *From Crisis to Coalition: The Conservative Party, 1997–2010*, Basingstoke: Palgrave Macmillan.

Eccleshall, R., Geoghegan, V., Hay, R. and Wilford, R. (1984) *Political Ideologies*, London: Hutchinson.

Elming, W., Emmerson, C., Johnson, P. and Phillips, D. (2015) *An Assessment of the Potential Compensation Provided by the 'New Living Wage' for the Personal Tax and Benefit Measures for Implementation in the Current Parliament*, London: Institute for Fiscal Studies.

Faucher-King, F. and Le Gales, P. (2010) *The New Labour Experiment: Change and Reform under Blair and Brown*, Stanford: Stanford University Press.

Gove, M. (2013) 'Please sir, I just want to learn more', *Standpoint*, 30 September, pp 28–31.

Gray, J. (2009) *Gray's Anatomy*, London: Allen Lane.

Green, E.H.H. (2002) *Ideologies of Conservatism*, Oxford: Oxford University Press.

Hay, C. (1999) *The Political Economy of New Labour*, Manchester: Manchester University Press.

Hayek, F.A. (1944) *The Road to Serfdom*, London: Routledge & Kegan Paul.

Hayton, R. (2012) *Reconstructing Conservatism? The Conservative Party in Opposition, 1997-2010*, Manchester: Manchester University Press.

Hickson, K. (2008) 'Conservatism and the poor: Conservative party attitudes to poverty and inequality since the 1970s', *British Politics* 4(3): 341–62.

Ishkanian, A. and Szreter, S. (eds) (2012), *The Big Society Debate*, Cheltenham: Edward Elgar.

Kwarteng, K., Patel, P., Rabb, D., Skidmore, C. and Truss, L. (2011) *After the Coalition*, London: Biteback.

Kwarteng, K., Patel, P., Rabb, D., Skidmore, C. and Truss, L. (2012) *Britannia Unchained*, London: Biteback.

Letwin, O. (2002) 'For Labour there is no such thing as society, only the state', in G. Streeter (ed) *There is Such a Thing as Society*, London: Politico's Publishing, pp 38–51.

Lowe, R. (2005) *The Welfare State in Britain since 1945* (3rd edn), Basingstoke: Palgrave Macmillan.

McManus, M. (2010) *Tory Pride and Prejudice: The Conservative Party and Homosexual Law Reform*, London: Biteback.

Montgomerie, T. (2004) *Whatever Happened to Compassionate Conservatism?* London: Centre for Social Justice.

Norman, J. (2010) *The Big Society*, Buckingham: University of Buckingham Press.

Office for Budget Responsibility (2014) *Economic and Fiscal Outlook*, Cm 8966, London: Stationery Office.

Olasky, M. (2000) *Compassionate Conservatism*, New York, NY: Free Press.

Osborne, G. (2015a) 'Budget Speech', *Financial Times*, 9 July, p 14.

Osborne, G. (2015b) 'Calling all progressives: help us reform the welfare state', *The Guardian*, 20 July, p 27.

Osborne, G. and Duncan Smith, I. (2015) 'Our fight to make work pay better than welfare has only just begun', *The Sunday Times*, 21 June, p 21.

Page, R.M. (2015) *Clear Blue Water? The Conservative Party and the Welfare State Since 1940*, Bristol: Policy Press.

Park, A., Clery, E., Curtice, J., Phillips, M. and Utting, D. (eds) (2012) *British Social Attitudes 28*, London: Sage.

Park, A., Bryson, C., Clery, E., Curtice, J. and Phillips, M. (eds) (2014) *British Social Attitudes 30*, London: Sage.

Powell, J.E. (1969) *Freedom and Reality*, London: Batsford.

Scruton, R. (2001) *The Meaning of Conservatism* (3rd edn), Basingstoke: Palgrave Macmillan.

Scruton, R. (2014) *How to be a Conservative*, London: Bloomsbury.

Seawright, D. (2005) 'One Nation' in K. Hickson (ed) *The Political Thought of the Conservative Party Since 1945*, Basingstoke: Palgrave Macmillan, pp 69–90.

Snowden, P. (2010) *Back from the Brink*, London: Harper Press.

Steadman-Jones, D. (2012) *Masters of the Universe: Hayek, Friedman and the Birth of Neoliberal Politics*, Princeton, NJ: Princeton University Press.

Timmins, N. (2012) *Never again? The story of the Health and Social Care Act 2012*, London: Institute for Government/Kings Fund.

Torrance, D. (2010) *Noel Skelton and the Property-Owning Democracy*, London: Biteback.

Williams, B. (2015) *The Evolution of Conservative Social Policy*, Basingstoke: Palgrave.

SIX

Exploring out-of-work benefit claimants' attitudes towards welfare reform and conditionality

Ruth Patrick

Introduction

In the May 2015 UK general election, confounding both the party's own expectations and the predictions of the pollsters, the Conservative Party returned to government, winning a parliamentary majority for the first time since 1992. During the election campaign, senior Conservatives pledged to continue their programme of welfare reform by cutting a further £12 billion from the annual 'welfare bill' (Syal, 2015). This approach appeared to win support from the public, with attitudinal surveys consistently showing enthusiasm for tough measures to address the 'problem' of a presumed 'welfare dependency' among many of those reliant on out-of-work benefits (Taylor-Gooby, 2015).

Public attitudes to 'welfare' need to be understood against the context of mainstream politicians' continued stereotyping and stigmatising of benefit claimants and the apparently endless growth in what some have termed 'Poverty Porn' (Jensen, 2014; Tyler, 2014a); television shows such as 'Benefits Street' that promise to show the 'reality' of what being on benefits entails. Combined with much of tabloid media's continued vilification of out-of-work benefit claimants, there is today a climate of hostility and suspicion towards those relying on out-of-work benefits. This climate creates a backdrop against which further reforms to social security often seem to be justified, even welcomed by the public, and regarded as politically necessary and desirable (Kellner, 2013).

While we hear a great deal about what needs to be done to out-of-work benefit claimants to make them responsible, hard working citizens (see Cameron, 2012; Duncan Smith, 2014), we hear rather less about their own attitudes and perspectives on the overarching direction of welfare reform. Drawing on findings from a study of out-of-work benefit claimants' experiences of welfare reform, this chapter explores whether and how far benefit claimants can see a logic for changes to the benefits system. Following an overview of the dominant narrative on 'welfare' and a brief summary of public attitudes towards 'welfare', the methods utilised in the study are introduced. The attitudinal findings are then explored, looking at broad positioning on welfare reform, attitudes to welfare conditionality and the extent of a related political disengagement in turn. A concluding discussion considers the possible explanations for the attitudes uncovered, and reflects on the implications of these attitudes for any future challenges to the status quo.

It should be noted that while the author prefers the term 'social security' to the Americanisation 'welfare' (Lister, 2011), the latter term is used here to reflect its adoption as the popular descriptor for social protection, mainstreamed in its usage by politicians, the media and – increasingly – many academics.

The new moral consensus on 'welfare'

Before exploring attitudes to welfare reform among out-of-work benefit claimants, it is first necessary to describe what is best understood as a 'new moral consensus on "welfare"'. Today, there is broad agreement among most politicians, the popular media and much of public opinion about what is characterised as the 'problem' of 'welfare' and the 'problems with' those who rely on it for all or most of their income. This problematising, which has a fundamentally moralising character, suggests that the provision and receipt of social security support, most particularly when not in paid work, is almost inherently negative and problematic, especially when it is provided to those judged as 'undeserving' and as having the 'capability' to participate in paid employment. Neat, if hard to sustain, divisions are created between 'deserving' and 'undeserving' populations within those reliant on 'welfare', which sit alongside a broader distinction between the 'hard working majority' and 'welfare dependants'; between 'strivers' and 'shirkers' (Patrick, 2014a; Tyler, 2014b).

While divisions between deserving and undeserving populations and a moralising critique of the poorest in our society have, of course, a long history (Hills, 2015), what is notable about the current period is the frequency with which these divisions are employed and recycled. Today, the majority of Westminster politicians seem united on the need to address the 'problem' of 'welfare', with welfare conditionality the preferred policy tool (Deacon and Patrick, 2011). Undoubtedly, the stability of this political agreement has been challenged by the election of Jeremy Corbyn as Leader of the Labour Party on an explicitly anti-austerity, pro-welfare stance. While his election suggests some appetite for a political voice that speaks for and positively about those reliant on social welfare, it remains the case that the dominant political narrative continues to regard 'welfare' as a policy problem requiring reform.

Certainly, Conservative politicians sometimes seem to be competing to use the most derogatory or stigmatising language to describe benefit claimants, whether it be George Osborne's critique of those who choose benefits 'as a lifestyle choice' (2010), Iain Duncan Smith's refusal to let claimants continue 'languishing on welfare' (2014) or, most recently, David Cameron's pledge to 'get rid of that well-worn path from the school gate, down to the Job Centre, and on to a life on benefits' (Wintour, 2015). At the same time as politicians continue to stigmatise and arguably (de)moralise benefit claimants, the media is an active participant in circulating and recreating ideas of claimants as undeserving, fraudulent and requiring of state intervention. Recent analysis of coverage of benefits in general (Baumberg et al, 2012), and disability benefit claimants in particular (Briant et al, 2013), shows a marked increase in the negative nature of such coverage.

The apparently endless growth in 'Poverty Porn' (Jensen, 2014; Tyler, 2014a) brings an additional dimension to the new moral consensus. Programmes such as 'Benefit Street' have a 'flattening effect on public discourse, crowding out critical and alternative perspectives' (Jensen, 2014). 'Benefits Street', 'Skint', 'On Benefits and Proud' and 'Benefits Britain: Life on the Dole' all create caricatures of 'welfare dependency' and shine attention on behaviours and practices that the audience are implicitly invited to judge and – most often – condemn. These television shows explicitly promise to give the 'real' picture (Plunkett, 2015), but are mediated by an editing process that sensationalises and distorts the lived realities of relying on out-of-work benefits in Britain today.

Taken together, politicians and the media drive forward a 'machine of welfare commonsense' (Jensen, 2014: unpaginated), such that viewing 'welfare' and those who rely on it as inherently problematic becomes doxic as it is taken for granted, and accepted as itself unproblematic and uncontentious. As Jensen has argued, this 'welfare commonsense' creates sharp dividing lines between those who do and do not participate in paid employment, and breeds resentment and discontent (2014). The extent of the acceptance of this new 'commonsense' is arguably apparent in the evidence on public attitudes to 'welfare' and it is to a brief summary of this that this chapter now turns.

Hardening public attitudes to 'welfare'?

Polling and qualitative findings from research consistently suggest that a majority of the public feel that current 'welfare' provisions are too generous, and actually discourage people from behaving responsibly by moving into work (Baumberg, 2014; Taylor-Gooby, 2015). Fifty-two per cent of respondents to the 2014 British Social Attitudes survey agreed with the statement that benefits for the unemployed are too high and discourage work, with the survey also finding substantial support for the Benefits Cap (Taylor-Gooby, 2015). Looking across Europe, it is notable that British attitudes are among the hardest on 'welfare', with the 2008 European Social Survey finding that people in Britain were the most likely of all countries surveyed to believe that the existence of benefits make people lazy, with around two thirds agreeing with this statement, compared with well under half in most other countries surveyed (cited in Hills, 2015).

In qualitative research into public attitudes to poverty, the Joseph Rowntree Foundation (JRF) found that people were frequently concerned about those who were seen to have 'chosen' a 'life on benefits' (Hall et al, 2014), showing the feedback and circulation of ideas of 'benefits as a lifestyle choice', which have meaning and currency for both politicians and members of the public. The JRF found a clear moralising dimension within attitudes to poverty (2014), with demarcations drawn between deserving and undeserving recipients of 'welfare'. At the same time as public attitudes show a concern that 'welfare' is often too generous and can discourage work, there are also signs that people are concerned for those living in poverty, with enduring support for the provision of social security, critically, though, to those deserving of support (Hall et al, 2014; Taylor-Gooby, 2015). Overall then, public attitudes to 'welfare' tend to correspond quite closely with the political presentation of 'welfare' and reliance on 'welfare' as inherently negative. Before exploring how these attitudes compare with those of individuals directly affected by welfare reform, it is first important to briefly detail the methodological approach taken in the study on which this chapter draws.

A methodological note – the lived experiences of welfare reform study

This chapter details findings from qualitative longitudinal research into the lived experiences of welfare reform (Patrick, 2014b). Between

2011 and 2013, a small group of out-of-work benefit claimants were interviewed three times as they experienced and responded to a range of welfare reforms. Twenty-two participants were initially interviewed, and of these, a smaller sub-sample of 15 were chosen to follow longitudinally (on the basis of those most likely to be affected by welfare reforms during the research period). These 15 were interviewed a further two times, approximately three and 16 months after the first interview. Of those followed longitudinally, 14 were interviewed all three times, with contact lost with just one participant between the second and third interview waves.

In adopting a qualitative longitudinal methodology, time was privileged as both a vehicle and object of study (Henwood and Shirani, 2012), with a particular interest in how experiences of welfare reform impacted upon how people lived in the present, thought about the past and planned for their futures. A purposively selected sample included young jobseekers affected by the reformed conditionality regime, disability benefit(s) recipients being migrated from Incapacity Benefit onto Employment and Support Allowance and single parents affected by changes to the age of a child at which eligibility for Income Support ends. The study was based in Leeds, and the researcher worked with two gatekeeper organisations to recruit possible participants.

The research prioritised good ethical practice, and ongoing informed consent was secured through a process of 'refreshing and reminding' participants about the research at each new interview encounter (Neale and Bishop, 2012). During the study, the researcher encountered a range of ethical dilemmas, some of which she has written about elsewhere (Patrick, 2012a; 2012b). Researching over time both magnifies and condenses the ethical challenges of the research endeavour (Thomson and Mcleod, 2015), and it is critical to consider the ethical plane throughout the research process. Findings from the research have provided rich data on both experiences and attitudes of those living with welfare reform, and it is to these attitudinal findings that this chapter now turns.

Findings from the research

Perspectives on welfare reform – 'the government has got to do something really'

In discussing their experiences of welfare reform, participants were very critical about its application to their individual cases, critiquing both the reforms they were experiencing and any threatened or possible extension of conditionality and sanctions:

'Especially single parents, this change from the age of 11 to seven [at which go onto Jobseeker's Allowance]... It's not fair. It's not practical... Even feeling that you're being pushed... I would have gone and worked, but not feeling I'm being pushed.' (Susan, Single Parent (SP), W1[1])

'It's quite irritating really because if you have a medical report saying one thing and then the system forces you to attend these interviews or have these appointments [to apply for Employment and Support Allowance]. You're thinking, I've got a piece of paper here that tells you, that you asked for this information, that I'm not fit for work. So why are you wasting time, effort and money forcing me to do these kinds of things, when life could be a lot simpler?' (Isobella, Disability Benefit(s) Claimant (DBC), W3)

'[On the work programme] they go, sign a little piece of paper, a little piece of paper of what jobs you've applied for and that's it. Then they give you another date. What's the point in that? There's no point.' (Robert, Young Jobseeker (YJS), W3)

However, many of the participants were receptive to the argument for the need for welfare reform, even at the same time as they were being directly affected by some of the changes that were introduced. Of the 15 participants followed longitudinally, nine expressed some agreement with aspects of the welfare reform approach. To understand this support, it is first necessary to emphasise that attitudes to welfare reform were almost always linked to, and themselves bound up in, distinctions being drawn between 'deserving' and 'undeserving' subsets of benefit claimants, which served to emphasise participants' own 'deservingness', while critiquing the behaviour and 'deservingness' of some 'other' (see Patrick, 2014b). A growing number of studies have highlighted the extent to which many of those living in poverty engage in this 'othering' (Garthwaite, 2011; Chase and Walker, 2013; Shildrick and Macdonald, 2013); where they describe their own entitlement to benefits at the same time as undermining and challenging that of some 'other'.

This 'othering' was much in evidence in this research:

'Some people choose it [benefits], some people think "I'll have a kid and go on benefits and that'll be me". Some people are used to it, but I'm not. Well, I never have been.' (James, YJS, W1)

'I know a few people who take Mcat and Ket [drugs] and they're just sat there off their faces day in, day out, and they're on Jobseekers so they lie and cheat and everything about what they're doing and it really annoys me.' (Josh, YJS, W3)

'I've met quite a few people who claim to have bad backs, and go to medicals with a Zimmer frame, and then next day you see them riding a bike. Some people will try it on really.' (Kane, DBC, W2)

It is possible that 'processes of othering', by identifying problematic and undeserving individuals and/or populations, create a ready-made target group for governmental welfare reforms that seek to ensure that people can no longer 'choose' benefits, and are compelled to take steps to enter paid employment where this is a realistic objective. Sometimes the link was explicit in people's accounts:

'There is quite a lot of people faking having bad backs and stuff. So I think [the government have] got to do something really.' (Kane, DBC, W1)

'In some ways [welfare reform] is a good idea because maybe there is people who don't need to be on certain benefits that could go out to work. Not like me but people that are just playing on it or something to get money out of the social.' (Amy, DBC, W1)

'There are some people that do look at it where they'll be no better off at work, they get their house paid for, they get the Council Tax, well stop it all. They do need to get a lot stricter.' (Sophie, SP, W3)

In these 'othering' narratives, individuals' own continued deservingness is emphasised, just as 'others' undeservingness is conceptualised as providing a justification for welfare reform.

Sometimes participants' attitudes to welfare reform seemed fluctuating and unstable. This could be linked to participants' conflicting perspectives as both observers of the benefits system as a whole and as individuals who were targeted by some of the changes. Adrian's views on the reforms fluctuated over time. In the first interview, he suggested that the reforms were necessary and needed:

> 'I think what they're doing is right. Everybody should have a job: the government's right really.' (YJS, W1)

But, in his second interview, he took a very different approach:

> 'Everything the government's doing at the moment is ridiculous.' (YJS, W2)

Adrian's position as both an advocate for welfare reforms targeted at 'others', and an individual adversely affected by the same reforms perhaps explains his changing and sometimes contradictory opinions.

Over time, there was also some evidence of support for welfare reform weakening, something which often occurred in tandem with the realisation that these reforms were causing significant hardship and difficulties for many, not least the participants themselves. This was particularly noticeable in the case of Isobella, who while critical of the pace of change, and its perceived targeting of many 'deserving' groups, did initially see some potential in the welfare reforms being introduced:

> 'I suspect there are lots of people who probably could go to work who are on something like Incapacity Benefit but on the other hand I think there are vastly more people who do need it who can't work. And so I think they're sort of being penalised for the fact there are some people who don't [deserve benefits], perhaps because in the past governments have been lax and the legislation hasn't been tight enough.' (DBC, W1)

However, over time, as Isobella saw her own entitlement to benefit questioned, she started to rethink her attitudes to the government's approach, becoming increasingly angry:

> 'I've got probably worse at feeling angry at what they're doing.' (W2)

> 'I am far more critical of the [government] of what they've done … and the problems that they've put people through.' (W3)

Taken as a whole, what was notable from this research was the extent of support for the 2010–15 coalition government's overarching narrative of welfare reform, an account of separating out the 'deserving' from 'undeserving' and instilling fairness in the benefit system, which had clear meaning and purchase for most of the participants. The government's behavioural reading of fairness, expressed most clearly in Cameron's statement back in 2010 that 'fairness means giving people what they deserve; and what people deserve can depend on how they behave' (Cameron, 2010: unpaginated) seemed to resonate with the participants in this study.

In explaining why they saw a need for welfare reform, individuals repeatedly described some problematic 'other', with implications for social solidarity and divisions both between 'the poor' and 'the non-poor' as well as within 'the poor'. There is the risk that, as welfare reforms continue, affected individuals' sense of anger and resentment to such 'others' will only grow, as they feel unfairly targeted and penalised due to the problematic behaviours of 'undeserving others'. This possibility is reinforced by Chase and Walker's research into shame and poverty, in which participants living in poverty described how they were not opposed to a 'crackdown' on 'others', but 'did feel that they often unfairly bore the brunt' (2013: 8) of the consequence(s) of such a crackdown.

Attitudes towards conditionality and compulsion

The 2010–15 coalition followed its predecessors in office in presiding over an extension and intensification of welfare conditionality, with reforms including new conditions, harsher sanctions, and a widening of the reach of conditionality (Deacon and Patrick, 2011; Dwyer and Wright, 2014). In defending the application of conditionality, politicians frequently draw on contractualist, paternalist and new communitarian arguments, as well as making regular recourse to the underclass thesis (Deacon, 2002). Arguably, the most popular and oft-used defence of welfare conditionality in government accounts is welfare contractualism, the now familiar 'something for something' refrain (Department for Social Security, 1998; Conservatives, 2010; Duncan Smith, 2010). Paternalist arguments are also regularly deployed, through an emphasis on the need to encourage and even compel people to behave in ways that are supposedly in their best interests. The underclass thesis can be mobilised to defend conditionality, by suggesting that claimants need intensive interventions to activate them from a state of passivity and idleness into one of 'work' and responsibility. The final theoretical defence of conditionality, communitarianism, suggests that the duty to enter paid employment should be understood to arise independently of government intervention (Etzioni, 1997; Deacon, 2005).

In the research reported here, attitudes towards conditionality and compulsion were explored and these theoretical defences were mapped onto the perspectives articulated by the participants, in order to see how these ideas are interpreted and understood by those directly affected by welfare conditionality. The focus here is on their perspectives of conditionality being applied to some 'other', with the effectiveness and applicability of conditionality to their individual cases explored elsewhere (Patrick, 2014b). In the first and third interviews, participants were presented with vignettes describing the application of work-related conditionality to a single parent, young jobseeker and disabled person. While altered between the first and third interviews to change small details, the vignettes were kept broadly the same, so that they could serve as a rough proxy to explore whether attitudes to conditionality changed during the course of the study.

In this exercise, support was most evident for conditionality being applied to single parents, with this often justified with recourse to paternalist and contractualist arguments. Participants were generally also positive about conditionality's appropriateness for young jobseekers, although there was some questioning of the lack of choice that the tightened conditionality regime could entail (particularly around demands that people take part in work experience programmes in areas where they might have no interest). There was most resistance to conditionality being applied to disabled people, with 13 of the 15 participants followed longitudinally concerned that this would cause substantial hardship and make individuals' impairments and health conditions worse. Participants often characterised the application of conditionality to a disabled person as based on a flawed assessment of capability, highlighting a growing awareness of the shortcomings with processes to assess eligibility for disability benefits. Across the different categories of participants, it was young jobseekers who were most likely to think that imposing conditionality was broadly fair, this despite their being the group most likely to experience work-related conditionality first-hand.

In their discussions about the applicability of conditionality to different groups, participants tended to engage in a consideration of the individual circumstances of the claimant in question, an assessment and exploration of their 'behaviour', and their 'deservingness'. There was comparatively little evidence of a broader questioning of the whole premise of attaching conditions to benefit receipt.

Chloe felt that it was fair for a young person to be compelled to take part in Mandatory Work Activity:

> 'Cause he's a boy, he's 19-year-old and he should go out to work... If I had a full-time partner and I lived with him I'd expect him to [work]... He's a young lad on his own. Get out to work you lazy little shit [laughs].' (SP, W1)

James defended conditionality's applicability to a single parent whose children were both at primary school:

> 'She could get a part-time job within them [school] hours. Ten till two or owt like that... I understand it would be hard for... but she should look for summat.' (YJS, W3)

In this way, it seemed that, perhaps through familiarity and repeated imposition, the overarching conditionality framework had become accepted and viewed as largely unproblematic. Some even called for conditionality to be extended further, with Josh arguing:

> 'I think a lot of support is offered to people that should be forced more than anything. Make them get help, make them get back into work, make them do this and that.' (YJS, W3)

In their descriptions of people who 'choose' benefits, participants frequently drew on ideas of intergenerational cultures of worklessness, depicting big families with 'lazy' adult members, who would rather sit around all day than enter paid employment. This depiction fits ideas of an underclass and has close correspondence with some of the harshest government rhetoric.

> 'There are people that abuse the system... A home where you find a grandmother, then the daughter then grandchildren all sat ... from morning watching TV and even buying booze on that money and all sorts... These parents are not even telling their children to go out and work.' (Susan, SP, W1)

'I know there is people that pop out kids left, right and centre 'cause they think they're gonna get the money for it.' (Sharon, DBC, W3)

Ideas of an underclass can link into justifications for welfare conditionality that emphasise a role for paternalism, as in Mead's argument that the poor are 'dutiful but defeated' (Mead, 1992: 122) and require compulsion if they are to be encouraged, supported, but ultimately compelled, to do the right thing. In this study, participants often seemed to be supportive of paternalist, conditional interventions, particularly when applied to young people with little previous working experience and no other caring responsibilities or commitments. In the vignettes based on a young jobseeker, there was an exploration of young men being compelled to participate in mandatory work experience programmes, with the threat of benefit sanctions designed to engineer continued engagement. Participants often drew on paternalist arguments to support the use of welfare conditionality in this instance:

'I can't see that being a bad thing because he's got no kids. He's only young and ... cleaning the streets and tidying up graffiti... There's nowt wrong with that and it will help him get into the work ethic.' (Cath, DBC, W1)

'At the end of the day he's a young lad, what else is he going to do? What's he doing, sat at home, smoking weed, drinking, chilling out on the street corners ... He's a young lad needs kicked up the arse.' (Sophie, SP, W1)

The notion of welfare contractualism had clear meaning for participants, and was in evidence in their discussions around welfare conditionality. Indeed, there was direct evidence of support for the idea of tying social rights to social responsibilities:

'If people refuse to work take their benefits off them, cos then they've got no choice but to work... And then if they do start looking for work put them back on [benefits].' (DBC, W1)

'If people aren't willing to look for jobs then why should they be allowed to get money for nothing?' (Josh, YJS, W1)

However, contractualism was perhaps applied more critically, with a particular interest in questions of the rights of the claimant under any such 'contract' and whether and how far the government was fulfilling its side of the bargain. Participants also questioned whether some of the work-related conditions were just, for example, requirements to work voluntarily in order to gain work experience, or to travel long distances for a job. Dissatisfaction with the support provided by the government, particularly around the promised help to enter and sustain paid employment, was frequently articulated, as was the enduring issue of an absence of jobs, which made fulfilling duties under any such welfare contract more difficult. Reflecting on negative experiences in his mandatory engagement with the Work Programme, and perhaps hinting at the power imbalance implicit in any 'welfare contract' (White, 2003; Patrick, 2011a), James drew on contractualist arguments:

> 'If you don't go [to appointments], if I don't stick to my part of arrangement, I lose me benefits, but if they don't stick to their part of the arrangement, it's like, "So what?"' (YJS, W3)

In terms of the communitarian defence of conditionality, many of the participants did speak of the responsibility to work, with this tied to the central aspiration of the large majority of the sample to make the transition into paid employment, where this was feasible and sustainable. At the same time, however, some participants took an alternative approach, instead emphasising what they felt should be the right to paid employment, a right that they identified as being absent in the contemporary context:

> 'There shouldn't be benefits in the first place, people should have a job.' (Adrian, YJS, W1)

The articulation of a right to paid employment is evidence of a challenge to the dominant government narrative, resting as it does on solidaristic and social democratic ideas. It turns the corrective lens to the demand side of the labour market, rather than welfare conditionality's lopsided focus on the steps individual claimants need to take to become more employable and job ready (Patrick, 2011a; 2011b).

Overall though, in thinking through their perspectives on conditionality, participants were most likely to engage in a questioning of whether particular individuals or categories of claimants were 'deserving' or exhibiting 'good' behaviour, with little evidence of a broader challenge to the tying of benefit entitlement to behaviour. Linked to this, participants were largely in agreement with an approach that privileges paid employment as the primary responsibility of the dutiful citizen, although they did often also mention demand-side barriers, which could sometimes make fulfilment of this duty more difficult.

Political (dis)engagement

Public attitudes to welfare reform and welfare conditionality will inevitably feed into the political process, but this will be mediated and affected by the extent of political (dis)engagement. There is a wealth of evidence on the inequality of electoral turnout, with substantial class, income and age divides in terms of electoral participation (Birch et al, 2013) that have grown in recent years. By 2010, individuals in the highest income group were 43% more likely to vote than those in the lowest income group. Young people are also disproportionately less likely to vote, and there is particularly low probability that young people living on low incomes (which included many of the participants in this research) will vote (Birch et al, 2013).

There was relatively little evidence of political participation among the participants in the study reported here, with nine of the 15 followed longitudinally not registered to vote, a finding which reflects the nationally low rates of formal political participation among those living in poverty (Flinders, 2014). When explaining why they did not vote, participants described voting as a pointless action, with no capacity to engineer positive change:

'I don't even vote. I don't think it's worth it.' (Chloe, SP, W1)

'Whoever I vote for, the country's going to the dogs anyway, so I don't bother.' (Sam, YJS, W3)

Participants spoke of being marginalised from the political process, while also feeling that their views and opinions were neither valued nor sought by officials and decision makers, reflecting the extent of their exclusion from mainstream political engagement. When asked whether there had been a time in the past two years when someone at the Job Centre or another official had been interested in their views on an issue, not a single participant said yes, hinting at the extent of this disenfranchisement. It was common to greet this question with laughter, as if the very idea of officials being interested in their views was comical. In Susan's response to this question, she laughed, saying:

> 'I haven't even tried because I'd probably think, hmm, who cares?' (SP, W3)

As well as signs of political disengagement, there was also evidence of substantial anger directed towards politicians and the broader political process. This anger was particularly apparent in threats of violence against the government, empty threats that perhaps illustrated participants' powerlessness in the face of welfare reforms:

> 'I think everyone [in government], all of them want shooting in the head.' (Chloe, SP, W3)

> '[Cameron's] another one that needs a machete... [What he says] make me want to go round and put my hands actually round his neck or shake him.' (Isobella, W3)

There was also a widespread distrust of politicians. As Terri put it:

> 'I don't have any faith in any of them because they're all alike. They say this, that and the other to get in and when it comes to the stick and lift, they don't deliver what they say.' (DBC, W1)

Participants described politicians' lives as far removed from, and out of touch with, the everyday lived experiences of struggling to 'get by' on benefits during times of welfare reform, a common criticism of politicians by those living in poverty (Perry et al, 2014; Roberts and Price, 2014). Isobella felt politicians 'haven't got a clue how people live. I don't know what planet they're on' (DBC, W2).

Indeed, in demarcating 'them' and 'us' and 'othering', participants also engaged in an 'othering' of politicians and powerful actors, who were conceptualised as making decisions with little regard or care for the negative impact they might have on individual lives. Participants spoke of the need for politicians to experience the lived realities of benefit reliance if they were to develop more effective policy. Responding to a quote from David Cameron about the need to change the benefits system, Cath suggested:

'Tell him "walk a year in my shoes" and then we'll talk about this statement that you've just made.' (DBC, W1).

Similarly, Karen reflected on politicians who ' 'aven't lived in our shoes. It's easy enough to judge' (SP, W1).

It was clear from this research that while participants were very angry and resistant to the way in which the government's reforms were affecting their own lives, this did not directly translate into political engagement, or broader challenges to the socio-economic context. In her exploration of the agency of people living in poverty, Lister (2004) points to the agency entailed in 'getting organised' to challenge the status quo. She observes that this is only rarely in evidence, reminding us that 'proud to be poor is not a banner around which many are likely to march' (Lister, 2004: 152).

While this is certainly the case, it is notable that recent years have seen examples of groups uniting in opposition to aspects of the government's welfare reform agenda, particularly evident among disability benefit claimants (see Gentleman, 2011; Tyler, 2014b). In the case of this study, following completion of the fieldwork, participants were given the opportunity to develop an animated film to disseminate this research (the Dole Animators project). A large number of the participants were enthusiastic, with seven sustaining engagement throughout the course of the project and remaining involved through media activities and attendance at events right up to the time of writing (Dole Animators, 2013). This engagement, and that of others living in poverty in the UK (see Atd Fourth World, 2014), suggests that when resources are made available and opportunities emerge to give voice to one's own experiences in a safe and confidential environment, and then to disseminate these experiences nationally, there is an appetite for 'getting organised' to articulate an alternative narrative on the lived experiences of welfare reform.

Discussion and conclusions

This chapter has explored the attitudes of a small group of out-of-work benefit claimants to welfare reform and the imposition of welfare conditionality, as well as highlighting the extent of their disengagement from mainstream politics. It has illustrated the ways in which the claimants in this study were often receptive to the case being made for welfare reform, at the same time as they problematised its application to their individual cases. Further, the research highlights widespread support for welfare conditionality, a policy approach, which is increasingly accepted as a central element of the contemporary social security offer, not just in the UK but throughout the OECD region.

These findings arguably point to both the reach and embeddedness of the 'new moral consensus on welfare' that sees mainstream politicians, popular media and much of public opinion in broad agreement about the inherent problematic nature of out-of-work benefits, and the lives of those who rely on them. This consensus creates an environment where it is very difficult for individual claimants to make a positive case for 'welfare' in general terms, and instead means that more negative, and inevitably divisive, forms of 'othering' become pervasive.

Importantly, this 'othering' provides a rationale for the overarching direction of welfare reform, and leads to a situation where some of those directly affected by the benefit changes still support them on the basis that they are necessary to address the 'problem' of 'welfare'. The defensive 'othering' in which participants engaged also creates division and antipathy among those in arguably quite similar social positions, divisions which make any collective challenge a less likely prospect (Chase and Walker, 2013; Clark, 2014; Walker, 2014). The disjuncture between individual resistance to welfare reform affecting oneself and broader support for welfare reform when targeted at some 'other', serves the government well in mitigating a sustained political challenge to their welfare reforms by those who are directly affected.

The attitudes to welfare reform and conditionality noted in this study, and the 'othering' of those judged undeserving, have implications for social citizenship and the in/exclusion of those who rely on benefits for all or most of their income. The narrative of creating and sustaining firm demarcations between the 'deserving' and 'undeserving' is an exclusive and excluding one that operates to further entrench the marginalisation of those on out-of-work benefits from mainstream society. Ironically, in seeking to assert their own deservingness by distancing themselves from 'others' judged less deserving, out-of-work benefit claimants recirculate and embed this excluding narrative (Chase and Walker, 2013); and further fuel the machine of welfare common sense (Jensen, 2014).

The marked differences in political participation among different groups leads to what IPPR have described as a 'divided democracy', where politicians can afford to almost ignore the views, needs and wishes of certain groups – most notably those living in poverty – given that they are comparatively unlikely to vote (Birch et al, 2013). Analysis of the impact of the 2010–15 coalition government's 2010 Spending Review shows that the cohorts (such as young people and those on low incomes) worst hit by the reforms introduced were those with the lowest rates of political participation, while those largely protected, most notably those past retirement age, have very high rates of political participation (Birch et al, 2013). Seeking to promote more equality in rates of electoral turnout is vital, but it is important to locate the problem not with individuals choosing not to vote, but with the broader political and electoral system that makes whole subsets of the population feel ignored, neglected and most certainly not listened to by politicians.

The 2015 general election campaign saw political parties clamour to be seen to represent the 'hard working' majority. As long as major political parties continue to seek to represent only those who conform to some 'hard working family' archetype, those who rely on out-of-work benefits will inevitably feel excluded from the political process. What is notable from this study is that despite this exclusion, and their broader distrust of politicians, out-of-work claimants often recognise and accept the dominant case being made for welfare reform and themselves articulate a similar argument when describing some 'undeserving' 'other'.

Note
[1] W1 denotes first wave of interviews, W2 second wave, and W3 third wave.

References
Atd Fourth World (2014) *The Roles We Play: Recognising the contribution of people in poverty*, London: ATD Fourth World, http://www.therolesweplay.co.uk/

Baumberg, B. (2014) 'Benefits and the cost of living: pressures on the cost of living and attitudes to benefit claiming', in C. Bryson, J. Curtice and A. Park (eds) *British Social Attitudes 31*, London: National Centre for Social Research.

Baumberg, B., Bell, K. and Gaffney, D. (2012) *Benefit stigma in Britain*, London: Turn2us/University of Kent.

Birch, S., Gottfried, G. and Lodge, G. (2013) *Divided democracy: Political inequality in the UK and why it matters*, London: IPPR.

Briant, E., Watson, N. and Philo, G. (2013) 'Reporting disability in the age of austerity: the changing face of media representation of disability and disabled people in the United Kingdom and the creation of new 'folk devils'', *Disability & Society*, 28(6): 874–89.

Cameron, D. (2010), 'Together in the national interest', *Speech to Conservative Party Conference*, 6 October, London: The Conservatives, http://www.conservatives.com/News/Speeches/2010/10/David_Cameron_Together_in_the_National_Interest.aspx

Cameron, D. (2012) 'Welfare speech', 25 June, London: HM Government, http://www.number10.gov.uk/news/welfare-speech/

Chase, E. and Walker, R. (2013) 'The co-construction of shame in the context of poverty: beyond a threat to the social bond', *Sociology* 47(4): 739–54.

Clark, T. (2014) *Hard Times: The divisive toll of the economic slump*, London: Yale University Press.

Conservatives (2010) *A New Welfare Contract*, London: The Conservatives.

Deacon, A. (2002) *Perspectives on welfare: ideas, ideologies, and policy debates*, Maidenhead: Open University Press.

Deacon, A. (2005) 'An ethic of mutual responsibility? Toward a fuller justification for conditionality in welfare', in C. Beem and L. Mead (eds) *Welfare reform and political theory*, New York: Russell Sage Foundation.

Deacon, A. and Patrick, R. (2011) 'A new welfare settlement? The coalition government and welfare-to-work', in H. Bochel (ed) *The Conservative Party and Social Policy*, Bristol: Policy Press.

Department for Social Security (1998) *New ambitions for our country: A new contract for welfare*, London: The Stationery Office.

Dole Animators (2013), www.doleanimators.org

Duncan Smith, I. (2010) 'Our contract with the country for 21st century welfare', Speech to Conservative Party Conference, 5 October, London: The Conservatives, http://conservative-speeches.sayit.mysociety.org/speech/601437

Duncan Smith, I. (2014), 'A welfare state fit for the 21st century', Speech to Centre for Social Justice, 28 January, London: Department for Work and Pensions, https://www.gov.uk/government/speeches/a-welfare-state-fit-for-the-21st-century

Dwyer, P. and Wright, S. (2014) 'Universal Credit, ubiquitous conditionality and its implications for social citizenship', *Journal of Poverty and Social Justice*, 22(1): 27–35.

Etzioni, A. (1997) *The New Golden Rule: Community And Morality In A Democratic Society*, New York, NY: Basic Books.

Flinders, M. (2014) 'Low voter turnout is clearly a problem, but a much greater worry is the growing inequality of that turnout', *London School of Economics*, 13 March, http://blogs.lse.ac.uk/politicsandpolicy/look-beneath-the-vote/

Garthwaite, K. (2011) "The language of shirkers and scroungers?' Talking about illness, disability and coalition welfare reform', *Disability and Society*, 26(3): 369–72.

Gentleman, A. (2011) 'Hardest hit march brings disabled people out on to the streets', *The Guardian*, 11 May, http://www.guardian.co.uk/society/2011/may/11/hardest-hit-march-disabled-people

Hall, S., Leary, K. and Greevy, H. (2014) *Public attitudes to poverty*, York: Joseph Rowntree Foundation.

Henwood, K. and Shirani, F. (2012) 'Researching the temporal', in H. Cooper, P.M. Camic, D.L. Long, A.T Panter, D. Rindskopf and K.J. Sher (eds) *APA handbook of research methods in psychology, Vol 2: Research designs: Quantitative, qualitative, neuropsychological, and biological*, Washington, DC: American Psychological Association Publications.

Hills, J. (2015) *Good times, bad times: The welfare myth of them and us*, Bristol: Policy Press.

Jensen, T. (2014) 'Welfare commonsense, poverty porn and doxosophy', *Sociological Research Online*, 19(3): 1–7.

Kellner, P. (2013) 'Welfare reform: who, whom?' *YouGov*, https://yougov.co.uk/news/2013/01/07/welfare-reform-who-whom/

Lister, R. (2004) *Poverty*, Cambridge: Polity Press.

Lister, R. (2011) 'Our social security system must guarantee real welfare', *The Guardian*, 29 August.

Mead, L.M. (1992) *The new politics of poverty: the nonworking poor in America*, New York, NY: Basic Books.

Neale, B. and Bishop, L. (2012) 'The ethics of archiving and re-Using qualitative longitudinal data: a stakeholder approach', in B. Neale and K. Henwood and (eds) *Timescapes Method Guides Series*, Leeds: Timescapes.

Osborne, G. (2010) 'Our tough but fair approach to welfare', Chancellor's Speech to The Conservative Party Conference, 4 October, London: The Conservatives, http://www.conservatives.com/News/Speeches/2010/10/George_Osborne_Our_tough_but_fair_approach_to_welfare.aspx

Patrick, R. (2011a) 'Disabling or enabling: the extension of work-related conditionality to disabled people', *Social Policy and Society*, 10(3): 309–20.

Patrick, R. (2011b) 'The wrong prescription: disabled people and welfare conditionality', *Policy and Politics*, 39(2): 275–91.

Patrick, R. (2012a) *The 'gift' relationship - an ethical dilemma in small-scale qualitative longitudinal research*, Leeds: Timescapes, http://www.timescapes.leeds.ac.uk/resources/knowledge-bank-for-ethical-practice-in-qualitative-longitudinal-research

Patrick, R. (2012b) 'Recruiting and sustaining sample populations over time: possibilities and challenges', in B. Neale and K. Henwood (eds) *Timescapes Methods Guides Series*, Leeds: Timescapes.

Patrick, R. (2014a) 'Welfare reform and the valorisation of work: is work really the best form of welfare?' in M. Harrison and T. Sanders (eds) *Social Policies and Social Control: New perspectives on the 'not-so-big society'*, Bristol: Policy Press.

Patrick, R. (2014b) 'Working on welfare: findings from a qualitative longitudinal study into the lived experiences of welfare reform in the UK', *Journal of Social Policy*, 43(4): 705–25.

Perry, J., Williams, M., Sefton, T. and Haddad, M. (2014) *Emergency Use Only: Understanding and reducing the use of food banks in the UK*, London: Child Poverty Action Group, The Church of England, Oxfam GB and The Trussell Trust.

Plunkett, J. (2015) 'Benefits Street series two to feature scenes of drug-dealing', *The Guardian*, 29 April, http://www.theguardian.com/media/2015/apr/29/channel-4-benefits-street-drug-dealing-series-two

Roberts, E. and Price, L. (2014) *Tipping the balance? A qualitative study on the cumulative impacts of welfare reform in the London Borough of Newham*, London: Community Links.

Shildrick, T. and Macdonald, R. (2013) 'Poverty talk: how people experiencing poverty deny their poverty and why they blame 'the poor'', *The Sociological Review*, 61(2): 285–303.

Syal, R. (2015) 'Tories may not reveal details of £12bn welfare cuts until after election', *The Guardian*, 29 March, http://www.theguardian.com/politics/2015/mar/29/tories-welfare-cuts-details-reveal-after-general-election

Taylor-Gooby, P. (2015) 'Benefits and welfare', in R. Ormston and J. Curtice (eds) *British Social Attitudes 32*, London: National Centre for Social Research Methods.]

Thomson, R. and Mcleod, J. (2015) 'New frontiers in qualitative longitudinal research: an agenda for research', *International Journal of Social Research Methodology*, 18(3): 243–50.

Tyler, I. (2014a) ''Being poor is not entertainment': class struggles against poverty porn', Manchester: Social Action and Research Foundation, http://mediapovertywelfare.wordpress.com/2014/10/30/being-poor-is-not-entertainment/

Tyler, I. (2014b) *Revolting subjects: social abjection and resistance in Neoliberal Britain*, London: Zed Books.

Walker, R. (2014) *The Shame of Poverty*, Oxford: Oxford University Press.

White, S. (2003) *The Civic Minimum: On the rights and obligations of economic citizenship*, Oxford: Oxford University Press.

Wintour, P. (2015) 'Unemployed will have to do community work under Tories, says Cameron', *The Guardian*, 17 February, http://www.theguardian.com/politics/2015/feb/17/unemployed-will-have-to-do-community-work-under-tories-says-cameron

SEVEN

The Troubled Families Programme: in, for and against the state?

Stephen Crossley

Introduction

> State institutions are often authoritarian, they put us down, tie us up with regulations. And many of the working class seem to be defined by the state as 'irresponsible', as 'troublemakers', 'scroungers'. If we are born out of wedlock, it defines us as illegitimate. All of these things leave us wondering: if the state is not providing these services in the way we want them, it cannot really be doing it for us. Why does the state provide them?' (London Edinburgh Weekend Return Group, 1980: 9)

In the aftermath of the Conservative general election victory of 1979, a group of 'state workers' published *In and against the state*. First a pamphlet and then a book, it outlined the contradictory positions they were often forced to take during their work in order to make government welfare policies meet the needs of the people they were working with. Although it is over 35 years since its publication, *In and against the state* undoubtedly retains its relevance.

It describes the struggle of people – who identified themselves as socialists – working within the state at a time when they felt that the state was not really theirs, if indeed it ever was. The authors noted that cuts to (and rhetoric surrounding) public sector spending were leading to their jobs becoming increasingly disciplined and tightly controlled, forcing them to be more 'accountable', in a way more akin to private sector work (London Edinburgh Weekend Return Group, 1980: 3). They also discussed at length the ways in which citizens' engagements with different parts of the state can be unsatisfactory and inadequate for both the service user and service provider:

The ways in which we interact with the state are contradictory – they leave many people confused. We seem to need things from the state, such as child care, houses, medical treatment. But what we are given is often shoddy or penny-pinching, and besides, it comes to us in a way that seems to limit our freedom, reduce the control we have over our lives. (London Edinburgh Weekend Return Group,1980: 8)

Fast forward 30 years to 2010 and the formation of a Conservative-led coalition government in the UK saw similar concerns expressed about welfare 'reforms' such as the Work Capability Assessment, the 'bedroom tax' and an overall 'cap' on the amount of benefits a single household can receive (see De Agostini et al, 2014: 10-13 for an introduction to the key tax-benefit policy changes). 'Street-level bureaucrats' (Lipsky, 1980) such as teachers, nurses and social workers and academics, as well as their unions, have protested about the impact of austerity measures and public sector job losses. More than 2000 teachers signed a petition criticising national curriculum reforms (Garner, 2013) and local government workers and college and university lecturers have taken industrial action over pay and changes to pensions. The Royal College of Nursing warned of the impact on child health if more school nurses were not recruited and trained (*The Guardian*, 2015) and junior doctors protested in Westminster in a dispute over a new contract (BBC, 2015).

Independent analysis has shown that it is deprived local authority areas that were hit hardest by local government finance settlements during the coalition years (Innes and Tetlow, 2015). Similar analysis suggests that it is families with children, and particularly groups such as lone parents and large families, which were disproportionately affected by the welfare and tax changes of the coalition (De Agostini et al, 2014). While the majority of these 'reforms' and cuts attracted criticism and were often controversial, one social policy established by the coalition managed to not only largely avoid criticism and controversy, but also generated positive coverage from both the media and politicians across the political spectrum.

The Troubled Families Programme (TFP), established in the aftermath of the 2011 riots, set out to 'turn around' the lives of the 120,000 most 'troubled families' in England. The relative lack of criticism surrounding the programme is interesting, given that the concept of 'troubled families' is arguably the latest version of the enduring 'underclass' thesis (Welshman, 2013). While some academics have highlighted the stigmatising language used to depict 'troubled families' (Levitas, 2012), political and media responses, at both local and national levels, have been overwhelmingly supportive. When the rhetoric surrounding 'troubled families' is closely examined, a number of competing, and often contradictory, messages begin to emerge, which may help to explain the strong support for the programme. In essence, there is something for everyone in the TFP – it is effectively a Janus-faced programme, at various times positioned as both for and against the state.

This chapter examines the ways in which the Troubled Families Programme has been positioned by central government and by local authorities and practitioners. Drawing on speeches by David Cameron and interviews with, and speeches by, Louise Casey, the Director General of the Troubled Families Unit, the article begins with an examination of how the programme has been positioned at a national level. The attention then turns to the implementation of the programme at a local level. All 152 local authorities in England are involved in the delivery of the TFP and the lack of statutory guidance in respect of the programme has allowed and encouraged a number of different local responses to the national rhetoric. Adopting a 'street-level lens' (Brodkin, 2011a), and drawing on the work of Pierre Bourdieu and Loic Wacquant, interviews with managers and workers in one local authority area are analysed to examine 'the complexity of interactions concealed beneath the apparent monotony of bureaucratic routine' (Bourdieu, 2005: 140). The chapter concludes with reflections on the Janus-faced nature of the Troubled Families Programme and a discussion of its role in the crafting of a new 'smart' business-like neo-liberal state in the UK (Crossley, 2015a).

The Troubled Families Programme – the national perspective

The Troubled Families Programme did not represent the coalition's first attempt to 'get to grips' with 'troubled' or 'troublesome' families. In December 2010, Cameron invited Emma Harrison, the chief executive of the welfare-to-work company Action 4 Employment (A4E) to help the government 'turn around' the lives of 'troubled families'. At this time, Cameron (2010) stated that he was 'as aware as anyone about the limits of what government can do in this area', suggesting that there were areas of people's lives that government shouldn't interfere with. He said, 'I loathe nanny-statism' and was 'not proposing heavy-handed state intervention'.

Instead, the Working Families Everywhere (WFE) scheme was to be a 'less bureaucratic' Big Society venture, headed by Harrison on a voluntary, unpaid basis. Cameron (2010) vowed to 'strip away the bureaucracy and give her, and the many others we hope will follow her lead, the freedom she needs to make a difference'. The WFE scheme was to be piloted in a small number of local authorities and was targeted at 100,000 'never worked' families. The scheme would see a number of volunteer 'family champions' supporting families with multiple disadvantages into work, with Harrison (2010) saying that 'every family will have their own "Emma", able to use every existing resource to help them get going, face up to and sort out their problems, whether they be parenting challenges, poor health, debt, addiction, dependency or lack of motivation'.

The scheme initially operated without much media attention but, following the riots in 2011, it was cast back into the spotlight when Cameron (2011a) announced that he believed that project was 'being held back by bureaucracy', promising 'Now that the riots have happened I will make sure that we clear away the red tape and the bureaucratic wrangling, and put rocket boosters under this programme'. Some commentators were less than supportive of the renewed impetus behind the scheme, with one arguing that the scheme 'conjures the image of workshy beasts lying in piles of Pringles and crack, waiting to be shouted at by Hyacinth Bucket' (Gold, 2011). Alice Thomson (2011), writing in *The Times* managed to pour scorn on the announcement that some government Ministers would be 'adopting' families under the scheme, while simultaneously perpetuating stereotypical and stigmatising views of families with no adult in work:

> Ah, lucky feckless family. One day soon there may be a knock at your door and a minister will stand before you and your brood of feral infants. 'I'm William Hague', he says. 'I've come to help you. Piano practice, Welsh verbs, international relations, I'm a dab hand at a few things', the Foreign Secretary will explain. 'Black belt in judo actually, but you may not need advice in that area.'
>
> Or it could be the Home Secretary teaching your Neets how to make a lasagne. Theresa May might bring a basket of organic goodies, turn a blind eye to the skunk your tattooed partner smokes, whisk out a bin bag to clear the congealed takeaways and give you a few of her leopard print kitten heels. (Thomson, 2011)

Just four months later, in December 2011, Cameron was launching a new scheme to 'turn around' the lives of the nation's 'troubled families' by May 2015, the end of the coalition's term of office. The approach of the Troubled Families Programme differed significantly from that of

WFE, which was quietly closed shortly after Harrison stepped down from her voluntary role amid allegations of fraud at A4E. Responsibility for the new scheme lay firmly with central government and a new Troubled Families Unit was created, based in the Department for Communities and Local Government (DCLG). Cameron (2011b), directly contradicting his views 12 months earlier, stated that 'only government has the power' to 'sort out' 'troubled families' and that the TFP was necessary to 'change completely the way government interacts with them; the way the state intervenes in their lives' and argued that it would 'take a concerted effort from all corners of Government'. The TFP would be delivered by all local authorities in England and would be accompanied by funding from across government departments, with Cameron name-checking six Ministers who had contributed 'hard cash from their budgets' towards the programme.

'Troubled families' were deemed to be those involved in crime and/or antisocial behaviour, whose children had poor school attendance or were excluded from school and where there was an adult in the household on out-of-work benefits. Each local authority was allocated an indicative number of 'troubled families' to turn around and were also allowed to use additional local filter criteria to help identify the requisite number of families. The programme was run on a Payment by Results (PbR) model, which meant that the majority of funding for work with 'troubled families' would be held by central government until families achieved certain outcomes. Local authorities would submit claims for funding from the government for families where either: children's school attendance had risen to over 85% and where crime and antisocial behaviour, where present, had fallen significantly, or; when any adult moved into work for three or six months, but not both (see DCLG, 2012b). Progress or improvements on other issues that may be affecting families such as poverty, poor housing, domestic violence or substance misuse were not recognised by the PbR model.

The assertive, muscular language used by Cameron in promising to 'sort out' and 'intervene' in the lives of workless or 'troubled families' is in keeping with Wacquant's argument that neo-liberalism should not be equated with 'small government' and should instead be understood as a remasculinisation of the state. He argues that, when concerned with issues of social control, neo-liberal governments reveal themselves to 'be fiercely interventionist, bossy, and pricey' as they endeavour to 'direct, nay dictate, the behaviour of the lower class' (Wacquant, 2010: 214). This new 'no-nonsense' intervention of the TFP was counter-posed by

Cameron (2011b) against the previous Labour government's approach to tackling disadvantage:

'The problem, particularly in the past ten years, has actually been an excess of unthinking, impersonal welfare. Put simply: tens of thousands of troubled families have been subjected to a sort of compassionate cruelty, swamped with bureaucracy, smothered in welfare yet never able to escape.'

'Troubled families' were portrayed as 'victims of state failures' (Cameron, 2011b) who were 'already pulled and prodded and poked a dozen times a week by government'. The Prime Minister went on to say that 'one of the reasons for their dysfunction is their hatred of 'the system', which they experience as faceless, disjointed and intrusive'. The TFP, then, would be a response to previous government approaches, which, all too often, according to Cameron, had 'simply failed':

So where it was impersonal – dealing with families like bureaucratic units, we will be human: engaging with families as the messy, varied, living, breathing groups of different people they actually are. Where it was disjointed – with a whole load of state agencies overlapping, we will have a single point of focus on the family: a single port of call and a single face to know. And where it was essentially top-down and patronising - keeping people sealed in their circumstances with a weekly welfare cheque and rock-bottom expectations, we will be empowering, not making excuses for anyone, but supporting these families to take control of their own lives. The message is this: 'we are not coming in to rescue you - you need to rescue yourselves, but we will support you every step of the way.(Cameron, 2011b)

The TFP would be based on an intensive model of 'family intervention' promoted by Casey when she headed up the Respect Task Force under the previous Labour government. The family intervention approach is based on a single keyworker who adopts a 'persistent, assertive and challenging' approach (DCLG, 2012a: 6) and can 'get to grips' with the whole family and look at the family 'from inside out rather than outside in' (DCLG, 2012a: 26). Family Intervention Projects (FIPs) were rolled out to 53 local areas under the Respect agenda in 2006 and were also positioned as a solution to the putative problem of traditional family services failing to 'get to grips' with 'troubled or 'problem' families (Parr and Nixon, 2008: 165). The often punitive, sanctions-based 'last chance' approach of FIPs, which largely ignores structural issues, has also attracted a large amount of criticism (Garrett, 2007; Gregg, 2010).

Casey, throughout the operationalisation of the 'troubled families' agenda, has continued to talk up the need for a new way of doing things. Speaking to the Association of Directors of Children's Services conference she criticised the 'reactive and uncoordinated approach [which] prevails across public services' (Casey, 2013). She argued that, 'we now have to change the services and systems around the families as much as turn the individual families around' and articulated the need for 'radical reform across all public services, not just local government'. In interviews with national newspapers, she has made the case for a different approach by characterising previous approaches in blunter terms. She has argued that the TFP is not 'some cuddly social worker's programme to wrap everybody in cotton wool' (quoted in Winnett and Kirkup, 2012) nor will it involve 'assessing the hell out of a family' (House of Commons Committee of Public Accounts, 2014: ev 25) where social workers 'turn up with clipboards' and 'monitor decline' but 'don't actually make any difference' (quoted in Bennett, 2012: 15).

Despite these concerns, Casey has also been a strident supporter of local authorities' involvement in the programme (see, for example, Smulian, 2014). At the same Association of Directors of Children's Services conference she told the audience that she 'went out during the spending round and fought to find more money to put together a new programme from 2015–16' (Casey, 2013). She claimed that the extension and expansion of the TFP was 'credit to your leadership within local government – you are making such good progress on the Troubled Families Programme that the government wants to build on the approach'. She finished her speech thus:

> I want though, to end with a thank you. Without colleagues in local authorities and especially colleagues in children's services as the leaders of this within local government, we would have really struggled with this work. Your heads have always been full of wise advice and guidance, your doors always open to dispense it and, I believe, your hearts fully committed to helping these families and their children. To quote one council chief executive talking about this programme:

> > "It is an appeal to both the head and the heart and it unites Whitehall and the Town Hall in common purpose."

The future of this programme is in your hands and I really hope you will use the considerable power you have to be leaders for change. And maybe we can give the children in these families a fighting chance. So I wish you well and stand ready to help. (Casey, 2013)

The TFP then, is full of contradiction and is 'a confusing agenda' (Hayden and Jenkins, 2013: 10). In direct contrast to the depoliticised approach of Working Families Everywhere, its immediate forerunner, it is a programme rooted firmly in the state. It is a centrally designed policy programme, which is driven by national government, but delivered locally during a period of alleged decentralisation and locally led solutions. Failing local services are cast as the 'accomplice' to the 'culprit' (Stone, 1984: 171) of 'troubled families', thus providing the government with the justification for a new approach, positioned against the state's previous attempts at working with 'troubled families'. And yet, the TFP is also positioned as being for the state, offering an empowering, enabling approach to public service delivery where the skills of heroic workers are allowed to flourish, free from the bureaucratic strait jackets, which previously constrained them.

It is this approach, which has, according to the government, worked successfully with 99% of 'troubled families' within the Prime Minister's desired timetable. In June 2015, the DCLG announced that the TFP had been an 'unprecedented success' and turned around the lives of 116,654 out of 117,910 families targeted and worked with under the programme (DCLG, 2015 – although see Bawden, 2015, Butler, 2015 and Crossley, 2015b for critiques of this 'miraculous' success). This 'success', achieved during a period of welfare restructuring and austerity, has seen local authorities praised by Cameron and Casey and enabled the TFP to be expanded before the independent evaluation reported any findings.

The Troubled Families Programme – a 'street-level' lens

From a street-level perspective, it is useful to think of organizational practices developing in the context of formal policy that establishes the playing field and governance that sets the rules of the game, leaving ample space for discretion in policy implementation. (Brodkin, 2011a: i258)

What politicians and senior civil servants believe should happen as a result of formulating any given policy does not necessarily translate seamlessly into action on the ground. Lipsky's (1980) concept of 'street-level bureaucrats' encouraged researchers and policy makers to consider the ways in which practitioners working on the 'frontline' in public services often have to negotiate, resist or subvert policies in order to make them work, and meet the needs of the citizens they encountered. The concept has since been widely used to investigate the daily life of welfare policies (see, for example, Evans and Harris, 2004; Ellis, 2011; Fletcher, 2011; Wright, 2012). Evelyn Brodkin has argued that the 'central task' of a 'street-level' lens in research is 'to expose the informal practices through which policies – and by extension social politics and social relations – are effectively negotiated, although rarely explicitly so. It seeks to make visible and understandable informal organisational practices that otherwise can escape analytic scrutiny and even recognition' (Brodkin, 2011b: i200).

This section draws primarily on interviews with managers and 'street-level' practitioners involved with the delivery of the TFP in a local authority in the North of England (referred to here as Northton). The research is part of a wider study examining the operationalisation of the TFP in three different local authority settings. The intention in using a single authority is not to suggest that it is representative of all local authorities, or indeed of the two other authorities involved in the study. At the same time, there is little to suggest that Northton represents an exceptional case or unique approach to the TFP. Instead, the intention here is to highlight 'the complexity of interactions concealed beneath the apparent monotony of bureaucratic routine' (Bourdieu, 2005: 140), as 'state workers' struggle to work with disadvantaged families under a programme many of them have at least some misgivings about. The names of research participants have been changed, and their job titles amended, to preserve anonymity.

Northton chose to deliver the majority of their 'troubled families' work in-house, primarily by utilising existing local authority structures and systems, rather than creating new ones. Managers and practitioners suggested that the 'new' approach was actually very similar to ones they had been using for many years, with only a small number of 'tweaks' being made to accommodate the central government criteria, data requirements and Payment by Results processes of the TFP. Many of the families identified as being 'troubled' were already known to services within the authority. This is perhaps unsurprising given the previous Labour government's exhortation for children's services practitioners to 'think family' (Cornford et al, 2013) and the similarities between the TFP and recent approaches to tackle antisocial behaviour among 'problem families':

"So we just thought, it's madness, don't reinvent the wheel. It's taken us six years to get where we are [in 2012], if you put another layer of something different, we'll lose everything we've done, and they're the same families." (Janet, Children's Services Manager)

"So there's no, honestly, no, apart from the assessments have changed, instead of Onset [an assessment form for young people entering the criminal justice system for the first time] it's the CAF [Common Assessment Framework – a multi-agency assessment for children where professionals have concerns], but there's no, we still liaise with the same professionals, go to the same meetings, have the same hassles in school. There's nothing, apart from delivering the [parenting] programmes, instead of referring them on. Instead of filling a form in, you've got to do it." (Alison, Family Worker)

New management arrangements were introduced, however, which included the establishment of a partnership board and an operational group to oversee the local delivery of the TFP. Lead practitioners sat in 12 different services across the authority, including children's social care teams, children's centres, education, the youth offending team, health and a disabled children's team. An existing family intervention style team also expanded. Workers filling these posts were largely recruited on fixed-term contracts through redeployment or secondment processes as a result of cuts to services such as youth offending, play, youth and community, and education. The extensive bureaucratic ensemble, which supported the implementation and subsequent delivery of the TFP, including data collection requirements and reporting arrangements, suggest that the positioning of the programme as a sleek and efficient 'smart' (Cameron, 2015) form of government does not sit easily with the local adjustments required to support the programme.

In Northton, the decision to align the TFP with existing work allowed the authority to resist using the term 'troubled'. While all 152 local authorities 'signed up' to deliver the Troubled Families Programme and their chief executives voted it their 'top government policy' (DCLG, 2013), many have chosen to rename their local 'troubled families' work to remove the stigmatising label (see Hayden and Jenkins, 2013). One manager in Northton was aware of the issues around the 'troubled' label and, while acknowledging Louise Casey's defence of the term, suggested it lacked a grasp of the problems the term created in practice:

> "I think what a practitioner can't do is go out to [name of neighbourhood] on a Tuesday morning and say 'you've been identified as part of the troubled families' agenda' on the doorstep, I think that's a different thing altogether, and I think it would hinder engagement." (Ben, Children's Services Manager)

The same manager highlighted contradictions within the national narrative around 'troubled families'. The strong 'no-nonsense' rhetoric of Eric Pickles (see Chorley, 2012 for an example) was eschewed in favour of what was seen as Louise Casey's more sympathetic portrayal of work with 'troubled families':

> "There was a big narrative around that, that reckless and feckless agenda. Louise Casey, I think, has been very skilful in bringing that onto her own terms and, err, making it something more genuine than that... And we're up for that, you know. We're not, we're not up for, you know, those kind of TV documentaries, the poverty porn around 'On benefits and proud' and all that sort of stuff. And, when we recruited our workers, they were very clear about that, you know, they were saying, 'We're not up for that agenda, but we're up for that one. We're up for Louise's, but we're not up for Eric's'. You know, and that was kind of interesting."

Participants in the research often expressed broad support for the aims of the programme and the discretion afforded by it. A number of the newly recruited family workers stated that it was work they would have been interested in doing even if there hadn't been cuts to the services they had been working in previously. Family workers sometimes positioned themselves against other services, with one stating that they were quick to tell families 'I'm not a social worker' and another referring to themselves as 'the good guys' with statutory social care services implicitly identified as 'the bad guys'.

Another manager in Northton stated that they 'just got it, got the agenda' and believed that the TFP was 'about improving outcomes for families, reducing the burden on the public purse and transformation'. They articulated how they dealt with 'resistance' from practitioners who were less supportive:

"I would say some of the ones that were really adamant that they didn't want to be involved, you know, it's a simple message. Well I tell you what, if you're not going to do this, you might as well say bye bye to your job." (Gill, Children's Services Manager)

As well as the support for – and negotiation within – the programme, there was also a strong sense of resistance among workers to elements of the programme itself and some of the rhetoric associated with it. One manager said they felt 'morally compromised' by the TFP, which was a 'flawed' but 'well-sold programme'. Their main concern related to the Payment by Results procedure, which considered a family to be 'turned around' if an adult in the household moved into 'sustained' employment, regardless of other 'troubles', such as domestic violence, that might still be affecting the family:

"How is it that work is top trumps? You can still be beating nine bells out of your wife and children, and your children may not be achieving anything at school because they don't attend because they're busy mopping the blood up off the floor. But actually, you went out and you got a job in a betting office or whatever you got. And that's top trumps and that hurts." (Janet, Children's Services Manager)

Other officers also expressed doubts about the design of the Payment by Results process with many of them ironically referring to getting an adult in a 'troubled family' back into work as a 'kerching' moment, or the 'golden ticket' or 'golden egg'. Practitioners also positioned themselves against the national narratives and sought to reinsert material deprivation and poverty into a local narrative around 'troubled families'. Louise Casey's *Listening to troubled families* report (Casey, 2012) does not mention the term 'poverty' once, despite it being an account of the lives of some of England's most disadvantaged families. Nationally, the poverty experienced by 'troubled families' may be marginalised, but a number of officers highlighted the centrality of this issue in their work:

"Yes, it is about poverty and a lot of young people don't actually have a decent bed to sleep on." (Sarah, Family Worker)

"There is absolutely no doubt that socioeconomic deprivation characterises the majority of families that we work with." (Ben, Children's Services Manager)

"I didn't know poverty existed the way that it does until I walked into this job. Honestly, you know, people have nothing, you know. And how degrading it must feel to have to ring somebody up and say, you know, 'will there be a chance that you could put £10 on my gas or £10 on my electric', you know." (Claire, Family Worker)

"Poverty. A lot of them ['troubled families'] are trapped in a cycle of poverty. And I know politically, we're not supposed to discuss things like that. But it's poverty underlying everything, it really is … If it's poverty we're dealing with, you call it poverty and you address it. You don't call it troubled families. It's families living in poverty, my opinion, a lot of the time." (Susan, Youth Worker)

However, other workers involved in the delivery of the TFP in Northton offered different, less sympathetic views on the issue of money and families' income and the perceived 'problematic' behaviours and dispositions of the families they were working with:

"I feel that sometimes I'm going out with, working with some families who are probably financially better off than what I am. I'm paying my own rent, paying, you know, erm, child, you know, maintenance and stuff like that, and I am struggling at the end of the month. And, you know, they're sitting there with, it is, you know, they do have their flat screen tellies, they do have, erm, their iPhones. I don't and that's frustrating." (John, Family Worker)

"I seem to spend a lot of time throwing money at them but because they're 'troubled families', we're allowed to do that." (Pam, Family Worker)

"I've got to go to work on time, that's basically, you know, why should you [a family member] get paid for sitting, when you do nothing all week and every two weeks you're late, you know, I'd sanction you as well." (Alison, Family Worker)

Numerous other examples of resistance and subversion of the national TFP took place in Northton. Cases were often co-allocated to two practitioners rather than the single keyworker model advocated by the government, generally when there were statutory responsibilities involved or where certain specialist skills were required that the family worker did not possess. One of the DWP secondees to the 'troubled families' work was primarily used to ensure full take-up of benefits within 'troubled families' rather than advice on how to move into employment, which was the original, central government intention. One worker, when discussing this, noted that, "clearly, one of the agendas of the programme is about, erm, cutting, reducing the amount spent on benefits". Officers also rejected the government's preferred 'data driven' approach to identifying 'troubled families' (DCLG, 2012b). This process, which was referred to as a 'data wash', produced a 'big list' of potentially 'troubled families', which often resulted in families being cold-called on the basis of out-of-date information. Northton's response was to wait for families to be referred into different services and then check them off against the 'troubled families' criteria.

Each example of resistance, however, was effectively a 'legitimated transgression, an official or semi-official dispensation, in the sense of an exception to the rule made within the rules, and a legally sanctioned privilege' (Bourdieu, 2005: 132). The design and rhetoric of the TFP encourages family workers to position themselves against their colleagues and creates the space to resist elements of the national programme while still fulfilling its objectives. The new, entrepreneurial 'persistent, assertive and challenging' (DCLG, 2012a: 6) 'family workers' of the TFP, positioned against social workers and other 'overlapping' state agencies, are thus supported to acquire a 'particular form of bureaucratic charisma that is acquired by distancing oneself from the bureaucratic definition of the civil service role' (Bourdieu, 2005: 132).

Discussion

Local authority officers working on the TFP were 'shot through with the contradictions of the State' (Bourdieu et al, 1999: 184) and 'enmeshed in relations of antagonistic cooperation' (Wacquant, 2009: 289) with central government. The 'success' of the TFP appears to owe as much to local officers' negotiation and subversion of the programme as it does to its original design. It is an exemplar of 'the rigidity of bureaucratic institutions' being 'such that ... they can only function, with more or less difficulty, thanks to the initiative, the inventiveness, if not the charisma of those functionaries who are the least imprisoned in their function' (Bourdieu et al, 1999: 191).

It is, of course, appropriate that state workers should work with 'troubled families'. Workers exercised the discretion offered by the TFP and often rejected the dominant national narrative of 'troubled families' being 'neighbours from hell', seeking to work with them in ways that owed more to 'support' and 'empowerment', than 'intervention' (see also Bond-Taylor, 2014). The transgressions described by workers, however, were those which were tolerated, if not encouraged, by the design of the TFP, which has a clear focus on what constitutes a 'troubled family' (those that represent a high cost to the state) and on what outcomes are required of families and local authorities. What exactly happens between 'troubled families' being identified and their being 'turned around' is, however, deliberately vague, and transgression, resistance or subversion in this area, matters little. The TFP allows local authorities, if they so wish, to name their local 'troubled families' work something different, adopt a supportive approach over a punitive intervention, and even claim for families it hasn't worked with (Bawden, 2015). But these are small, 'quick wins', 'partial revolutions' against the TFP, that do not 'call into question the very foundations on which the whole game is based' (Bourdieu, 1993: 74).

These transgressions, then, occur under the radar and do little to trouble the national narrative of an assertive central government policy working successfully with troublesome families. They are not permitted to distract from the portrayal of the TFP as a unique way of working that can 'turn around' the lives of 'troubled families' and can also be applied to other service areas, saving 'the taxpayer' substantial significant sums of money. Local authorities have already begun commissioning 'troubled adults' services (Calkin, 2015), the public policy think tank IPPR has produced a report on a proposed 'Troubled Lives Programme' (IPPR, 2015) for individuals and, in the 2014 Budget, the government committed to exploring ways 'to further reduce the waste and complexity of public services' and exploring ways of extending the TFP approach to other groups of people (HM Treasury, 2014: 25).

The idea of 'transforming' public services is at the heart of the TFP, a public policy arguably more concerned with 'turning around' state services to marginalised groups than it is about the lives of any 'troubled families' (Crossley, 2015a). Cameron's (2014) belief that 'whatever the social issue we want to grasp – the answer should always begin with family' is instructive and needs to be examined alongside wider welfare reforms and his concomitant argument that there exists an opportunity to craft a 'smarter', more business-like state (Cameron, 2015). The 'smart state' vision is one which espouses the private sector virtues of entrepreneurship, efficiency and innovation. Returning to *In and against the state*, the preface to the first edition highlights how cuts in public funding 'are pushing us all into positions and attitudes that are similar to those of workers for private capital' (London Edinburgh Weekend Return Group, 1980: 3).

Significantly, Cameron argued that the size of the state does not matter, a statement that supports Wacquant's (2009; 2010) thesis that neo-liberal governance is not predicated on a small, retreating state, but that it instead requires an expansive and intrusive apparatus to 'unfurl disciplinary supervision over precarious factions' (Wacquant, 2009: 307), and marginalised populations. It is, Wacquant (2009: 305) argues, no surprise that 'the populations most directly and adversely impacted by the convergent revamping of the labour market and public aid [such as large families and lone parent families in the UK] turn out also to be the privileged "beneficiaries"' of the states 'new' approach to working with troublesome groups.

The overly simplistic framing of the TFP as an 'unprecedented success', built on a new and more efficient way of delivering public services belies the expansive bureaucratic apparatus supporting the programme and the daily complications and negotiations that street-level bureaucrats face in making it work. The political and rhetorical focus on austerity and public sector savings helps to deflect attention away from the ways in which the reach of the UK government is growing and becoming more 'involved' in the daily lives of 'troubled families'. The TFP is a programme that is therefore reliant on 'institutional bad faith', one where the UK government engages in 'a collective double game and double consciousness' (Bourdieu et al, 1999: 204-5). The antagonistic positioning of the TFP as being both for and against the state, thus serves to highlight the Janus-faced nature of the programme and, by extension, the governments that have promoted it as a near-perfect social policy intervention and a model for a new 'smarter' form of public service provision.

References

Bawden, A. (2015) 'Is the success of the government's troubled families scheme too good to be true?' *The Guardian,* 11 November, http://www.theguardian.com/society/2015/nov/11/troubled-family-programme-government-success-council-figures

BBC (2015) 'Health secretary to meet doctors over contract row', *BBC,* 28 September, http://www.bbc.co.uk/news/health-34383670

Bennett, R. (2012) 'Local Authority Officials 'should scrub floors', *The Times,* 27 April, p15.

Bond-Taylor, S. (2014) 'Dimensions of Family Empowerment in Work with So-Called 'Troubled' Families', *Social Policy and Society*, 14(3): 371–84.

Bourdieu, P. (1993) *Sociology in Question*, London: Sage.

Bourdieu, P. (2005) *The Social Structures of the Economy*, Cambridge: Polity.

Bourdieu, P., Accardo, A., Balazs, G., Beaud, S., Bonvin, F., Bourdieu, E., Bourgois, P., Broccolochi, S., Champagne, P., Christin, R., Faguer, J.P., Garcia, S., Lenoir, R., OEuvrard, F., Pialoux, M., Pinto, L., Podalydès, D., Sayad, A., Soulié, C. and Wacquant, L. (1999) *The weight of the world: Social suffering in contemporary society*, Stanford, CA: Stanford University Press.

Brodkin, E. (2011a) 'Policy work: street-level organizations under new managerialism', *Journal of Public Administration Research and Theory*, 21(2): 253–77.

Brodkin, E. (2011b) 'Putting street-level organizations first: new directions for social policy and management research', *Journal of Public Administration Research and Theory*, 21(2): 199–201.

Butler, P. (2015) 'Troubled families scheme outcomes: miraculous success or pure fiction?' *The Guardian*, 22 June, http://www.theguardian.com/politics/2015/jun/22/troubled-families-scheme-outcomes-miraculous-success-or-pure-fiction

Calkin, S. (2015) 'Districts and county launch tender for 'troubled adults' service, *Local Government Chronicle*, 20 May, http://www.lgcplus.com/news/health/social-care/districts-and-county-launch-tender-for-troubled-adults-service/5085128.article

Cameron, D. (2010) 'Speech on families and relationships', 10 December, https://www.gov.uk/government/speeches/speech-on-families-and-relationships

Cameron, D. (2011a) 'PM's speech on the fightback after the riots', 15 August, https://www.gov.uk/government/speeches/pms-speech-on-the-fightback-after-the-riots

Cameron, D. (2011b) 'Troubled families speech', 15 December, https://www.gov.uk/government/speeches/troubled-families-speech

Cameron, D. (2015) 'Prime Minister: My vision for a smarter state', 11 September, https://www.gov.uk/government/speeches/prime-minister-my-vision-for-a-smarter-state

Cameron, D. (2014) 'Speech at the Relationships Alliance Summit', 18 August, https://www.gov.uk/government/speeches/david-cameron-on-families

Casey, L. (2012) *Listening to Troubled Families*, London: DCLG

Casey, L. (2013) 'Troubled Families Programme', 16 July, https://www.gov.uk/government/speeches/troubled-families-programme

Chorley, M. (2012) 'Problem families told - 'Stop blaming others'', *Independent,* 10 June, http://www.independent.co.uk/news/uk/politics/ios-exclusive-problem-families-told-stop-blaming-others-7834235.html

Cornford, J., Baines, S. and Wilson, R. (2013) 'Representing the family: how does the state 'think family'?', *Policy & Politics,* 41(1): 1–18.

Crossley, S. (2015) 'Realising the (troubled) family', 'crafting the neoliberal state', *Families, Relationships and Societies,* http://dx.doi.org/10.1332/204674315X14326465757666

Crossley, S. (2015) 'The Troubled Families Programme: the perfect social policy?', *Centre for Crime and Justice Studies,* Briefing 13, http://www.crimeandjustice.org.uk/sites/crimeandjustice.org.uk/files/The%20Troubled%20Families%20Programme%2C%20Nov%202015.pdf

DCLG (2012a) *Working with Troubled Families,* London: DCLG.

DCLG (2012b) *The Troubled Families programme: Financial framework for the Troubled Families programme's payment-by-results scheme for local authorities,* London: DCLG.

DCLG (2013) 'Troubled Families programme receives extra £200 million boost', 24 June, https://www.gov.uk/government/news/troubled-families-programme-receives-extra-200-million-boost

DCLG (2015) 'PM praises Troubled Families programme success', 22 June, https://www.gov.uk/government/news/pm-praises-troubled-families-programme-success

De Agostini, P., Hills, J. and Sutherland, S. (2014) 'Were we really all in it together? The distributional effects of the UK coalition government's tax-benefit policy changes', *Social Policy in a Cold Climate Working Paper 10,* London: Centre for Analysis of Social Exclusion.

Ellis, K. (2011) 'Street-level bureaucracy revisited: The Changing Face of Frontline Discretion in Adult Social Care in England', *Social Policy and Administration,* 45(3): 221–44.

Evans, T. and Harris, J. (2004) 'Street-Level Bureaucracy, Social Work and the (Exaggerated) Death of Discretion', *British Journal of Social Work,* 34(6): 871–95.

Fletcher, D. (2011) 'Welfare Reform, Jobcentre Plus and the Street-Level Bureaucracy: Towards Inconsistent and Discriminatory Welfare for Severely Disadvantaged Groups?' *Social Policy and Society,* 10 (4): 445–58.

Garner, R. (2013) 'Teachers speak out against Michael Gove's 'list of facts' curriculum', 14 April, *The Independent*, http://www.independent.co.uk/news/uk/politics/teachers-speak-out-against-michael-goves-lists-of-facts-curriculum-8572623.html

Garrett, P. (2007) "Sinbin' solutions: the 'pioneer' projects for 'problem families' and the forgetfulness of social policy research', *Critical Social Policy*, 27(2): 203–30.

Gold, T. (2011) "Problem families' do not need an army of Hyacinth Buckets shouting at them', *The Guardian*, 26 August, http://www.theguardian.com/commentisfree/2011/aug/26/working-families-everything-scheme-tanya-gold

Gregg, D. (2010) *Family intervention projects: A classic case of policy-based evidence*, London: Centre for Crime and Justice Studies.

Harrison, E. (2010) 'Working Families Everywhere is announced', *Working Families Everywhere,* 10 December, https://web.archive.org/web/20110818180930/http://www.workingfamilieseverywhere.com/news/10/12/2010/working-families-everywhere-is-announced/

Hayden, C. and Jenkins, C. (2013) 'Children taken into care and custody and the 'troubled families' agenda in England', *Child and Family Social Work*, 20(4): 459–69.

HM Treasury (2014) *Budget 2014*, London: HMSO.

House of Commons Committee of Public Accounts (2014) *Programmes to help families facing multiple challenges, Fifty-first Report of Session 2013-14*, London: The Stationery Office.

Innes, D. and Tetlow, G. (2015) *Central cuts, local decision-making: Changes in local government spending and revenues in England, 2009-10 to 2014-15*, IFS Briefing Note BN166, London: Institute for Fiscal Studies.

Hunter, J. and McNeil, C. (2015) *Breaking boundaries: Towards a 'Troubled Lives' programme for people facing multiple and complex needs*, London: IPPR, http://www.ippr.org/files/publications/pdf/breaking-boundaries_Sep2015.pdf?noredirect=1

Levitas, R. (2012) There may be trouble ahead: what we know about those 120,000 'troubled families', *Poverty and Social Exclusion*, 21 April, http://www.poverty.ac.uk/system/files/WP%20Policy%20Response%20No.3-%20%20'Trouble'%20ahead%20(Levitas%20Final%2021April2012).pdf

Lipsky, M. (1980) *Street-Level Bureaucracy: Dilemmas of the Individual in Public Services*, New York: Russell Sage Foundation.

London and Edinburgh Weekend Return Group (1980) *In and Against the State*, London: Pluto Press.

Parr, S. and Nixon, J. (2008) 'Rationalising family intervention projects', in P. Squires (ed) *ASBO Nation: The criminalisation of nuisance*, Bristol: Policy Press.

Smulian, M. (2014) 'Eligibility criteria set for expanded Troubled Families work', *Local Government Chronicle*, 2 September, http://www.lgcplus.com/news/services/childrens-services/eligibility-criteria-set-for-expanded-troubled-families-work/5074393.article

Stone, D. (1984) *The disabled state*, Basingstoke: Macmillan.

The Guardian (2015) 'Escalating child health crisis feared due to lack of school nurses', *The Guardian,* 24 August, available at: http://www.theguardian.com/society/2015/aug/24/child-health-school-royal-college-nursing-obesity

Thomson, A. (2011) 'Mentored by a minister? It might just work,' *The Times*, 24 August, p 18.

Wacquant, L. (2009) *Punishing the Poor: The neoliberal government of social insecurity*, Duke University Press: Durham and London.

Wacquant, L. (2010) 'Crafting the neoliberal state: workfare, prisonfare and social insecurity', *Sociological Forum*, 25(2): 197–220.

Welshman, J. (2013) *Underclass* (2nd edn), London: Bloomsbury.

Winnett, R. and Kirkup, J. (2012) 'Problem families have 'too many children'', *The Telegraph*, 20 July, http://www.telegraph.co.uk/news/politics/9416535/Problem-families-have-too-many-children.html

Wright, S. (2012) 'Welfare-to-work, Agency and Personal Responsibility', *Journal of Social Policy*, 41(2): 309–28.

EIGHT

What counts as 'counter-conduct'? A governmental analysis of resistance in the face of compulsory community care

Hannah Jobling

Introduction

The treatment and control of individuals with severe mental health difficulties in the community has long been positioned as a problem in need of a solution. Community treatment orders (CTOs), enacted under the Mental Health Act (2007) are one recently introduced 'solution' in English mental health services. CTOs give mental health professionals the power to impose conditions on how service users live in the community, particularly in regards to medical treatment, and provide a mechanism for hospitalisation and treatment enforcement, called recall, if these conditions are not met or if the service user's mental health has deteriorated to the extent that they are deemed to be a risk to their own health and safety or that of others. CTOs tend to be aimed at particular groups of service users, especially those who have been described as 'revolving door', meaning they regularly stop their medication and experience relapse, leading to continuous movement between hospital and the community. The large majority of individuals placed on CTOs have been given a primary diagnosis of a psychosis-related disorder, and are on antipsychotic medication (Churchill et al, 2007), which the CTO is intended to ensure they adhere to. Although CTOs are regularly reviewed they can be renewed indefinitely, and so the individuals who are placed on them can be under compulsion in the community for an unlimited period of time.

CTOs have spread persistently across different jurisdictions over the last 30 years, and yet remain a much debated addition to the landscape of community mental health wherever they have been enacted. Modern mental health services, both in the community and in hospital, have always contained elements of compulsion and coercion, which can be seen as forming a continuum, from informal persuasion through to formally mandated hospital treatment (Monahan et al, 2001). However, a distinction can be made between the undefined and discretionary use of treatment pressure in the community and the legislatively defined role of CTOs. As Churchill et al (2007: 20, emphasis in original) state, CTOs are qualitatively different from what has gone before in the countries where they have been implemented because they, 'enforce community treatment outside (and independently) of the hospital, contain specific mechanisms for enforcement and/or revocation and are authorised by statute'. In this sense, CTOs have expanded the boundaries of legally mandated compulsion in mental health, and in doing so, have galvanised debates on where the balance should be struck between rights or risk, and freedom or coercion for individuals within the mental health system. Therefore, although CTOs are premised on distinctive historical and cultural contingencies, they also bring into sharp focus the longstanding moral balancing acts that frame the treatment (in the broadest sense of the word) of individuals diagnosed with severe mental health difficulties. Opinion on CTOs is strongly divided, with opponents arguing that an extension of compulsion into the community results in an unnecessary and stigmatising focus on risk, a loss of liberty and rights for service users, and the neglect of alternative, less coercive methods of engagement (Brophy and McDermott, 2003; Geller et al, 2006; Pilgrim, 2007). Conversely, supporters of CTOs argue that they help to engage service users who are hard to reach and/or considered a risk, facilitate community-based care, reduce rates and length of compulsory hospitalisation, encourage better treatment, improve clinical outcomes and promote recovery (Munetz and Frese, 2001; O'Reilly, 2006; Lawton-Smith et al, 2008;).

Given the controversial nature of CTOs and the concerns that have been raised about their potentially coercive effects, the experiences of those individuals who are made subject to them seem particularly important to understand. In this chapter the findings of an ethnographic study of CTOs in action are reported on, focusing on how individuals made subject to CTOs perceive the role the CTO has in their lives, and their subsequent responses to its imposition. Empirical work on CTOs has rarely been theorised, and in order to gain a deeper and more nuanced understanding of individual responses to compulsory intervention, Foucault's notion of governmentality is drawn upon to elucidate the diverse connections between 'practices of the self', 'conduct' and 'counter-conduct' in the face of compulsion. It will be argued that individuals' conceptions of self in relation to disciplinary policy interventions can lead to complex, ambiguous and perhaps unexpected responses to compulsion, which are not easily categorised into binary forms of compliance and resistance. The chapter begins with an exploration of governmentality and the useful role it can play in making sense of policy interventions, particularly those where compulsion of some form is integral to their function. The intended purposes of CTOs are discussed next, as to understand how individuals respond in varied ways to the CTO, it is important to first understand what rationalities they are responding to. This provides context for a series of 'cases', which highlight how the personal 'ends and means' of those made subject to the CTO coalesce or diverge from the 'ends and means' of the CTO.

Governmentality and subjectification

Governmentality originates in Foucault's critique of sovereign power, in which he contested the idea that power is operationalised in a centralised, repressive and hierarchical way. Instead, Foucault contended that 'power is everywhere' (Foucault, 1990: 93), being omnipresent and dispersed. As such, power is not 'possessed' by a few but is a force that is relational in nature and in constant flux within society; Foucault therefore 'challenges the polarisation of such categories as "powerful" and "powerless"' (Pease, 2002: 139). Consequently, Foucault argued that power does not have to be thought of solely in coercive terms, but can also be productive and indeed necessary – an integral part of how societies work (Gaventa, 2003). Such a conceptualisation of power shifts the focus from an analysis of sovereign power to disciplinary power and how it manifests at a 'micro-political' level.

Foucault derived disciplinary power as a particularly modern invention, emanating and evolving from the Enlightenment period: "The Enlightenment', which discovered the liberties, also invented the disciplines' (Foucault, 1977: 222). Disciplinary power is thus reliant on scientific discourses regarding the nature of human thought and behaviour, and associated techniques and strategies of objectification and subjectification, which are not premised on the use of force. In contrast to sovereign power then, disciplinary power is 'a modest, suspicious power [which] regards individuals both as objects and as instruments of its exercise' (Foucault, 1977: 170). The aforementioned techniques and strategies that underpin disciplinary power consist of various systems of surveillance and categorisation, made possible through the creation of the human sciences and associated expert-based disciplines such as social work, psychiatry, psychology and criminology. In this way a 'disciplinary society' is created, where individuals are measured against normalising judgements, and are disciplined, or discipline themselves accordingly.

As inferred here, Foucault's conceptualisation of disciplinary power is entwined with another of his central ideas, that of 'power/knowledge'. While Foucault did not conflate knowledge and power, he was interested in the complex and inextricable relationship between them, arguing that 'power produces knowledge ... power and knowledge directly imply each other' (Foucault, 1977: 27). The formation of a 'disciplinary society' is reliant on particular 'regimes of truth', which as dominant discourses constitute normalising judgements and in turn the regulation of conduct, as Foucault (1977: 27) goes on to say:

> Knowledge linked to power, not only assumes the authority of 'the truth' but has the power to make itself true. All knowledge, once applied in the real world, has effects, and in that sense at least, 'becomes true'. Knowledge, once used to regulate the conduct of others, entails constraint, regulation and the disciplining of practice. (Foucault, 1977: 27)

The question that therefore arises is how discourse – via power/knowledge – constitutes the subject, in particular through the human sciences and the accompanying application of expertise. Accordingly, power is locally dispersed rather than centrally coordinated, using small-scale rather than hegemonic means.

Foucault also posits how subjects might interact with and work at their own constitution through ethical 'practices of the self'. Foucault's view of what 'the self' might mean is not easily categorised. He rejected humanism and the idea of an unchanging and universal human nature, which allows each of us primacy over our selves and in a greater sense, our destinies and our world. However, in his development of 'practices of the self', which is based on a 'self-self' reflexive relationship, Foucault does not take a nihilistic position. His focus is not on defining human nature, but as Hacking (2004: 288) posits, on how people become who they are; the 'dynamics of human nature'. This presupposes that a flat, rather than vertical relationship exists between self-government, government by and of others, and government of the state (Dean, 1994: 196). If we accept that particular moral codes have held sway at particular junctures, and in turn interact with how we relate to ourselves and others via ethical practices, then the focus is on how we choose to form ourselves through a variety of means and in relation to a multiplicity of moral codes in the present. What this means is that: 'Foucault – most assuredly, not a sociologist – offers us a thoroughly sociological sense of self that does not reduce the self to the social' (Dean, 1994: 216).

In this sense, Foucault is not quite as far removed from an existentialist perspective on the role of agency as has sometimes been supposed (Hacking, 2004). His 'practices of the self' refers to four dimensions necessary for ethical self-work: 'ethical substance' or the focus for moral conduct; the external stimulus that leads to recognition of moral obligation; 'ethical work' or the means by which we attempt change; and the telos of such work, the end person that is aspired to (Foucault, 1997). Governmentality thus brings together disciplinary and reflexive power, connecting the processes by which we work on ourselves to broader governance processes by which we might be worked on. Governmentality has subsequently been developed as an analytical framework to illuminate the process of governing across a continuum that stretches beyond sovereign power, to a dispersed disciplinary 'microphysics of power', to reflexive power via reformation of identity and regulation of the self.

Specifically, an 'analytics of government' is focused on delineating various manifestations of the 'conduct of conduct' (Foucault, 2007: 192), which can be defined as 'any attempt to shape with some degree of deliberation aspects of our behaviour according to particular sets of norms for a variety of ends' (Dean, 2010: 10). Mckee (2009: 466, emphasis in original) draws out the dual foci of thought and action that an analytics of government explores as:

> Both the discursive field in which the exercise of power is rationalised – that is the space in which the problem of government is identified and solutions proposed; and the actual interventionist practices as manifest in specific programmes and techniques in which both individuals and groups are governed according to these aforementioned rationalities. (McKee, 2009: 466)

Governmentality then is concerned with both how conduct is problematised and how such rationalities are subsequently put to work through technologies that direct and reform conduct. However, the 'conduct of conduct' can be understood not only in relation to how others are governed, but as highlighted in 'practices of the self', how we govern ourselves. In other words, how 'individuals recognise themselves as particular kinds of persons and ... work upon and transform themselves in certain ways and towards particular goals'

(Hodges, 2002: 457). Individuals make choices in how they integrate influences; logically an individual who can respond positively to external mandates and techniques can also respond negatively. Foucault (2007: 75) terms such responses as 'counter-conducts', which he defines as 'the will not to be governed thusly, like that, by these people, at that price'. 'Counter-conducts' therefore are not rejections of government in itself, but an expression of seeking different forms and means of government. Within governmentality, forms of conduct and counter-conduct reflect each other and are interdependent – they both rely on the same processes of rationalities, technologies and reformation. As such, counter-conduct does not translate to resistance in terms of a revolutionary and emancipatory 'stepping outside' of pre-existing power structures. Disciplinary power operates at the micro-level and Foucault posited that so did counter-conducts. 'Thus there is no grand refusal, only dispersed and shifting points of resistance' (Death, 2010: 239), which draw on 'subjugated knowledges' to form alternative ways of thinking and going about governance.

Where governmentality has been empirically applied, such research has been criticised for being overly concerned with the 'discursive' aspect of governmentality and a corresponding neglect of the realisation of rationalities in practice (Clarke, 2004; Stenson, 2005; Marston and McDonald, 2006; Parr, 2009). This focus on discourse analysis emphasises a view of the '"social as a machine" reforming and constituting everything it comes into contact with' (Hunter, 2003: 331), which does not account for the techniques and technologies of government. That argument can be extended further to suggest that the focal point of governmentality – conduct itself – requires more detailed empirical exposition. The emphasis placed on discourse foregrounds power/knowledge while neglecting power/knowledge/ethics and the relationship between conduct, counter-conduct and 'practices of the self'. Specifically, this would involve study of the complex, unpredictable and contradictory nature of life as it is lived with agency and as embedded in variable social relations and institutions.

As Marston and McDonald (2006: 7) suggest then, 'an analytics of government is particularly relevant to the re-emerging genre of "street-level" policy evaluation … because it focuses attention away from the institutions of government towards the actual practices of government'. Policy interventions which rely on some form of compulsion are especially suited to a governmental approach given their often dual foci on reformation as well as control of the individual. Although Foucault decentred the role of sovereign power, Dean (2010: 8) has argued that governmentality still allows for the elucidation of 'sovereign and coercive rationalities and techniques' alongside and in interaction with disciplinary and reflexive forms of power, based on Foucault's (2000) contrasting notions of the 'city-citizen' and the 'shepherd-flock'. The individual as citizen can be defined as operating within a juridico-political structure, on equal footing with other citizens in the exercise of freedom, rights and responsibilities. By its nature, this conception relies on there being a boundary between those who could be classed as citizens (due to their ability to exercise freedom, rights and responsibilities) and those who cannot. Within the 'shepherd-flock' concept, the individual can be understood in pastoral terms as 'a living being who can be known in depth, whose welfare is to be cared for as an individual and as part of a population, as one submits to integration within complex forms of social solidarity' (Dean, 2010: 100, emphasis in original). Such an understanding is based on the belief that all individuals should be cared for. Notions of pastoral care and citizenship bring between them inherent tensions for the administration of liberal government because they depend on 'human beings as both self-governing individuals within a self-governing political community and clients to be administered, governed and normalised with respect to governmental objectives' (Dean, 1994: 209).

This brings us to what Foucault deemed the potential 'demonic' possibilities inherent in liberal government, which can arise from the interaction between discourses of citizenship and welfare (Foucault, 1988). It is Dean's (2010: 156) argument that such tensions, if sharp enough, can lead to the paradox of 'liberal illiberality', whereby the subject is managed via 'dividing practices' along the axes of responsibilisation and control: 'the subject is either divided inside himself or divided from others' (Foucault, 1983: 208). Such divisions often have a strong biopolitical element, which can be seen from extreme manifestations such as forced sterilisation of particular members of a society 'for their own good' and for the perceived good of everyone else, through to pervasive 'whole-population' messages on self-care and well-being. Certainly, CTOs can be seen as an example of a biopolitical intervention, as they are based on a particular understanding of embodied madness and their foundational function is to ensure the management of such madness via medical means. The intended 'ends' of CTOs are discussed in more detail next, as in order to fully make sense of the responses of those made subject to the CTO, it is necessary first to understand to what they are responding.

The rationalities for CTOs: risk and recovery

In recent decades, community care for those with severe mental health difficulties has become associated with public fears about insufficiently controlled individuals presenting a risk of harm to the community at large (Stuart, 2003; Pilgrim, 2007). CTOs as a tool for regular monitoring and medication compliance can therefore be posited as a political response to public concerns, most obviously in the North American practice of naming their introduction after the victim of homicide by a mentally disordered individual (for example, Brian's Law in Ontario, Kendra's Law in New York and Laura's Law in Florida). A similar narrative for CTOs was evident in England, beginning in 1998 when the then Secretary of State for Health, Frank Dobson proclaimed that 'community care has failed'. A spate of much reported homicides committed by individuals in contact with mental health services provided impetus for policy reform, with the Home Office as well as the Department of Health shaping mental health policy based on public safety. The public inquiries that arose from these killings attracted substantial media attention, particularly in relation to their key findings, which drew attention to common service failures and made a range of recommendations, including that legislation should be examined, particularly in regards to compulsory treatment and supervision in the community (Blom-Cooper et al, 1995; Sheppard, 1997). The government made it clear early on in the reform process that they believed the existing legislation for community supervision was outdated, and had failed to either benefit service users or to protect the public (Department of Health and Home Office, 2000). As the then Minister for Health Services, Rosie Winterton made clear, the argument for CTOs was closely linked to risk:

> There are 1,300 suicides every year and 50 homicides by people who have been in contact with mental health services. We believe that supervised community treatment is vital to helping patients continue to take treatment when they leave hospital and to enable clinicians to take rapid action if relapse is on the horizon. (HC Deb, 18th June 2007, Vol 461, Col 1193)

However, it would be simplistic to suggest an overriding concern with risk was the sole driver behind policy making on CTOs. CTOs have also been associated, albeit much less overtly, with a somewhat paternalistic version of the recovery approach in mental health, where it has been surmised they can act to provide a secure foundation for individuals to operate from and to encourage self-efficacy. Dawson (2009: 29) argues that an understanding of CTOs as enabling self-direction and choice is philosophically grounded in the concept of positive liberty (Berlin, 1969), which he defines as 'our capacity for self-governance ... our ability to set goals and have some chance of meeting them, and to maintain important relationships, without being dominated by internal constraints that prevent this occurring'. The framing of CTOs as a conduit for individual growth and empowerment is most evident in Munetz and Frese's (2001) assertion that CTOs are reconcilable with the recovery model and indeed, can act as an opportunity for individuals to become 'well enough' through long-term medication compliance to start the recovery process. In this way, they suggest longer-term outcomes of being on a CTO could include service users sustaining meaningful activity in the community, experiencing better quality of life and holding better relationships with significant others. The result of this thinking is that arguments for individual freedom are constructed as morally hazardous, as it is not enough to simply offer services and medical care which service users are free to reject (Kinderman and Tai, 2008). Munetz et al (2003: 178) go as far as to say that practitioners who do not accept the necessity for compulsory community treatment are negating their 'obligation as helper and healer'. Although less prominent as a rationale than risk in policy debates, CTOs were nevertheless defended with recourse to recovery in parliament: 'Supervised community treatment ... will allow patients, so far as possible, to live normal lives in the community. This will reduce the risk of social exclusion and stigma associated with detention in hospital for long periods of time or with repeated hospital admissions' (Roll and Whittaker, 2007: 21).

Recovery in these terms requires that strong boundaries are put in place in order for individuals to overcome internal constraints, so that they are able to develop the discipline to comply, maintain stability and manage their lives. From this perspective, CTOs can be seen as a typical governmental practice which is aimed at influencing what individuals may become; the limitation of freedom through control in the short term encourages individuals' capacity for freedom in the longer term.

Returning to the concept of 'dividing practices' discussed earlier, CTOs can therefore be characterised as differentiating and categorising 'low-risk' individuals who are 'empowered' to become responsibilised, autonomous, and self-regulating members of society from 'high risk' individuals who require external regulation (Kemshall, 2002). CTOs enable the reformation of individuals and their conduct if possible, but also allow for control and separation of the individual from society and the application of sanctions, should this transformative optimism prove unwarranted. Within this framework, CTOs contain both inclusionary and exclusionary facets so as to both manage risk and bring individuals into the fold of citizenship. The terminology of CTOs reflects these dual objectives. They have a highly contractual flavour, most specifically in the use of the term 'conditions' which service users must 'agree' and adhere to, or otherwise face the consequence of recall to hospital. Behaviour control in this sense is concerned with risk management in both a concrete and an abstract sense, the latter meaning prudent individuals are expected to make their own way in society while complying with complex rules and requirements, or as Rose (2002: 19) puts it in regards to mental health, '"play the game" of community care'. Citizenship is therefore defined conditionally, and 'irregular citizens' (Zedner, 2010) are expected to earn their way to full citizenship through conforming to prescribed expectations. As Zedner (2010: 397) describes, the use of 'contractual devices', specific to the individual, subvert 'the universalism of the ... law and [delegate] considerable quasilegislative powers to the public officials who determine their precise terms'. In this way, CTOs change the state of play in regards to the rights that those who are placed on them hold, as compared to 'regular citizens'.

There are connections here with a broader narrative that describes an intensification in recent decades of a behaviourist trend in social policy and an associated turn to 'coercive support' across a range of welfare domains, aimed at ensuring individual responsibility (Rodger, 2008; Flint, 2009). Both the recovery and risk agendas as played out in mental health policy and specifically in relation to CTOs locate the problem and the solution within the individual, thus individualising social problems. In these terms, it is the individual's refusal to comply with medication, which leads to their riskiness and/or lack of recovery, and the underpinning argument for using CTOs has been the ability they would bring to enforce medication compliance. There is little acknowledgement in this explanatory framework of the complex reasons why individuals might be non-compliant with medication, or the societal and institutional factors, which mediate risk and pathways to recovery. In the next section, the complexities of individual responses to CTOs are explored via a series of four cases drawn from research findings.

Conduct and counter-conduct in response to CTOs

The findings reported here come from an ethnographic study of CTOs, which traced the pathways of 18 CTOs in two English mental health trusts over a period of eight months. Interviews were carried out with 18 individuals who were on a CTO and the professionals who were working with them. Case file analysis and observations of key meetings such as CTO reviews and appeals also took place, and unstructured time was spent within community mental health services in order to examine the day-to-day use of CTOs. In this way, a picture was formed of CTOs over time, within context and through a variety of methods utilised to capture both meaning and action in their everyday practice[1].

The following cases are drawn from these 18 CTO cases and have been chosen to highlight the various connections that can be made between service users' conceptions of self as related to the CTO and how they responded to it as an intervention in their life. Service users can be placed along a spectrum from acceptance to resistance of CTOs, and the cases discussed take different points on this continuum. If we revisit Foucault's (1997) dimensions of ethical self-work, we can see that they relate to: external impetus for change, the means by which we act upon ourselves to bring about such change, and the end person we seek to become through these means. In formulating forms of conduct and counter-conduct, the CTO acts as the external stimulus, and the task here is to delineate how the means and ends service users have conceived for themselves relate to the means and ends – the practices and rationalities – of the CTO.

Acceptance of CTO means and ends: Nick[2]

Nick can be described as a service user who wholeheartedly accepted the CTO and who expressed strong respect for the authority of the professionals who worked with him. He had not experienced recall to hospital under the CTO, as he had adhered to its conditions and practitioners saw the role of the CTO in his case being for boundary-setting rather than active intervention. In a superficial sense, he is a CTO 'success' story, particularly regarding behaviour change. However, there are interesting nuances that can be drawn out which are not quite as clear-cut, beginning with how the CTO related to the changes he wanted to see in himself. Nick aligned himself with a particular aspect of the CTO agenda, corresponding to how he saw himself and his relationships to others.

Nick expressed extreme anxiety about what he thought he was capable of in relation to harming others, particularly those who he was close to, and the CTO for him performed an important psychological function through imposing control when he did not feel able to exercise self-control. As he said: "being on a CTO if the truth's known, I know deep down I'll never ever get to the point where I've totally lost control like I've done in the past." Nick's self-conception was refracted through a 'risk' identity and he aligned himself with the risk mandate of CTOs: "I don't think it's something for everyone, it's something that is good for violent, psychotic people like me." Therefore, he accepted one particular 'end' of the CTO – risk management – as it related to the kind of individual he wanted to become. As such, Nick was very clear that he did not want to be discharged from the CTO, and talked about it as being necessary for the foreseeable future, for the safety of others as well as his continuing and relative autonomy in the community.

Nick's compliance to the CTO and insistent dependence on its continuation can, however, also be seen as a form of resistance to practitioners' attempts to 'move people on' to independence and in this way he was not entirely an exemplar of conduct. For Nick, the idea of the CTO being removed generated similar feelings associated with coercion that study participants who were resentful of the CTO described, such as not having their view respected, anxiety and a lack of control. In Nick's case, a pattern of uncertainty surfaced in practitioner discussion of how and if to bring about CTO discharge. He had been on the CTO for three years by the time of the fieldwork, and his care coordinator thought it was time to try him without the CTO, but was also aware of the distress such a decision would cause. It is possible to see in this dilemma some of the tensions inherent in the purposes of CTO. While Nick can be positioned as having internalised both CTO means and ends in his appreciation of its boundaries and its risk-oriented rationality, he was also thinking and acting in opposition to a recovery narrative that emphasises the avoidance of ingrained dependency. A professed need for dependence can be seen as inimical to an intervention that foregrounds individual autonomy.

Resistance to CTO means but acceptance of ends: James

James, conversely, had taken on board the messages about responsibilised recovery inculcated in the CTO and expressed in a literal sense the transformation he felt the CTO had brought: "Compared to when I first came on the CTO and now, it's like two different people... I mean from negative to positive. That's the difference... I mean my feelings towards people, my actions towards people." He saw himself very much in relation to the broader mental health system and network of support he received from practitioners, family and friends. In this sense he felt it was his 'duty' and responsibility to use the CTO to recover and live what he viewed as a productive and independent life. James related this to the contractual nature of the CTO, with him upholding his side of the bargain: "And the CTO, if you're not compliant to it, you're wasting people's time. You're abusing the system. You're responsible for yourself. That's what the CTO is about, isn't it? So the responsibility for taking your meds, for coming to your appointments, for seeing your doctor, I mean, yes, it's a huge responsibility."

Although James was different from Nick in terms of which CTO purpose he related to, it appeared he had also strongly accepted the place of the CTO in his life. Again, however, by following James through the CTO it became evident that his case was not entirely straightforward. While James accepted the ends of the CTO, he had contested its means and in particular how he had his medication given under its remit, whereby he was placed on an injection for the first time rather than self-administered oral medication. As he says here: "I had a bit of negativity towards my nurse. There wasn't a bond; there wasn't a friendship. It was like, 'no, you're the nurse and you're the injection and that hurts, I don't like it and I'm tired of it'." It seems that James's care coordinator's role in giving him the injection under the CTO created a professionalised distance and conflated her with the painful intervention she administered.

Consequently, in order to reach acceptance of the CTO, James shaped its means in a way which was coherent with his understanding of it. James did not see the CTO as being 'done' to him, and he demonstrated considerable agency in making the reality of the CTO fit with his responsibilised conception of it, which revolved around him taking control for his recovery. He did this by making a unilateral decision on how and where he should receive his medication, arranging for the injection to be administered through his GP practice instead of by his care coordinator. Here we can see that an element of the CTO that would be 'taken for granted' by practitioners as being inherent to how the CTO worked, was viewed very differently by James as being in opposition to how he saw it. He explained: "I felt that the CTO and my injections were in conflict because I didn't feel in control of my injections. I was being told you've got to have them. It felt like the responsibility had been taken out of my hands. It was in the hands of the nurses and the doctors here and I thought, 'well, that's not fair because my CTO says I've got to be responsible, I've got to be in charge' and then, when I went up to the medical centre and they started doing it, I settled down a bit better." For James, his actions allowed him to 'settle down' and achieve stability on the CTO. In making this choice, James reduced his treating team's ability to monitor his medication and consequently created some 'space' for himself within compulsion. Through buying into the recovery vision for CTOs, James also rejected and effectively resisted the control-oriented means by which the CTO functioned.

Resistance to CTO ends but acceptance of means: Simon

Resistance to CTO ends but acceptance of its means meant in Simon's case, 'playing the CTO game' for his own ends, which did not cohere with the CTO drivers of risk or recovery. This was based on Simon's ambivalent feelings towards the CTO: on the one hand the CTO was antithetical to his dreams of achieving 'normality' and to a life lived without feeling 'different'; on the other, the functions of the CTO allowed him to carry on using particular support mechanisms. Simon had developed a pattern over the years of seeking admission to a respite facility as a coping strategy, but with the closure of this service and increasingly limited access to beds in acute services, his coping strategy had been disrupted. To this end, Simon regularly attempted (and at least initially succeeded) in triggering recall to hospital under the CTO by refusing his medication and avoiding contact with services. He explained this as a way for him to get admission to hospital, which he saw as a significant safety net: "And so for me it is like most people who have mental health problems, hospital is a safe environment, away from society, away from everything. You don't have to worry about somewhere to stay and whether you are going to get kicked out."

Simon's care coordinator was sympathetic to why Simon might do this, as a natural response to the changes and subsequent limitations of services: "I think he doesn't like the CTO and he would like to be in control of it himself. He'd like to be able to say, 'I need a break now', when he's had enough of dealing with living alone, and that's how he was managed previously. But unfortunately we don't have respite care anymore ... so the only way he can get respite is by becoming non-compliant, deteriorating and getting into hospital that way, where he feels safe." Indeed, practitioners generally felt that the recall function of the CTO could provide a much-needed protective 'short-cut' to hospital in overstretched services where admission was often difficult to attain. However, at the same time Simon's actions did not fit with the mandated use of recall, which was directed by when practitioners thought it was necessary. Nor did his behaviour adhere to the priorities of inpatient services – self-perceived welfare needs were not viewed as an acceptable reason for acute care, and service users were usually quickly discharged if this was deemed the reason for their being admitted. As Simon's CTO went on, it became increasingly difficult for him to be recalled; in his case notes it was requested that practitioners no longer initiated recall unless absolutely necessary, and in an appeal report it was noted: 'His social worker felt that the CTO was not necessary since if anything Simon was too demanding of support.' Simon had effectively undermined the use of the CTO by making it difficult for practitioners to decide when they thought he 'needed' recall and consequently his CTO was eventually discharged.

By subverting the key component of the CTO – recall – Simon had found a way of meeting his self-prescribed needs and retaining some kind of agency. Simon thus used the means of the CTO as a way of maintaining the level of care he felt he required. However, Simon did not align his actions with CTO policy aims as he was opposed to such principles applying to him, and certainly his use did not fit with either of the policy agendas for CTOs. In particular, the recovery narrative for CTOs can be viewed as not only premised on encouraging independence but also on managing levels of service use. This suggests that the development of CTOs for 'revolving door' service users such as Simon was also partly resource-driven, particularly within the context of the continuing rollback of inpatient services and residualisation of state support more generally. In this sense, CTOs can be understood as aimed at maintenance through the enforced delivery of medically-focused 'bare minimum' provision. What is interesting is that despite this – in a paradoxical sense – Simon turned the CTO to his advantage by forcing access to resources via the obligations practitioners held under the CTO. In terms of conduct then, Simon acted within the remit of the CTO, but in a way which destabilised its agendas, and in a way which eventually rendered the CTO void in his case.

Resistance to CTO ends and means: Andrew

At the furthest end of the spectrum were those individuals who rejected both the means of the CTO and what it stood for. Resistance to CTO ends and means meant a complete rejection of the 'service user role', and Andrew provides interesting insights into how this might play out. Andrew did not believe the CTO had any place in his life – he resented both the compulsion it placed him under, and the sense that it was aimed at shaping his attitude and behaviour, when he wanted to be 'left alone' by services. He believed that the CTO was in place, "… just so they [services] can keep an eye on me, so I can't operate, and to protect professional interests: It's a way of controlling the situation or controlling someone's behaviour, which puts people's minds at ease and [sarcastically] I think everybody's minds have got to be at ease."

Andrew would continue to have occasional meetings with his care coordinator who he had known for some years, but avoided appointments to have his injection where possible, and refused to meet his psychiatrist. Because of this, he was an individual who was made to undergo monthly recalls to hospital in order to enforce medication compliance. These 'recall cycles' were at the sharp end of compulsion under the CTO. One of the characteristics of CTOs across all countries where they are enacted is that none of them cross the ethical 'Rubicon' (Dawson, 2005) of enforced treatment in a community setting – people are always brought back into hospital for enforced medication. The cycling of individuals in and out of hospital on a monthly basis to receive their depot means that the concept of 'crossing the Rubicon' loses its potency, as the boundary between community and hospital became porous and enforced treatment in the community happened by proxy.

For those individuals like Andrew whose resistance to the CTO regularly triggered recall, practitioners might think of it as a 'failed CTO' because of the problematic ethical questions it raises, and because it brings less stability for individuals in the community, damaging the therapeutic relationship and costing time and resources. An alternative view was if repeat recalls means service users are regularly taking medication and subsequently staying relatively well, then the CTO was working in lowering their risk to others and ensuring they are protected from the worst of relapse. A combination of Andrew's forensic history and because recall in his case tended to be relatively straightforward, meant that his treating team had decided on balance that his CTO was worth retaining indefinitely even though it had a significant psychological negative effect on him personally. Out of all the cases described thus far, Andrew's thoughts and actions in relation to the CTO can most typically be seen as 'counter-conduct', but his experience is also most redolent of the 'dividing practices' of liberal governmental rationalities and technologies. This meant that his attempts at shaping the CTO were also the least effective; his actions meant he was placed very firmly within the parameters of the CTO by practitioners. Agency and resistance are often closely linked in research and theory on the responses of those made subject to coercive policy interventions, and yet in Andrew's case, the latter significantly limited the former.

Discussion

These cases have illustrated the non-dichotomous forms conduct and counter-conduct can take to governmental programmes. Dawson et al (2003: 253) suggest that the CTO has the capacity to 'both advance and limit [an individual's] freedom, in different respects and at different times in their lives'. This complex and fluctuating interaction between compulsion – as characterised by the CTO – and freedom was certainly reflected in participant experiences. The CTO is a compulsory measure, but how much room for manoeuvre participants believed they had within the CTO varied, both individually and in relation to different aspects of the CTO. As noted earlier, conduct and counter-conduct are two sides of the same coin and mutually constitutive – neither involves 'stepping outside' of existing power structures, but instead responding to disciplinary power in differential ways, as related to both individual and social means and ends. Removing this 'either/or' distinction from discussions of power and resistance means that such responses can be seen in a more variegated sense, which does not look 'beyond government' (Rose, 1999: 281) but at how individual action plays out within the strategies and techniques of government (Death, 2010). As Death (2010: 236, emphasis in original) comments, forms of conduct 'have the potential to reinforce and bolster, as well as and at the same time as, undermining and challenging dominant forms of ... governance'.

With CTOs, it is possible to see where conduct and counter-conduct contain continuity and movement between them: with Nick who although accepting of the risk agenda for CTOs and compliant in every sense to the CTO, highlights the challenges practitioners might face when individuals resist the lifting of compulsion; James, whose personal 'ends' aligned with the recovery-oriented aim of the CTO even if he resented and reformed the means of the CTO in itself; Simon who although opposed to the CTO in principle took the means of the CTO to achieve his own ends of support; and with Andrew, who became further entwined in systems of conduct the more he attempted to resist the CTO. It is also possible to see the significance that needs to be placed on personhood when considering the effects policy interventions have on individuals. As Sayer (2005: 51) explains, interpreting this normative dimension of everyday life is necessary to avoid a representation of 'bloodless figures who seemingly drift through life, behaving in ways which bear the marks of their social position and relations of wider discourses, disciplining themselves only because it is required of them, but as if nothing mattered to them'. These cases illustrate the potent psychological responses service users could have to the CTO as premised on the way it keyed into their sense of identity and reflected their sense of self and self in relation to others as an articulation of being and belonging in society. 'Thin' theorisations of change through policy programmes framed as 'carrots, sticks and sermons' (Bemelmans-Videc et al, 1998) do not account for the individual they are imposed on – their history, hopes and self-conceptions, or the reflexive work such factors instigate. A governmental analysis of how service users think and act in response to disciplinary and coercive forms of power has implications for why CTOs follow particular pathways. The CTO cannot be understood as transformative in and of itself, but instead as acting in conjunction with ethical 'self-work'. Consequently, simplistic policy theories about the responses of 'target' groups to intervention cannot predicate what programme outcomes will be. It seems that both the multifaceted motivations and challenges service users bring to CTOs, coupled with the complex ways they interact with CTOs, mean such expectations are not always fulfilled. In this way the process of subjectification via governmental means is complicated by how people are 'made up' from below via communicative action and the application of lay normativity as well as from above via discourse (Hacking, 2004: Sayer, 2005).

Indeed, the responses of service users to CTOs highlight the 'inconvenient facts' about discontinuities between explicit governmental rationalities and their strategic effects (Dean, 2010). Foucault argued that programmes of government include the seeds of their failure, which inevitably leads to on-going strategies and mutations in forms of government, and we can see how that plays out with the evolution of CTOs. As Lemke (2000: 9) suggests, struggles and compromise are integral to governmental programmes, 'actively contributing to ... "fissures" and "incoherencies" inside them'. Specifically, the cases of Nick and James exemplify that the dual risk management and responsibilised version of recovery for which CTOs are intended to work, carry tensions, which are not easily reconciled. Further, the cases of Nick and Simon in particular bring to the surface a further 'ground-level' rationality, which is missing from the dual risk/recovery narrative for CTOs – that of dependency and associated care – which does not align easily with 'contemporary practices of government ... which have come to rely on the governed themselves' (Dean, 2010: 82). It is difficult to separate out the responsibilised individual from the networks of support which sustain them and within which they are entwined (Trnka and Trundle, 2014). Flint (2009) suggests that the public positioning of policy programmes aimed at behavioural change as premised on coercion can hide the provision of enhanced support such programmes may provide to the individuals made subject to them, particularly when more universal provision is becoming increasingly restricted. The responses of individuals in the face of CTO means and ends particularly demonstrates that they do not necessarily perceive the CTO in terms of their own 'power and powerlessness, consent and constraint, subjectivity and subjection' (Dean, 2010: 84). An analysis of conduct and counter-conduct thus also moves the debate on CTOs beyond the opposing positions that are prevalent in discussions of their use.

Notes

[1] For more detailed information on methodology, see Jobling (2014).

[2] All participants have been given pseudonyms.

References

Bemelmans-Videc, M., Rist, R. and Vedung, E. (1998) *Carrots, Sticks and Sermons: Policy Instruments and their Evaluation*, New Jersey: Transaction Publishers.

Berlin, I. (1969) *Four Essays on Liberty*, Oxford: Oxford University Press.

Blom-Cooper, L., Hally, H. and Murphy, E. (1995) *The Falling Shadow: One Patient's Mental Health Care 1978-1993*, London: Gerald Duckworth & Co Ltd.

Brophy, L. and McDermott, F. (2003) 'What's driving involuntary treatment in the community? The social, policy, legal and ethical context', *Australasian Psychiatry*, 11(1): 84–88.

Churchill, R., Owen, G., Singh, S. and Hotopf, M. (2007), *International Experiences of Using Community Treatment Orders*, London: Institute of Psychiatry, Kings College London.

Clarke, J. (2004) *Changing Welfare, Changing States: New Directions in Social Policy*, London: Sage Publishing.

Dawson, J. (2005) *Community Treatment Orders: International Comparisons*, Dunedin: Otago University Press.

Dawson, J. (2009) 'Concepts of liberty in mental health law', *Otago Law Review*, 12(1): 23–36.

Dawson. J., Romans. S., Gibbs. A. and Ratter. N. (2003) 'Ambivalence about community treatment orders', *International Journal of Law and Psychiatry*, 26: 243–55.

Dean, M. (1994) *Critical and effective histories: Foucault's methods and historical sociology*, London: Routledge.

Dean, M. (2010) *Governmentality: Power and Rule in Modern Society* (2nd edn), London: Sage Publishing.

Death, C. (2010) 'Counter-conducts: a Foucauldian analytics of protest', *Social Movement Studies*, 9(3): 235–51.

Department of Health and the Home Office (2000) *Reforming the Mental Health Act*, (Cm 5016), London: The Stationery Office.

Flint, J. (2009) 'Governing marginalised populations: The role of coercion, support and agency', *European Journal of Homelessness*, 3: 247–60.

Foucault, M. (1977) *Discipline and Punish: the Birth of the Prison*, New York, NY: Pantheon.

Foucault, M. (1983) 'The subject and power', in H. Dreyfus and P. Rabinow (eds) *Michel Foucault: Beyond Reason and Hermeneutics* (2nd edn), Chicago: University of Chicago Press.

Foucault, M. (1988) *Politics, Philosophy, Culture*, L. Kritzmann (Ed), New York: Routledge.

Foucault, M. (1990) *The History of Sexuality. Volume 1: An Introduction*, London: Vintage.

Foucault, M. (1997) 'The ethics of the concern of the self as a practice of freedom', in P. Rabinow (ed) *The Essential Works of Michel Foucault, volume 1*, New York: The New Press.

Foucualt, M. (2000), 'Omnes et singulatum: towards a critique of political reason', in J. Faubion (ed) *Power*, New York: The New Press. Foucault, M. (2007) *Security, Territory, Population*, London: Palgrave.

Gaventa, J. (2003) 'Power after Lukes: An overview of theories of power since Lukes and their application to development', unpublished briefing paper.

Geller, J., Fisher, W., Grudzinskas, A., Clayfield, J. and Lawlor, T. (2006) 'Involuntary outpatient treatment as 'deinstitutionalised coercion': the net-widening concerns', *International Journal of Law and Psychiatry*, 29(6): 551–62.

Hacking, I. (2004) 'Between Michel Foucault and Erving Goffman: between discourse in the abstract and face-to-face interaction', *Economy and Society*, 33(3): 277–302.

HM Government (2007) *The Mental Health Act 2007*, London: The Stationery Office.

Hodges, I. (2002) 'Moving beyond words: therapeutic discourse and ethical problematization', *Discourse Studies*, 4(4): 455–79.

Hunter, S. (2003) 'A critical analysis of approaches to the concept of social identity in social policy', *Critical Social Policy*, 23(3): 322–44.

Jobling, H. (2014) 'Using ethnography to explore causality in mental health policy and practice', *Qualitative Social Work*, 13(1): 49–68.

Kemshall, H. (2002) *Risk, Social Policy and Welfare*, Maidenhead: Open University Press.

Kinderman, P. and Tai, S. (2008) 'Psychological models of mental disorder, human rights, and compulsory mental health care in the community', *International Journal of Law and Psychiatry*, 31(6): 479–86.

Lawton-Smith, S., Dawson, J. and Burns, T. (2008) 'Community treatment orders are not a good thing', *The British Journal of Psychiatry*, 193(2): 96–100.

Lemke, T. (2000) 'Foucault, governmentality and critique', Rethinking Marxism Conference, 21-24 September, University of Amhurst.

Marston, G. and McDonald, C. (eds) (2006) *Analysing Social Policy: A Governmental Approach*, Cheltenham: Edward Elgar Publishing.

McKee, K. (2009) 'Post-Foucauldian governmentality: What does it offer critical social policy analysis?' *Critical Social Policy*, 29(3): 465–86.

Monahan, J., Steadman, H., Silver, E., Appelbaum, P., Robbins, P., Mulvey, E., Roth, L., Grisso, T. and Banks, S. (2001) *Rethinking Risk Assessment: The Macarthur Study of Mental Disorder and Violence*, New York: Oxford University Press.

Munetz, M.R. and Frese, F.J. (2001) 'Getting ready for recovery: Reconciling mandatory treatment with the recovery vision', *Psychiatric Rehabilitation Journal*, 25(1): 35–42.

Munetz, M.R., Galon, P.A. and Frese, F.J. (2003) 'The ethics of mandatory community treatment', *Journal of the American Academy of Psychiatry and the Law*, 31(2): 173–83.

O'Reilly, R.L. (2006) 'Community Treatment Orders: This Emperor is Fully Dressed!' *Canadian Journal of Psychiatry*, 51(11): 691.

Parr, S. (2009) 'Confronting the reality of anti-social behaviour', *Theoretical Criminology*, 13(3): 363–81.

Pease, B. (2002) 'Rethinking Empowerment: A Postmodern Reappraisal for Emancipatory Practice', *British Journal of Social Work*, 32(2): 135–47.

Pilgrim, D. (2007) 'New 'mental health' legislation for England and Wales: some aspects of consensus and conflict', *Journal of Social Policy*, 36(1): 79–95.

Rodger, J.J. (2008) *Criminalising Social Policy: Anti-Social Behaviour and Welfare in a De-Civilised Society*, Devon: Willan Publishing.

Roll, J. and Whittaker, M. (2007) The Mental Health Bill [HL], House of Commons Library Research Paper 07/33, 30 March.

Rose, N. (1999) *Powers of Freedom: Reframing Political Thought*, Cambridge: Cambridge University Press.

Rose, N. (2002) 'Society, madness and control', in A. Buchanan (ed) *The Care of the Mentally Disordered Offender in the Community*, Oxford: Oxford University Press, pp 3–25.

Sayer, A. (2005) *The Moral Significance of Class*, Cambridge: Cambridge University Press.

Sheppard, D. (1997) *Mental Health Inquiries published during 1997.* Institute of Mental Health Law.

Stenson, K. (2005) 'Sovereignty, biopolitics and the local government of crime in Britain', *Theoretical Criminology*, 9(3): 265–87.

Stuart, H. (2003) 'Violence and mental illness: an overview', *World Psychiatry*, 2(2): 121.

Trnka, S. and Trundle, C. (2014) 'Competing responsibilities: Moving beyond neoliberal responsibilisation', *Anthropological Forum, A Journal of Social Anthropology and Comparative Sociology*, 24(2): 136–53.

Zedner, L. (2010) 'Security, the State, and the Citizen: The Changing Architecture of Crime Control', *New Criminal Law Review*, 13(2): 379–403.

Part Three
Individualised budgets
in social policy

Catherine Needham

The shift to individualised funding is a trend within a range of social policy sectors and across many countries. This is evident in the move to personal budgets in adult social care and personal health budgets in the English NHS, as well as the trialling of individualised funding for rough sleepers, for parents of children with special educational needs and for adoptive parents (Needham and Glasby, 2014). Scotland is developing its own version of self-directed support, with an individualised budget element, and many countries already offer so-called 'cash for care' schemes (Manthorpe et al, 2015).

Contributions to this themed section explore these changes in different international settings, and also explore the validity of the underlying assumptions, which have driven the shift towards greater use of individualised funding. Individualised funding can have a range of justifications – is it about giving citizens 'the power of the purse' to stimulate a better range of support services; is it about empowering citizens as autonomous choice agents, within a rights agenda; is it about challenging 'expert knowledge' and downgrading professionalism; is it about transferring risk and responsibility to the users of services, while masking funding cuts and reductions in support? It is useful to explore how far these perspectives are borne out in the experiences and outcomes of people receiving budgets and those working to support them.

The chapters in this section offer a range of empirical lenses through which to examine these debates. For Purcal et al it is the emerging context of the National Disability Insurance Scheme, a new approach to disability support that is being piloted in Australia. For Brown it is in the context of individualised financial support for people who are homeless, drawing primarily on a study undertaken in Wales. The chapter by Karen Jones and colleagues reports findings from a national evaluation of the personal health budget pilot programme in England, funded by the Department of Health. Christensen's chapter discusses the user-controlled personal assistance scheme in Norway. In Locke and West's chapter, they explore individualised budgets for older people in England, taking a feminist ethic of care approach.

Across these different territories and services, there are a number of similar insights: that rights-based approaches based on freeing people up to make financial choices risk underestimating the relational context within which people experience care and make choices. Locke and West critique the notion that choice is best exercised by autonomous individuals who can free themselves from dependency, and all of the chapters in different ways support this point. The importance of providing support and information for people to use individualised budgets effectively comes out in all of the contributions. The empirical studies cited here do not present examples of confident choice agents, itching to use the 'power of the purse'. Rather, people are diffident and uncertain about whether they have a budget, and what that budget might be used for: as one of Purcal et al's interviewees puts it, "There are more people set up to help you find the answer, but not so many to help you find the questions". What is also evident in all of the studies is that the implementation of standardised national approaches or pilot studies results in very different local practices in relation to eligibility for budgets or rules around what budgets can be spent on. Such observations get in the way of neat generalisations of the impact of personalised funding within a national context. All of these findings resonate with existing literature on the broader tensions surrounding personalisation, particularly as it is developed in a context of funding reductions and very limited support, and information for people as they make choices about support (Needham and Glasby, 2014).

As well as similarities between the chapters there are also a number of differences. In Norway, access to individualised funding has been open to most people with long-term care needs, whereas the Australian proposals limit access to individualised packages to people with very high support needs. Many of the articles on care services affirm the importance of keeping people embedded in their local networks, whereas one aim of individualised budgets in the context of homelessness was to break existing social networks where these were found to be increasing behaviours associated with homelessness.

Together these chapters help to deepen an understanding of individualised approaches within social policy. They are methodologically diverse and draw on different theoretical perspectives, but together they present a compelling account of the ways in which individualised budgets can be a means to getting a better life – but only as part of a broader set of supports and an adequate financial settlement.

References

Manthorpe, J., Martineau, S., Ridley, J., Cornes, M., Rosengard, A. and Hunter, S. (2015) 'Embarking on self-directed support in Scotland: a focused scoping review of the literature', *European Journal of Social Work*, 18(1): 36–50.

Needham, C. and Glasby, J. (eds) (2014) *Debates in personalisation,* Bristol: Policy Press.

NINE

Social insurance for individualised disability support: implementing the Australian National Disability Insurance Scheme (NDIS)

Christiane Purcal, Karen R. Fisher and Ariella Meltzer

Introduction

Australia is implementing an ambitious new approach to individualised disability support based on a social insurance model. In a world first, the National Disability Insurance Scheme (NDIS) is funded through a levy on income and general taxation and gives Australians with disability an entitlement to social service support. It does not affect access to income support, which remains organised and funded through the general taxation system. Can the new scheme work in practice?

Constraints on the NDIS are whether people are eligible and what the size of their individual package might be. The estimate is that about 10% of people with disability will receive packages when the NDIS is fully implemented by 2019. Most people will continue to be pointed towards general social services, which will likely remain in short supply. Questions arise about the availability of mainstream and specialised services; coverage for people with complex needs; and information gaps to access support. The feasibility of the scheme remains under question during this establishment stage.

This chapter describes the NDIS approach and implementation so far and summarises concerns and challenges about the NDIS discussed in the literature. It then uses data from an action research project to inform these feasibility questions about how people find out about and receive the individualised support they need. Some people who took part in the research lived in NDIS pilot sites and others accessed other individual packages or contributed their expectations for future access when the NDIS is fully implemented in 2019. The research focused on whether they had sufficient knowledge and support to make use of that opportunity. This question has important implications for the position of individual packages relative to other social services.

In Australia, disabled people are currently referred to as people with disability and social care is referred to as social services or disability support; this is the terminology used in this chapter.

NDIS development to date

Individualised approaches to organising disability support are increasingly common internationally, whether driven by consumer sovereignty or citizen's rights (Needham and Glasby, 2014). Australia too has shifted in this direction over the last three decades, with various programs, pilots and eventually state-wide arrangements (Laragy et al, 2015). In 2013, national legislation was passed to introduce the NDIS, a social insurance model of disability support. The history and consequences of that change are discussed here.

The NDIS was conceived in the context of Australia's ratification of the United Nations Convention on the Rights of Persons with Disabilities (CRPD, 2008), committing Australian governments to a human rights framing of policy affecting people with disability. Plans to meet government obligations under the Convention were articulated in the National Disability Strategy (NDS) 2010–2020, in which the Australian national government and those of the eight states and territories expressed their 'shared vision [...] for an inclusive Australian society that enables people with disability to fulfil their potential as equal citizens' (Commonwealth of Australia, 2011: 8). One of the policy planks of the Strategy was to investigate whether and how to implement an NDIS.

The NDIS was first seriously mooted by the Disability Investment Group (Price WaterhouseCoopers, 2009), which had been assembled by the government to explore innovative disability funding ideas from the private sector. In response, the government referred the question to its independent research and advisory body, the Productivity Commission. The Commission's inquiry recommended a social insurance design for the NDIS (Productivity Commission, 2011). It argued that without significant reform of disability support, people with disability and the people in their lives were constrained in their capacity for active participation in society and the economy, and that the cost of current support arrangements was unmanageable for them and governments. In the words of the Productivity Commission, the system at the time was 'underfunded, unfair, fragmented, and inefficient, and gives people with a disability little choice and no certainty of access to appropriate supports' (Productivity Commission, 2011: 2).

The Productivity Commission recommended an insurance model because of the widespread recognition in the Australian public and political spheres that the previous, state-based system – which was highly rationed and largely based on fixed funding to disability service providers – achieved poor outcomes and was financially unsustainable. An insurance model, on the other hand, could be costed and needs-based and, being a universal system, could be supported by the wider community (Productivity Commission, 2011; Walsh and Johnson, 2013).

The National Disability Insurance Scheme Act 2013 followed the design advice of the Productivity Commission and achieved bipartisan support (Whalan et al, 2014). Implementation of the scheme began in trial areas in July 2013. Currently, eight location or age-based trials are under way. Full national implementation is expected by 2019, accelerated in some states through national-state agreements. Implementation and funds management are the responsibilities of the National Disability Insurance Agency (NDIA), an independent statutory agency set up for the purpose.

As a social insurance scheme, the NDIS targets all Australians by funding specialist disability support packages, information and referral. Initially this was framed as three tiers of different groups of 'customers' and has since been renamed. Up to 10% of people with disability, that is about 460,000 people, are expected to have sufficiently high support needs to be eligible for individual funding packages (Bonyhady, 2014). The individual packages are the most developed part of the NDIS so far, and the part that people colloquially refer to as the NDIS. These packages extend and generalise a policy trend in Australia that has seen limited, state-based individual funding programs developed over the last 30 years (Purcal et al, 2014a), reflecting the shift to individualised funding models in social care around the world.

The other 90% of people with disability who have support needs are expected to access other community and mainstream services, either through referral from NDIA or by entering social services through other routes. The NDIA is contracting organisations to provide information and referrals, known as Local Area Coordinators (LAC). All other Australians are also expected to benefit from the NDIS, through their entitlement to seek information about disability support for their family members, and through their potential eligibility for NDIS support packages or referral to other social services if they become disabled. This part of the NDIS is the least developed to date.

In the trial sites, an NDIA assessor determines whether someone is eligible for an individual package due to their 'significant and ongoing support needs' (Productivity Commission, 2011: 166). If a person is assessed as eligible, they develop an individual plan with an NDIA planner. The plan sets individualised outcome goals in the areas of choice and control, daily activities, relationships, home, health and wellbeing, lifelong learning, work, and social, community and civic participation. It includes reasonable and necessary supports to achieve the goals, which are costed according to a price guide. The NDIS funds a range of disability supports but not if the supports are part of mainstream universal services like health, housing or education. The individual funding package is allocated to the person, who has the choice to self-manage their funds (or with a nominee), which provides the highest level of individualisation; or to allocate the package to a financial intermediary agency. The funds can be spent on support from workers employed by the person, service providers registered with the NDIA or other mainstream services and equipment. The package is reviewed annually or more frequently as required.

The expected cost of the NDIS is AUS\$13.5 billion per year in 2011 dollars (\$2=£1 approximately). Given that national, state and territory governments already spent about half that amount on disability support, the additional annual cost of the scheme is about AUS\$6.5 billion, or AUS\$290 per citizen. The NDIS is financed through a fund managed by the NDIA, with an increase to public health care contributions (the Medicare levy) from 1.5 to 2% of personal income tax (Medicare Levy Amendment (DisabilityCare Australia) Act 2013), and with other federal and state revenue from reorganising former disability-specific payments to the states. The question of the financial viability of the scheme remains open. Analysing estimates and evidence available in 2014, Purcal and Boyce (2014) concluded that it was too early to tell whether the scheme would be sustainable, because it was developing as it grew. By mid-2015, NDIS costs remained in line with expectations (NDIA, 2015b).

As at June 2015, approximately 17,000 people had an NDIS package, averaging \$34,000 per year, although most packages were under \$30,000 (71%; NDIA, 2015a). Most people had chosen to allocate their package to an agency, although 6% of people with a package self-managed it and 33% had a mix of agency and self-management arrangements. Participant satisfaction with the scheme was high, at an average rate of 1.64 out of 2. According to the NDIA and a national disability advocacy organisation, people with disability in the NDIS trial sites found that they were benefiting from the amount of the support the package could buy and the additional control it enabled (People With Disability Australia, 2015).

While this chapter concentrates on the NDIS, it should be mentioned that the scheme legislation includes a second strand, the National Injury Insurance Scheme (NIIS) (Productivity Commission, 2011). The NIIS is planned as a state-based, fully funded, no-fault accident compensation scheme that covers people with permanent injury who may require high-cost support, due to injuries from motor vehicles, workplaces, medical treatment and others[11]. Implementation has been slower than for the NDIS. Some states already have schemes covering some NIIS injury types. These states are considering how to build from their existing schemes. Other states, particularly the smaller ones, are considering a direct arrangement with the NDIA or the larger states.

Concerns and challenges regarding the NDIS

An overall design of the NDIS is outlined in the legislation and described above, but the details are being developed through the trials and remain unclear. A review of the published literature about the NDIS shows that the uncertainty weighs on people with disability, who hope to benefit from the new approach to their support. The literature focuses on three broad issues:

- First, it poses questions about the availability of quality support services, for example: Will there be service gaps, especially in rural and remote areas? Will people find enough workers with the skills to provide person-centred support? For people who are not eligible for an individual package, will states provide sufficient social service support and mainstream services like health, education and housing?
- Second, equity of access to the NDIS for marginalised groups of people with disability is in question, such as people with multiple and complex needs, people with intellectual disability or mental illness, Aboriginal people and those from culturally and linguistically diverse backgrounds.
- Third, how will the information needs of people with disability be met? How will they be supported to develop the knowledge, skills and experience necessary for planning how to use individualised funding and, for some, how to self-manage their funds? To exercise choice about their support, people need to know and understand

their options and have a chance to develop the necessary experience and skills. Information gaps are a risk.

Current literature about these three issues is reviewed here as background to the latter part of this chapter, which explores through action research findings what information people with disability need as they prepare to enter the scheme.

Regarding the first question about the availability of quality support, concern has been raised that the centralised design and bureaucracy of the NDIS might stymie innovation in the service sector (Duffy, 2013). Providing adequate services in remote locations may not be economically viable for organisations, thus diminishing people's choice (Fawcett and Plath, 2014). At a personal level, people with disability need a workforce with the new skills to provide person-centred support (Koop, 2014) who 'stop deciding for the consumer' (Collins, 2014: 14). At the same time, people with disability are accountable for how they spend their package and manage their support workers, including ensuring safe working conditions (Dickinson et al, 2015).

The 90% of people with disability who will not qualify for an individual package face uncertainty about the continuation of existing support services. For example, in the state of Victoria, community-based psychiatric rehabilitation and support services will shift to the NDIS, yet in New South Wales none of the state-funded mental health programmes are in scope for the scheme. Such inconsistencies may be revisited in state-national agreements or state legislation but currently add to the uncertainty for people with disability (Koop, 2014; Smith, 2014).

The NDIS interface with mainstream services such as health, justice, housing and education is similarly uncertain. As mentioned above, the NDIS funds only specialist disability support and otherwise refers people to mainstream services. Therefore, the capacity of mainstream services – which are mainly state funded – to meet the needs of people with disability is central to the design of the NDIS (Bigby, 2013; Madden, 2014). However, the boundaries between NDIS and mainstream service responsibilities have not been clearly defined (Williams and Smith, 2014), and the impact of the NDIS on the demand for mainstream services is not yet understood (KPMG, 2014).

One mainstream service area that is already overstretched is housing. In Australia generally, declining affordability is a barrier to accessing adequate housing, but even more so for people with disability (Wiesel et al, 2015). The NDIS funds people's housing modifications and housing support and assists with public housing applications, but it does not cover housing costs. There is additional concern for Indigenous people in remote areas, whose housing may be unsuitable for modifications and who may move frequently for cultural and kinship reasons and to support relatives in distant hospitals (Grant et al, 2014).

The second question, about equity of access to NDIS support, stems from the design of the NDIS: it is a rationed programme that limits eligibility, and it is a market-based model that relies on individuals to initiate NDIS assessment processes and make informed choices about support options. These elements have raised concerns about how marginalised groups within the disability population might access the scheme and how they might achieve positive outcomes (Fawcett and Plath, 2014). These marginalised groups include people with intellectual disability, whose NDIS assessment process may require the support of family members or advocates, as well as time and patience, to communicate their needs and aspirations (O'Connor, 2014). Many people with intellectual disability have multiple and complex needs, sometimes due to mental illness, drug and alcohol use, poverty, poor education, contact with the criminal justice system and/or cultural and language barriers (Department of Justice, 2007). They experience barriers to accessing disability support anyway (Ethnic Disability Advocacy Centre, 2011; Baldry and Dowse, 2013). Risks are that they will not initiate NDIS assessments, especially if they have not used support services before (Soldatic et al, 2014; Springgay and Sutton, 2014).

Indigenous people with disability, especially in remote communities, are another marginalised group that might not be well served by a market-based model. Issues such as limited service capacity, high cost of service provision, insufficient transport infrastructure, and NDIS assessment tools that are designed for use with Western, English-speaking populations lead to concerns that Indigenous people will not benefit equitably from the NDIS (Stephens et al, 2014). Finally, people with mental illness are at risk of missing out on NDIS support due to their fluctuating support needs: most people with periodic severe mental illness but who are usually well in-between may not be eligible for an individual package (Smith, 2014; Williams and Smith, 2014).

The third question concerns the information needs of people with disability under the NDIS, especially those with an individual package. They (or their nominee or financial intermediary) need to know which services are available to them and how suitable they might be. They need skills and systems for recording their expenditure, documenting their experiences, managing their support workers, understanding the safety and administrative aspects involved and deciding between options, and they need to assess how well the support has helped them towards reaching their goals. To achieve this, capacity building, information and skill development are needed. Martin (2011; cited in McLaughlin et al, 2014) distinguishes between a 'personal information space' for recording and reviewing an individual's supports, and an 'information economy' for accessing registers of providers and other people's stories and recommendations. The concern is that many people with disability – especially if they are marginalised and not accessing support services – may not know enough about the NDIS to consider applying (for example, O'Connor, 2014), and that people who do apply may neither be given adequate information to prepare for the individualised planning process nor be provided with comprehensive service lists, thus limiting informed choice (PWDA, 2015).

While the literature highlights risks about NDIS service provision, equity of access and information needs, as previously discussed, the authors acknowledge that the NDIS includes design elements to minimise those risks from the outset, such as local area coordinators, financial intermediaries and development of personal plans. How well these design elements are implemented will determine the scheme's success. A strength of the NDIS implementation is that its gradual introduction until 2019 has the expressed purpose of identifying and addressing these risks.

Until then, people with disability remain unsure at best and fearful at worst about how effectively the NDIS will work for them. The remainder of this chapter considers whether the experience of people with disability who have or would like to have individualised funding bear out these expected problems and how they attempt to solve them. It does this by analysing data from an action research project conducted at the time the trials of the NDIS were beginning. The research found that the third concern discussed above, namely unmet information needs, is central to the experience that many people currently have with individualised funding options. It also shows how limited knowledge and experience, in turn, constrain people's options regarding the other two challenges previously discussed, namely adequate service provision and equitable access to support.

Action research project

The research, conducted in 2013, was supported by a grant under the Australian government's National Disability and Development Agenda and led by a partnership between university-based researchers and a national disabled person's organisation (DPO). It used a participatory action research approach (Balcazar et al, 2004), where university researchers and community members collaborated to develop knowledge and effect change. The action research process focuses on being useful for research participants. It may provide peer support, where participants learn from each other and may feel empowered to advocate for their interests, in this case, for improved disability support. It may also develop people's research capacity, for example for employment or when deciding and advocating about new disability support options.

In this project, the action research groups were called community action research disability groups (CARDs). The national DPO organised with eight local DPOs and community contacts to form one group in each of the eight Australian states and territories. Each group included people with disability, using disability support through individualised or traditional funding arrangements, as well as people not using formal disability support. The groups were coordinated by the national DPO. A group facilitator who worked for each local DPO recruited participants to the group, organised group meetings and forwarded and discussed research data with the university researchers for analysis.

Local group formation enabled diversity, depending on local needs and priorities. The groups made arrangements to enable a variety of people to take part, such as providing transport and offering inclusive participation methods. The groups included people who had more or less experience of action research and/or peer support, and people of different ethnic and language backgrounds (12% from countries other than Australia), ages (ranging from 19 to 73 years), gender (55% women, 45% men), types of disabilities and levels of support need (80% physical disability; 11% each for psychological, sensory and intellectual disability; 18% cited multiple disabilities). The groups had between three and 12 participants. In most groups, the membership changed during the course of the project, as people left and others joined. Due to the change in group membership, the demographic statistics cited above are from 45 core participants, drawn from seven of the eight groups who completed the demographic surveys.

Each group met about six times, usually monthly, between May and December 2013. Participants came together for about two hours each month to explore the overarching research question: What are your experiences with your disability support, and what kind of support do you wish for? Meetings usually focused on one or more of six suggested topics:

- characteristics of the support;
- organising support services;
- social life;
- community participation;
- relationships with support workers;
- reflections on the research process.

Research methods and other activities in the group varied according to each group's preferences. They included art, discussions, photos, recordings, conversations, surveys and fun activities, such as sharing a meal. The university researchers and national DPO developed resources for the group facilitators, including research ethics guidance, topic guides with prompts and discussion ideas, 'how-to' guides for inclusive research methods and easy-read resources (for example, Meltzer et al, 2014). They also provided ongoing support for facilitators while the groups were meeting, through telephone and email discussions and an online forum to share experiences. More detail about the methodology is in the project report (Purcal et al, 2014b).

Experience of individualised support

The groups were an important opportunity for participants to share views about using individualised support. This was because the groups included a mix of people: some who had individualised packages, some who had other support arrangements and some who had no formal disability support. With the planned expansion of individualised funding arrangements under the NDIS, the group discussions were important for understanding what people with disability thought about individualised support and what assistance they might need to use this type of support in the future. The participants shared experiences about two main areas: finding out about individualised support, and organising the support.

Finding out about individualised support

One of the most thoroughly discussed topics in the groups was how to access individualised support. This included finding out about available packages, getting a package that they were entitled to and, if they did get a package, how to find out about the mechanics of managing it. These were key concerns, as individualised support was new to many people in the groups.

Several group members felt they were constrained in even deciding whether individualised funding might be beneficial for them because they had limited experience and knowledge about this type of funding and how it might differ from their current support. Yet they also felt there was an expectation that they already had this knowledge and were able to advocate for their own support needs. Among the people who did not yet have individualised support, several felt that they would have to actively advocate to get it. One participant said, "It is important to be able to advocate for yourself." However, they also felt that such self-advocacy required sophisticated skills, such as being 'pushy' and 'personally strong' or needing to draw on background knowledge about rights and entitlements that they did not have. One participant said, "If you don't know your rights, what you are entitled to, it is hard to negotiate with the agency."

People who already had individualised support felt that it had benefited them, citing increased flexibility, choice and control. Like the knowledge about how to access support, they felt that managing the support also came with expectations that they had the skills and understanding required to manage their package. One person said, "Being on self-directed funding means being a lot more on top of things." Some people wanted more assistance to develop the skills and understanding to manage their support. One person had found it difficult to find the information needed, as he said he "did not know what questions to ask". He explained, "There are more people set up to help you find the answer, but not so many to help you find the questions." Others felt they became more cognisant of what to ask for and how to ask for it over time. For example, one person explained how she had learnt to tailor her message when asking for what she needed. She said, "It helped to be creative in what you call things in order to get grants and when to keep your mouth shut."

In general, both the participants who had individualised support and those who did not mentioned topics on which they wished to receive more information. This included what support services were available, the process of how to access individualised funding and what government policies supported the self-managed approach. They also wanted more information about how individualised support would work in practice, for example, how to self-manage administrative aspects such as payment and insurance for support workers, whether unused money or hours could be rolled over to the next year and how to best use the package to meet their goals and aspirations. Other areas where participants wanted further information included the relationship between individualised funding, self-management and the NDIS, including what would happen to supports funded from other sources, such as subsidised taxi schemes.

Participants also identified information resources that would assist them. These included lists of commonly used acronyms, lists of suggested 'interview questions' for choosing their own service providers and support workers, reporting templates, and a hotline to assist with the administrative aspects of self-management. Participants thought that these resources should be adapted to different cultures, languages and literacy levels in order to be effective for different people. They indicated that they preferred to receive this information through other people with disability, independent advocacy services, disability advocacy organisations and peer support, rather than government agencies and service providers. Their reasoning was that they had found these preferred sources of information to be the most useful and trustworthy.

Organising individualised support

People who were already receiving individualised support had learnt important lessons about how to best use it to meet their goals and aspirations. These lessons were mainly around allocating the funding and managing the support relationships involved. In the groups, people shared lessons around the items and types of support they funded from an individualised package. Some had discovered that they could use funding left over at the end of the year to make large purchases, such as a hoist for a car. Others had put in place innovative arrangements, such as using their funds to pay someone for each kilometre of transport they provided; or people had purchased specialist equipment that allowed them to fulfil their goals, such as a man who bought a modified ironing board so that he could do his wife's ironing and 'be a good husband'. In each of these cases people tested out the possibilities and limits of their individualised package to make arrangements that suited their individual aspirations.

Other lessons were around the relationships involved in organising individualised support, especially when people with disability were self-employing their support workers. Participants appreciated the increased level of contact they had with support workers under self-management and the increased control they had over scheduling support, without an agency as an intermediary. However, they also recognised that increased contact with workers came with relational risks and responsibilities. Participants reflected on the need to manage their relationships with support workers by respecting them but also remaining in control of their own lifestyle and daily arrangements. People commonly found that clear communication and mutual respect between themselves and support workers were vital. One participant said, "If you want the support workers to treat you with respect, you have to treat them with respect."

In some instances, this meant maintaining respectful but clear boundaries with support workers on particular lifestyle issues, such as beliefs and practices around food, alcohol and accessing sex workers. For example, conflicts over food choices were a common issue. One participant, while acknowledging the need to be respectful, recommended to others in the group, "Always keep control of the shopping, because then you can keep control of the kitchen." The mention of both respect and boundaries highlights the combination of relational skills that group members found to be involved in individualised funding arrangements.

Implications

Australia is introducing individualised funding of disability support nationally under a social insurance approach, to be fully implemented by 2019. This chapter reviewed the three types of risks of the approach identified by other authors, namely availability of services, equity of access and information needs. Action research with groups of people with disability found that to even get to first base of accessing individualised support, people with disability needed information of various kinds and as basic as what packages were available, what funding they were entitled to and how it might be different from their current support. They felt their limited experience and knowledge constrained their decisions on even whether to apply for individualised support and whether to self-manage a package.

Participants who had made the change and taken up an individual package talked about their further information needs concerning how to best implement individualised support to meet their aspirations. In the groups they shared the learning they had gained, usually through trial and error and imaginative testing of the limits allowed by their package. During the action research process, people were eager to share their questions and experiences, so that they could extend their own knowledge and be in a position to make the most of any opportunities for more control over their support.

These findings highlight that limited experience and knowledge are serious constraints on the take up of individualised support and its potential for improving the capacity of people with disability to articulate and achieve their aspirations. Exchange through peer support also demonstrated that, with information and support from trusted sources, the confidence and skills of people with disability to contribute to decisions about support arrangements or to manage their own support can develop over time. While this was a small qualitative study, it showed that people in different Australian states, of different ages and with different types of disabilities had similar experiences, concerns and aspirations in the lead up to the NDIS.

Conclusion

The findings of this chapter have implications for information sharing, insurance-based social support schemes and the position of individualised funding packages relative to fixed funding of social services. Previous research has focused on the risk of people not having sufficient information that the NDIS exists, about how to apply and how to choose support providers. This chapter has highlighted a more basic gap in people's familiarity with what individualised support even is, how it works and how they might benefit from the new approach.

A policy implication is that, with the expansion of individualised support, the public is likely to need various opportunities and forms of information sharing, to explore and learn from each other about what the new approach is, how to do it and what its possibilities are. This applies especially when the approach is a national social insurance scheme like the NDIS, where any member of the public can potentially come in contact with the scheme, either for themselves or their friends and family.

Controlling one's own support funding is not a concept that most citizens are familiar with, because they cannot draw on parallels or transfer experience from other social services, which largely remain controlled by the government or service providers. As individualised funding is expanded across social services over time, familiarity with the needs for information, skills and integration with other services may become more transferrable. In the meantime, investment in creating intentional opportunities for sharing experiences about how to make the most of personal control over support will be needed to assist people to reconceptualise their relationship with the state and the way it funds services.

Acknowledgements
Ngila Bevan, Rosemary Kayess, Sally Robinson.

Note
[1] www.treasury.gov.au/Policy-Topics/PeopleAndSociety/National-Injury-Insurance-Scheme

References
Balcazar, F.E., Taylor, R.R., Kielhofner, G.W., Tamley, K., Benziger, T., Carlin, N. and Johnson, S. (2004) 'Participatory action research: General principles and a study with a chronic health condition', in L.A. Jason, C.B. Keys, Y. Suarez-Balcazar, R.R. Taylor, and M.I. Davis (eds) *Participatory community research:Theories and methods in action,*Washington, DC: American Psychological Association, pp 17–35.
Baldry, E., and Dowse, L. (2013) 'Compounding mental and cognitive disability and disadvantage: police as care managers', in D. Chappell (ed) *Policing and the mentally ill: international perspectives*, Boca Raton: CRC Press Taylor and Francis Group, pp 219–34.
Bigby, C. (2013) 'A National Disability Insurance Scheme—Challenges for Social Work', *Australian Social Work*, 66(1): 1–6.
Bonyhady, B. (2014) 'Tides of change: the NDIS and its journey to transform disability support', *New Paradigm Australian Journal on Psychosocial Rehabilitation*, Summer 2014: pp 7–9.
Collins, I. (2014) 'What do consumers want, need and deserve from the NDIS?' *New Paradigm Australian Journal on Psychosocial Rehabilitation*, Summer 2014: pp 13–15.
CRPD (2008) *UN Convention on the Rights of Persons with Disabilities*, United Nations, http://www.un.org/disabilities/default.asp?id=259
Commonwealth of Australia (2011) *National Disability Strategy 2010-2020. An initiative of the Council of Australian Governments*, Canberra: Commonwealth of Australia, https://www.dss.gov.au/sites/default/files/documents/05_2012/national_disability_strategy_2010_2020.pdf
Department of Justice (2007) *Intellectual disability in the Victorian prison system. Characteristics of prisoners with an intellectual disability released from prison in 2003-2006*, Melbourne: Department of Justice,Victoria.
Dickinson, H., Needham, C. and Sullivan, H. (2015) 'Individual funding for disability support: what are the implications for accountability?' *Australian Journal of Public Administration*, 73(4): 417–25.
Duffy, S. (2013) *Designing NDIS. An international perspective on individual funding systems*, Sheffield: Centre for Welfare Reform.
Ethnic Disability Advocacy Centre (2011) *Response to the WA primary health care strategy consultation*, Perth, WA: EDAC.
Fawcett, B. and Plath, D. (2014) 'A National Disability Insurance Scheme: what social work has to offer', *British Journal of Social Work* (44): 747–62.

Grant, E., Chong, A., Beer, A. and Srivastava, A. (2014) 'The NDIS, housing and indigenous Australians living with a disability', *Parity*, 27(5): 25-26.

Koop, K. (2014) 'NDIS and state mental health reform: opportunities and risks for Victoria', *New Paradigm Australian Journal on Psychosocial Rehabilitation*, Summer 2014: 10–12.

KPMG (2014) *Interim report: Review of the optimal approach to transition to the full NDIS*, Canberra: National Disability Insurance Agency.

Laragy, C., Fisher, K.R., Purcal, C. and Jenkinson, S. (2015) 'Australia's individualised disability funding packages: when do they provide greater choice and opportunity?', *Asian Social Work and Policy Review*, 9(3): 282–92.

Madden, R. (2014) 'NDIS costs and the budget', presentation, *CADR Research to Action Conference*, Sydney.

Meltzer, A., Fisher, K.R., Purcal, C., Bevan, N. and Cooper, S. (2014) *What can we do in our research group? Different ways to do research, SPRC Resource 1/2014*, Sydney: Social Policy Research Centre, UNSW Australia.

McLoughlin, I., Bayati-Bojakhi, S., Purushothaman, K. and Sohal, A. (2014) 'Informational requirements and client-centred disability care: issues, problems and prospects in Australia', *Social Policy and Society*, 13(4): 609–21.

NDIA (National Disability Insurance Agency) (2015a) *Eighth Quarterly Report to COAG Disability Reform Council*, http://www.ndis.gov.au/sites/default/files/Q4-Report-to-COAG-Disability-Reform%20Council.pdf

NDIA (2015b) *Report on the sustainability of the scheme, prepared by the Scheme Actuary*, http://www.ndis.gov.au/sites/default/files/Report-on-the-sustainability-of-the-scheme.pdf

Needham, C. and Glasby, J. (eds) (2014) *Debates in personalisation*, Bristol: Policy Press.

O'Connor, M. (2014) 'The National Disability Insurance Scheme and people with mild intellectual disability: Potential pitfalls for consideration', *Research and Practice in Intellectual and Developmental Disabilities*, 1(1): 17–23.

PriceWaterhouseCoopers (2009) *Disability Investment Group: National Disability Insurance Scheme Final Report*, Canberra: Australian Government.

Productivity Commission (2011) *Disability Care and Support. Report no. 54*, Canberra: Australian Government.

Purcal, C., Fisher, K.R. and Laragy, C. (2014a) 'Analysing choice in Australian individual funding disability policies', *Australian Journal of Public Administration*, 73(1): 88–102.

Purcal, C., Bevan, N., Cooper, S., Fisher, K.R., Meltzer, A., Wong, M. and Meyer, P. (2014b) 'Self-directed disability support: Building people's capacity through peer support and action research', *Final report, SPRC Report 7/2014*, Sydney: Social Policy Research Centre, UNSW Australia.

Purcal, S. and Boyce, K. (2014) *Is the NDIS sustainable?*, Sydney: Macquarie University Centre for the Health Economy.

PWDA (2015) *National Disability Insurance Scheme Citizens' Jury Scorecard for the National Disability Insurance Agency and People with Disability, Australia*, Sydney: People With Disability Australia, http://www.pwd. org.au/admin/ndis-citizens-jury-scorecard-project.html

Smith, T. (2014) 'Further unravelling psychosocial disability: experiences from the NSW Hunter NDIS launch site', *New Paradigm Australian Journal on Psychosocial Rehabilitation*, Summer 2014: 20–22.

Soldatic, K.V., Toorn, G., Dowse, L. and Muir, K. (2014) 'Intellectual disability and complex intersections: marginalisation under the National Disability Insurance Scheme', *Research and Practice in Intellectual and Developmental Disabilities*, 1(1): 6–16.

Springgay, M. and Sutton, P. (2014) 'Psychosocial disability: the urgent need for reform in assessment and care', *New Paradigm Australian Journal on Psychosocial Rehabilitation*, Summer 2014: 16–19.

Stephens, A., Cullen, J., Massey, L. and Bohanna, I. (2014) 'Will the National Disability Insurance Scheme improve the lives of those most in need? Effective service delivery for people with acquired brain injury and other disabilities in remote Aboriginal and Torres Strait Islander communities', *Australian Journal of Public Administration*, 73(2): 260–70.

Walsh, J. and Johnson, S. (2013) 'Development and principles of the National Disability Insurance Scheme', *The Australian Economic Review*, 46(3): 327–37.

Whalan, J., Acton, P. and Harmer, J. (2014) *A review of the capabilities of the National Disability Insurance Agency*, Canberra: National Disability Insurance Scheme, http://www.ndis.gov.au/sites/default/files/documents/capability_review_2014_3.pdf

Wiesel, I., Laragy, C., Gendera, S., Fisher, K.R., Jenkinson, S., Hill, T., Finch, K., Shaw, W. and Bridge, C. (2015) *Moving to my home: housing aspirations, transitions and outcomes of people with disability, AHURI Final Report No.246*, Melbourne: Australian Housing and Urban Research Institute, http://www.ahuri.edu.au/publications/projects/p71040.

Williams, T.M. and Smith, G.P. (2014) 'Can the National Disability Insurance Scheme work for mental health?' *Australian and New Zealand Journal of Psychiatry*, 48(5): 391–94.

TEN

Right time, right place? The experiences of rough sleepers and practitioners in the receipt and delivery of personalised budgets

Philip Brown

Introduction

This chapter outlines one way in which personalisation has been implemented within the field of homelessness within the United Kingdom (UK). The chapter draws on research findings from a longitudinal study, which evaluated the delivery of an approach to allocate 'individual budgets' to people experiencing homelessness. The chapter outlines the effectiveness of the approach both in terms of outcomes for those who participated as recipients and its operationalisation by workers. The chapter makes a number of central points. First, individual budgets, as described here, can be a particularly effective tool in reducing the length of time homelessness is experienced. Second, how such budgets are delivered is as important as the budget themselves. The skill of workers to work in innovative and creative ways is crucial to their success. Finally, there are inspiring findings arising which point to the pragmatic yet frugal approach by rough sleepers towards the use of individual budgets.

The 'personalisation turn' in health and social care policy within the UK appears to have had two main drivers. First, it is a coping response by services seeking to adapt to the economic austerity measures introduced by the coalition government. Second, it is an ideological shift in the way policies influencing the commissioning and delivery of health and social care services were formulated. However, a shift to new ways of working and a movement towards more targeted services was no doubt hastened by an economic necessity largely as a result of the ending of the ring fence around the Supporting People Programme and the subsequent overall reduction in funding available for adult social care. As McCabe (2012) highlighted, many services, as early as 2012, were experiencing the same or higher caseload but with fewer staff available to meet the need. This has meant that organisations have had to prove their cost-effectiveness to funders, particularly the government, by focusing on ensuring the 'recovery' (that is, reintegration into the labour market) of clients (Scullion et al, 2015).

An apparent consequence of this is that those people with the most complex needs were also the ones finding it less easy to access support due to the challenging nature of their cases for already overstretched workers (Cornes et al, 2015). At the same time an ideological shift to the discourse of personalisation has been gaining momentum. However, as Spicker (2013) points out, although the term 'personalisation' is relatively new, the concepts underpinning the ideology are not; pointing to the establishment of the quasi-market in social care in the 1980s and 1990s (Hudson 1992; Le Grand and Bartlett, 1993) and the discourse utilised within the Department of Health's report *Community care: Agenda for action* (Griffiths, 1988) as early manifestations of personalisation. Nonetheless, early policy documents more fully embracing the discourse of 'personalisation' included *Improving the life chances of disabled people* (Cabinet Office, 2005), *Opportunity age* (Department for Work and Pensions, 2005) and *Independence, well-being and choice* (Department of Health, 2005). The publication of *Putting people first: A shared vision and commitment to the transformation of adult social care* (Department of Health, 2007) most fully affirmed the commitment to personalisation within social care policy.

Although developed under the previous Labour government, the principles of the personalisation movement gained momentum within the work of coalition government policy. Personalisation is now embedded as a key principle in the provision of care for specific groups within the Care Act 2014 (Cornes et al, 2015). The aim is to replace paternalistic, reactive care with high quality, personally tailored services; its philosophy is to give clients maximum choice, control, and power over the support services they receive and increasingly shape and commission their own services. The agency of the individual is often seen as pivotal to the personalisation approach by putting 'the person who needs support in control' of the services they receive (In Control, 2009).   However, the centrality of 'individual choice' does not account for all the conceptualisations of personalisation. According to Spicker (2013: 1261), the definition for what personalisation means in terms of health and social care services can draw upon any of three competing interpretations:

- those which refer to individualised assessments and responses;
- those which draw on the preferences of the user;
- those which attempt to reconcile both individualised process and individual preference.

Spicker (2013) goes on to explain that in this latter interpretation 'the task of professionals is to facilitate and inform personal choice' (p 1262). Personal budgets are considered a key practice within the wider personalisation agenda and these are supposed to help ensure that people receiving public funding use available resources to choose their own support services. As the Department for Health guidance states:

> Personal budgets also need to be included in the law as they are important for making care and support personalised. If they are not in the law, it will be more difficult to offer them to everyone. While some local authorities are already making great progress in this area, legislation is needed to make it happen everywhere. (Department of Health, 2014: 2)

Although it is argued that the concept of personal or individual budgets is not new (Spicker, 2013), individual budgets are intended to put the person who needs support in closer control of the services they receive (In Control, 2009).

Individual budgets and homelessness

Homelessness has been a priority for policy in the European Union (EU) and the UK for some time. Successive governments have invested considerable resources attempting to reduce the variety of manifestations homelessness takes. As Johnsen et al (2014) have outlined, over time there has been a steady increase in 'tough love' responses towards homelessness and those more recently characterised by increasing conditionality and assertive 'interventionist' approaches. Concerns have been raised as to the use of such approaches as those who are most excluded often have the most complex needs, thus these approaches can lead to increasing vulnerabilities. However, as Johnsen et al (2014) have documented, there has also been a rise in the development of approaches that have taken a less conditional approach particularly to working with those most 'entrenched' or who could be regarded as multiply excluded homeless.

In the homelessness sector, a commitment to personalisation was asserted in the Department for Communities and Local Government's (DCLG) rough sleeping strategy document *No one left out: Communities ending rough sleeping in 2008*. Within this, a range of measures were introduced including a commitment to pilot personalised support to long-term rough sleepers (Hough and Rice, 2010). The DCLG subsequently funded four national pilots in London, Nottingham, Northampton, and Exeter and North Devon. In social care, there are typically three elements of personalisation: a needs assessment; resource allocation to determine entitlement; and the development of a support plan. The pilot projects for homeless individuals receiving personalised support, however, were not bound to this method: in the London pilot, for instance, formal needs assessment and resource allocation were removed and replaced by an obligation to appoint a broker and a commitment to spend their budget on things that would help them move into and retain accommodation (Hough and Rice, 2010). The London pilot scheme aimed to test personalised budgets as a new way of working and showed that it can contribute to moving entrenched rough sleepers away from the streets.

The target recipients of this pilot service were 15 individuals who were perceived as very resistant to moving off the streets and for whom standard services did not work. The project intended to find out if this group of people, who had been sleeping rough for between four and 45 years, would move off the streets, stay off the streets, and make positive changes to their lives. Thirteen people out of the 15 that were offered a personalised budget accepted it. They created a support plan with the project coordinator outlining what they would spend the budget on and how it would help them find and keep their accommodation (though they were not told what the maximum budget was). Clients bought things like bed and breakfast accommodation (if they preferred not to stay in hostels), pieces of furniture, a television, mobile phone, clothes, passport, a hearing aid, courses and travel costs. Purchases had to be approved by a commissioner but administration was kept to a minimum and decisions were usually made within a day.

Though professionals expected clients to spend the money without making any commitment to finding accommodation, the opposite actually happened: clients found it hard to identify what they should spend the money on, spent little, and were reluctant to buy more expensive items. The outcome of the pilot was that seven people remained in accommodation four to 11 months after moving in. Two more were planning to go into accommodation but the remaining four had disengaged. For those that maintained their accommodation, there were additional benefits such as new welfare benefits claims, improvements in mental and physical health, engagement with substance misuse services, reduced alcohol use, and several were making plans away from the streets, re-engaging with family members, and were developing independent living skills such as cooking and budgeting. However, it was the choice and control that the budgets offered, combined with intensive work from a single trusted worker, that were seen as critical to the success of the pilot (Hough and Rice, 2010). Overviews of the design, process and outcomes from the Exeter and North Devon, Northampton, and Nottingham pilots can be found in Homeless Link (2012a, 2012b, 2012c).

The Individual Budget projects in Wales

Following on from these initial pilots, the Welsh Local Authority Homelessness Network sought to explore new ways of tackling long-term homelessness by embracing the individual approach. Five areas, which mapped onto local authorities across Wales, were allocated funding. The projects within each of these areas were asked to focus their work on the most difficult to accommodate individuals. Working within existing support structures, each area would have access to an individual budget. Each area was encouraged to develop their work in ways which suited their client group, the service structure in their area and the broader context of their locality. Each project had a budget of around £20,000 and these were to be used as budgets for individual rough sleepers. Some small additional funds were available to cover limited management and/or staffing costs incurred by the lead organisations. Workers selected to work on the project were already in post and in all except one case merged the work on the project with their existing (if reduced) caseload.

An evaluation of the projects in Wales was undertaken by the author and the full report contains a detailed account as to the design, process and achievements of the project (Brown, 2013). The evaluation employed a predominantly qualitative longitudinal approach, which was contextualised by integrating secondary information and embracing a collaborative approach where emerging findings were relayed to practitioners within learning and sharing workshops over the course of the evaluation. Interviews were carried out with both the managers/coordinators of the project in each area (five people) and a selection of the support workers in each project area (a total of 13 support workers). Efforts were made to interview them at three separate intervals of the project: commencement, mid-term (around nine months), and the end of the projects. In total there were 41 consultations with service providers over the period of the evaluation. In addition, a total of 17 people in receipt of individual budgets were interviewed. The research team worked with support workers to identify respondents for the study. Where possible, attempts were made to interview people twice over the course of the projects: at or near their initial engagement and finally at or near the end of the project. However, not all clients were able to take part in both consultations. Eleven respondents took part in both initial and final interviews with the remaining six respondents only able to take part in the initial interviews. A total of 28 separate interviews were carried out with clients over the course of the evaluation. Quotes are presented below to illustrate particular points, which the identity of the speakers protected by the use of pseudonyms.

The vast majority of those people involved in the evaluation had been rough sleeping immediately prior to being attached to the project. A number of coordinators and support workers described the 'model' participant as someone for whom all other attempts at helping people secure stable accommodation had failed and who had other complex needs and interdependencies. Most could easily be described as experiencing multiple exclusion homelessness (see McDonagh, 2011). Those people who were selected for the project by services had very often spent periods in prison, were heavy alcohol drinkers and/or significant substance misusers. Most people were well known to many agencies within the areas in which the project was based. Those selected were often characterised as having exhausted every other option for financial and housing support. The people involved in the interviews for the evaluation certainly reflected this background. For example, from the interviews with individual budget recipients, Bob talked about how he spent two years living in a tunnel, Carl talked about trying to live in a local park and Harry talked about how he tried to find places in and around a local church.

Did it work?

Asserting the effectiveness of the projects is far from simple as the end point of the evaluation coincided with the conclusion of the funding for the initiative therefore long-term successes are, at this point, impossible to ascertain. However, in terms of their success in getting the most excluded into stable accommodation, there were some clear immediate successes. A total of 79 people were involved in the individual budget projects. Of these it was estimated that a total of at least 33 (42%) were in a position of having achieved relatively stable accommodation (living in some form of low support accommodation, living with a partner or supported by their family, living in own accommodation with no or little support etc) at the conclusion of the project. Of the remainder, a large number (around 40%) were accommodated in some form of temporary accommodation. In addition to achieving accommodation there were also non-accommodation-related successes noted by workers such as a reduction in alcohol and substance misuse, increased self-esteem and self-confidence, an increase in trust and engagement with support services, more appropriate engagement with health and support services. It was difficult for the evaluation to achieve a definitive conclusion as to the cost-effectiveness of the projects due to the scale of the evaluation carried out. However, in the very broadest sense the projects did appear to offer good value for money. As an example, although it was initially envisaged that around £80,000 would be spent on implementing the projects as a whole, the actual spend was less than half at just over £34,000. It was also anticipated that this would be spent on around 50 individuals when in practice 79 people were affiliated with the projects. This resulted in average expenditure per recipient of the budget across all areas of £434. This, of course, is in addition to staffing costs, which were not quantified. In addition, workers cited savings to the public purse as a result of reduced levels of criminality and reactive health care as a result of their work, but these were not able to be quantified by the evaluation.

In terms of the difference the approach made to individuals, those clients who were aware that they were on a 'special' programme (it should be noted that some clients were in the early stages of recovery from a range of issues and were not always cognisant that they were in receipt of an individual budget) and had 'gone in' to settled stable accommodation often directly attributed this success to the project. Where stable accommodation had not been achieved it could be argued that the individual budgeting approach might not have been successful. However, from consultations with staff and clients it was repeatedly stated that their accommodation status at the end of the projects often hid a complexity of positive personal developmental experiences. In almost all circumstances – even where people were still rough sleeping – there were tangible improvements reported to their overall situation. Examples of individual successes included:

- the development of new and more positive social networks not defined by mutual drug and/or alcohol use;
- a reduction in levels of alcohol and substance intake which, for the individuals concerned, was often an enormous success given what tended to be described as their significant and relentless use prior to engaging in the projects;exercising an ability to save some of their income;
- more regular positive contact with family members and dependants;
- cessation of sex work;
- increase in ability to engage in personal care;
- volunteering at hostels, as peer mentors and at local schools;
- noticeable improvements in self-esteem and self-confidence when in social interactions.

Although there was overwhelming positive support for the individual budget approach, attributed largely to its usefulness of developing person-centred solutions to problems, there was a strong message from workers, and clients themselves, that the approach would not be suitable for everybody. Indeed, there were a number of occasions where things had not gone as anticipated. Common downsides of the use of the budgets included:

- accommodation being damaged by the client;
- bought items being damaged or stolen by 'friends' and associates;
- selling bought items on.

According to the support workers interviewed, such eventualities appeared few and far between. Still we see evidence of what Padgett et al (2015) see as 'small victories' in that in the majority of occasions the clients remain engaged both with the individual budget approach and, perhaps most importantly, with their support worker.

Organisation and administration of the individual budgets

In most cases the support and the money received worked in coordination, either explicitly or implicitly, with a support plan that was developed between a support worker and the client. The budget within one of the areas however was reported as not being tied to a support plan as it was designed in order to be flexible to best respond to individual needs. None of the pilot areas discussed the total amount of money available with their clients.

> "You've got to remember they know we can get funds for them. They don't know how much we can get. They don't know where it's coming from. They don't really know it's solely for them." (Support worker)

Furthermore, it was apparent as time went on that as new clients were brought onto the project that not all clients were informed that they had access to an individual budget. Instead the project was often referred to in more ambiguous terms, for example, a new scheme, new programme, and so on. The way in which support workers framed the individual budget project was reflected in the responses provided by clients in the interviews. A number of people said that they had become aware of the project over time. People sometimes said their support worker had not told them about it, or not gone into details or they simply assumed it was another fund to help them pay for housing costs. For example, a number of clients expressed confusion about why they were being consulted in such depth about the funding they had received, such as Alistair:

> "Like I say, I had a brief meeting with her. We had a brief discussion about bonds and then they said, bed and breakfast as well. I don't see this as a pot of money which I've got control of. I don't know the limits of it all or whatever."

Such practice raise questions as to whether the approach described here accurately reflects the principles of personalisation outlined earlier in the chapter or whether this approach might be best seen as 'personalisation-lite'.

On the other hand, there were other people who appeared fully aware of the project as well as the principles and scope of the individual budget approach, for example Karen:

> "Thinking about it, I thought it was good. It helped me get back onto my feet without like, with obviously how to use it wisely and what to do with it and not obviously right now with the shared accommodation, there is not a lot we can do with budgeting just yet. When I was transferred into my safe place, they had more with budgeting than with everything else, with decorating and things

like that. I'm still in the programme with it at the minute. I think it's – I thank the people who have helped them to help others like myself and others in the same situation as I'm in."

At the outset there was some concern, by workers, about the lack of guidance as to what the budget could be spent on. People often wondered about what the right thing to be purchasing was and whether certain items would be allowed. Workers in one of the localities took a very broad inclusive view of what was permissible and workers here were encouraged to think broadly and adhere to being pragmatic by allowing spending on a range of areas, the guiding principle was that the money, "… can't be spent on anything immoral or illegal". However, in a couple of other localities there was some initial uncertainty as to whether the budget could be spent on repaying debts or on deposits for accommodation. However, over time, once coordinators and workers had become more experienced with the individual budget concept, it appears many of the initial restrictions were relaxed. Once the initial anxiety subsumed, where possible, ideas began to be co-produced with clients in order to try and facilitate the unlocking of some of the complexities. For example, one support worker recounted their particularly successful work with one of their clients:

> "He didn't say, can I have a bus pass. It was like, what's your main sort of hurdle in moving on with things and it was he couldn't access his family, he's got a young son and sister, because he couldn't afford to go backwards and forwards to see them. We thought, well, maybe we could do a bus pass for him to be able to do that and then it just went from there really and he rebuilt relationships which then has knock on effects. He now since moved closer… That was one of the things that he was really struggling with at that point and felt that if that was improved then other things may improve, which it did." (Support worker)

For this client, the bus pass was subsequently replaced with a bicycle, in order for there to be a more sustainable solution preparing for the end of the pilot, which was purchased out of the individual budget funds.

There were a variety of reasons support workers gave for purchasing the items they did with their clients. Many of the workers who supported clients through the project reported that the strength of the individual budget approach was the access to funds to address housing costs which their clients would otherwise not have recourse to. This, for some, meant that a route into accommodation could be provided for clients when the individual budget was spent on providing bonds and settling housing debts. Similarly, landlords were also seen as more amenable to the notion of clients living in their properties when they came with the added support provided by workers. On at least one occasion the budget was used to help a client remain within bed and breakfast accommodation while the local authority decided whether they had a duty towards him. The authority eventually decided in his favour and he was able to obtain independent accommodation, the alternative would have meant a return to rough sleeping. Mitigating the potential for clients to exercise their 'negative agency' (Hoggett, 2001) was a central reason for suggesting or encouraging the purchase of certain items. Purchasing things that would keep clients distracted and away from, what was perceived as, negative social networks was a major reason for using the budget. Items such as TVs, fishing tackle, DVD players, and so on. were all purchased with the aim of keeping people away from boredom, breaking up existing social networks and generally occupying people's time in a non-self-destructive way.

However, using the budget as part of an effort to develop and maintain trust with the client was a core use of the budget in almost all cases. Being able to agree to a purchase of an item and actually follow through with it was a core component in the development of trust, as well as a shared shopping experience to purchase items. As such, common areas of expenditure tended to be practical and essential things, often inexpensive, including food, sensible footwear, waterproof jackets, phones, and so forth:

'It's all similar items that come up again and again that people want, phones, jackets, boots, footwear. Very basic stuff. There is nothing apart from the lampshades here and there, everything is essential. That's not surprised me about it, but I think that's really stood out that nobody wants anything frivolous at all. Everything that people want is practical. It's just practical. Literally, my shoes are falling apart, so I need a new pair of shoes. I will keep the old ones for begging, because I get more money then, which I think is good. That is what people want. It's practical stuff.' (Support worker)

Engaging in the pilot and making progress

Much of the support for the individual budget approach from workers was grounded in the perception that it was seen as a welcome turn to an assertive outreach role (Witheridge, 1989). Having access to the budget was seen as an important part of the approach and regularly described as the 'hook' or 'carrot' that helped get people engaged with the support worker. As one coordinator explains:

> "It doesn't matter what you are actually buying with the money, but it's a carrot to bring people into support when they wouldn't normally be engaging with support workers. We've got support available now, but for whatever reason they are not engaging with it because it's not what they want or it's provided in the way that they want and the budget basically allows us to sort of get involved with that rough sleeper, because if they tell us they want something we can go ahead and provide it." (Coordinator)

It was clear that having access to a new way of resourcing potential interventions, or even covering basic incidental expenditure for people, gave workers options that had not before been available to them.

Although the focus of the projects was the introduction of the individual budget, what emerged as the crucial element in making the projects operationally effective was the person-centred increase of time and support from a support worker, a key finding shared with Hough and Rice (2010). Such rapport was seen as a prerequisite to allow for a trusted relationship to develop between support worker and client. Similarly, the Association of Directors of Adult Social Services (ADASS, 2012), in the context of older people, suggests that what matters most is not who provides the support, but the nature of the support and the rapport established with those providing it. Many workers spoke of the value that having meaningful time with their clients had on the co-development of effective interventions; this was enacted in various ways. To some it meant accompanying clients to appointments, to others it included shopping trips to help them make decisions and follow through with their purchases. The relationship clearly meant a lot to many of the people. Notions of 'respect', 'support' and 'trust' were some of the key concepts mentioned by clients about their relationship with their support worker. Although the time spent with each client differed on a case-to-case basis, it was reported that there was a noticeable increase in the time devoted to clients on the project when compared with 'regular' clients. As one support worker describes, this was as much as 30-40% more time per client:

"My clients, my regular clients I see every day. However, because he's here every day, I do visit him in his tenancy as well, which I wouldn't do with my other clients, necessarily ... Percentage wise, I suppose you would call it 30%, 40% more." (Support worker)

Once the initial anxiety around what was permissible under the individual budget approach had subsided, workers described a whole range of ways in which they had begun to work and feel more creative in their approaches to dealing with the challenges clients were facing. As one support worker reported:

"I've learned to be more flexible and look outside the box for things. People are all different. There are little things that you can do that will make a big impact on people and finding what suits them, if you can do it in your role, then try and do that." (Support worker)

As well as becoming more creative, workers, who were used to working within a more reactive service, began to adopt more assertive preventative practice in order to attempt to stop challenging situations getting worse. Often, this brought to light frustrations workers had with what they perceive as the 'revolving door' of their usual practice where clients simply present at one service and then another with few apparent sustainable successes. One way in which the creativity was made possible was via a certain degree of supported autonomy provided for workers by the coordinators, or management structure. This was seen, by support workers, as an important part of the structure in order to allow for immediate and creative responses to take place. At the same time however, it was also noted that a support network should be wrapped around workers as a way in which people, who are working with individual budgets, could draw upon support and professional stimulus if required. One support worker in particular, reported feeling isolated in their work and needing some input to help shape her decisions:

"I think it's been a bit hard for me, because I don't have anyone else to bounce off, you know, the problems that they have and even though I do have supervision with my line manager, how is IB [individual budgets] going? It's fine. Whereas I know if I was in an office and if I'm working with people that were on the same project as we'd be talking about things and maybe give each other advice or support.'" (Support worker)

Partnership working

As Cornes et al (2011) have stated, some people, particularly those seen as experiencing multiple exclusion homelessness, do not fit neatly into the compartments provided by many services. Many people have multiple or polyphonic identities (Hermans, 2001) and it is, unfortunately, not unusual to find people who are homeless, drug users, sex workers, and have mental health issues all at the same time. As such, homelessness is seen as presenting particular difficulties for joint working. Indeed, as Oldman (1997: 241) suggests, 'assessing need and delivering health and social care services to an itinerant population is immensely difficult'. Within a UK context, Roche (2004) highlighted the difficulties that exist for both service users and providers in terms of navigating through the various services available. There are also issues around the different ethos of organisations and cultures of provision, which can create problems when looking at the integration of services (Roche, 2004).

All areas involved in the individual budget pilots recognised the existence of multiple identities and complex lives and attempted to bring together a range of partner agencies in order to help with the delivery of the project. However, there were challenges faced in certain areas and differences between the areas as to how effective these partnerships were. It appears that the effective delivery of the projects was more straightforward in areas where inter-organisational partnerships were already strong or where the activity was coordinated by a single full-time support worker, as was the case in one of the areas. However, it was clear that with careful planning, a range of support work models could work effectively. One area relied on a small number of support workers within particular agencies to deliver the project. This appeared well coordinated, with evidence of significant communication between the partners and a distinct sense of joined-up working. However, a small number of workers did make note of the added strain the individual budget work had on their workloads. Workers talked about how it was manageable as a pilot scheme but expressed concern about the sustainability of the approach if there was no added capacity built into their work. There was no evidence of the fear expressed by Williams and Sullivan (2010) that collaborative working was seen as a 'bolt on' activity as a result of a reduction of available resources. Although agencies appeared very content to work together and communicate effectively, it is possible that as these were time-limited projects, this may have contributed to staff remaining engaged and adopting special arrangements in order to deliver the projects effectively. For instance, one organisation talked about having some 'windfall capacity' as a worker had her hours increased from part-time to full-time during the delivery of the project.

One of the interesting ways the individual budget project contributed to more productive partnership working was the framing of the project as a 'special programme'. Such framing by workers to 'external' agencies and organisations (for example, landlords) seemed to create confidence that 'high risk' clients would get extra support. This ultimately allowed the support workers to have access to a greater range of accommodation options than would otherwise be the case:

> "The one thing we have found with the IB [individual budgets] is that it's actually opened doors for people. It's seen as this strange project that other agencies don't really know that much about. It's allowed us to carry on working with people so there is none of this cross funding thing. Agencies sometimes say that, 'we don't want to be abandoned with this person, because they are very very difficult' and we could say, 'well, no, we will support them as well'. They then have multi-agency support whereas people had said, 'well in that case, we will take them on'. And we say, 'We will work with them. We will find them accommodation. But you must do the support as well'. And so it's opened a lot of doors with people. All these people that we've accommodated we wouldn't have done without the IB." (Support worker)

In one of the areas, however, the project was not successful and did not really get under way. Here, once the project had concluded we took the opportunity to review the outcomes in this locality and it was clear that the design of the project in the area meant that there was ineffective inter-agency partnership working and a lack of staff capacity:

> "I think perhaps we were a bit naïve in thinking that there would be enough capacity in these different projects to be able to do it, working with chaotic people. When they go from one place to another everything changes... With hindsight it would have been good to look at the makeup of the projects [existing activities] beforehand and any possible duplication or whatever. At the last stage before finishing we were saying, let's try and get this money and we were saying to the partners, look, can you reconfigure at all? Can you reconfigure what you are doing or can you release some hours or whatever. There was a pressure on it to do it then, because we could lose the funding. They managed to come up

with it, because there was that pressure. That would have been good at the beginning, I guess." (Project coordinator)

Conclusions

By drawing on the experiences and views of those involved in designing, delivering and receiving individual budgets, this chapter has raised several issues for how the turn to personalisation in social care is being delivered in practice within the context of homelessness. The material provided here demonstrates that individual budgets can be seen as a particularly effective tool in both reducing some of the structural barriers in place and enhancing the agency of those in receipt of budgets. The projects carried out in Wales indicate potential cost-effectiveness and positive outcomes for getting people off the streets, away from precarious housing and reducing a wide range of harmful issues. There was also qualitative evidence of a range of psychosocial benefits such as increasing self-esteem, disrupting negative social networks and a reduction in substance misuse.

It is not clear how much of the success is due to the selection of the support workers chosen to work on the pilot by the lead organisations. However, what is clear is that the approach and skills of the support worker is crucial. It was seen that those workers most entrenched in their current practice, and who are less open to innovating in their work, would not necessarily have the same level of positive outcomes seen by other workers. As a consequence, the individual budget approach places significant demands upon the skills and professionalism of staff. Workers require patience and capacity in order to remain in contact with individuals in spite of speed bumps and crisis. These findings compliment previous research, which has emphasised the crucial role played by such workers in the delivery of support to people with complex interdependent issues (Cornes, et al, 2011). Furthermore, a large part of the successes of these pilots is down to the ability of support workers to balance responsiveness with proactive working. These findings continue to point to the need of untapped potential within 'housing support workers' to make material differences to the lives of the most excluded and who, as Cameron (2010) argues, continue to feel the vacuum left by qualified social workers.

However, there was a general lack of awareness from clients as to presence of the programme, the budget and the size of the resource they have recourse to. As such, this individual budget approach excludes many of the key factors intrinsic within the ideology of personalisation.

Although this did not appear to present many disadvantages to the delivery of the pilots, it is not known how far the factors of choice, control and power were mobilised. This perhaps suggests that not all areas of social care suit a 'pure' approach to implementing personalisation. Instead the ideology could be adapted in order to tailor approaches along a spectrum of personalisation in order to suit a specific context. Furthermore, a number of the issues around the inability of systems to respond quickly, difficulties associated with permitting creative working and tensions around inter-agency working raise questions about the ease with which a pure approach to personalisation can be operationalised in the homelessness sector.

Moreover, this experience of individual budgets highlights that the process of expenditure is as important, if not more so, than the item being purchased. This study illuminated the frugalness of people who are homeless and have relatively few personnel possessions. It showed the act of shopping for mundane items such as clothes, a bed and cutlery can have reportedly life changing and emancipatory meanings for people. At the same time the process of sharing the experience of exercising choice with someone helps shape trust between the worker/organisation and individual, and gradually supports the ability of people to self-direct their own lives. The findings discussed here would tend to concur with the thoughts of Blackender and Prestige (2014) and Cornes et al (2015) that it is '"person-centred care" and not "personal budgets" that people want' (Cornes et al, 2015: 9). As such, the individual budget approach cannot be separated from the role of the support worker in their care of clients. Where there were positive outcomes the budget and support work role appears symbiotic and any reduction in one of these factors may impact on the effectiveness of the other. These findings support the assertion by Homeless Link (2013: 30) that, 'Personalised approaches seem to be most effective where workers are given time and flexibility to support clients as they require, with no time bound targets to achieve results with small case loads'.

As such, the projects in Wales provide a good example of what Cornes et al (2011: 4) have called the so-called 'holy grail' of community care policy.

References

Association of Directors of Adult Social Services (2012) *The Case for Tomorrow*, London: ADSS

Blackender, L. and Prestige J. (2014) 'Pan London personalised budgets for rough sleepers', *Journal of Integrated Care*, 22(1): 23–26.

Brown, P. (2013) *Right time, right place? An evaluation of the Individual Budget approach to tackling rough sleeping in Wales*, Cardiff: Welsh Government and University of Salford, http://usir.salford.ac.uk/35792/1/ Individual%20budget%20report.pdf

Cabinet Office (2005) *Improving the Life Chances of Disabled People*, London: HMSO.

Cameron, A.M. (2010) 'The contribution of housing support workers to joined-up services', *Journal of Interprofessional Care*, 24(1): 100–10.

Cornes, M., Joly, L., O'Halloran, S. and Manthorpe, J. (2011) *Rethinking Multiple Exclusion Homelessness: Implications for workforce development and interprofessional practice*, Swindon: Economic and Social Research Council.

Cornes, M., Mathie, H., Whiteford, M., Manthorpe, J. and Clark, M. (2015) *The Care Act, Personalisation and the New Eligibility Regulations: A discussion paper about the future of care and support services for homeless people in England*, London: Kings College London. Available at: http:// eprints.lse.ac.uk/61135/1/Clark_%20discussion_paper_about_the_ future_of_care_author.pdf

Department for Work and Pensions (2005) *Opportunity Age: Meeting the challenges of ageing in the 21st century*, London: HMSO.

Department of Health (2005) *Independence, Well-Being and Choice*, London: HMSO.

Department of Health (2007) *Putting people first: a shared vision and commitment to the transformation of adult social care*, London: HMSO.

Department of Health (2014) 'Factsheet 4 The Care Act: personalising care and support planning', https://www.gov.uk/government/uploads/ system/uploads/attachment_data/file/268681/Factsheet_4_update.pdf

Griffiths, R. (1988) *Community Care: Agenda for Action*, London: Department of Health and Social Security.

Hermans, H.J.M. (2001) 'The Dialogical Self: Toward a Theory of Personal and Cultural Positioning', *Culture and Psychology*, 7(3): 243–81.

Hoggett, P. (2001) 'Agency, rationality and social policy', *Journal of Social Policy*, 30(1): 37–56.

Homeless Link (2012a) *Exeter and North Devon Council's Individual Budget Pilot*, http://homeless.org.uk/Exeter-north-devon-pilot (accessed 11/11/13).

Homeless Link (2012b) *Northampton Personalisation Pilot with Socially Excluded Groups*, http://homeless.org.uk/northampton-personalisation-pilot (accessed 11/11/13).

Homeless Link (2012c) *Nottingham City Pilot and Framework HA Pilot*, http://homeless.org.uk/Nottingham-personalisation-pilot (accessed 11/11/13).

Homeless Link (2013) *A High Cost to Pay: the impact of benefit sanctions on homeless people*, London: Homeless Link.

Hough, J. and Rice, R. (2010) *Providing personalised support to rough sleepers: An evaluation of the City of London pilot*, York: JRF/Broadway.

Hudson, B. (1992) 'Quasi-markets in health and social care in Britain', *Policy & Politics*, 20(2): 131–42.

In Control (2009) *An Introduction to Self-Directed Support. Factsheet 1*, http://www.in-control.org.uk/media/16696/01.%20introduction%20to%20self-directed%20support%202011%20v1b.pdf

Johnsen, S., Fitzpatrick, S. and Watts, B. (2014) *Conditionality Briefing: Homelessness and 'Street Culture'*, York: University of York.

Le Grand, J. and Bartlett, W. (1993) *Quasi-Markets and Social Policy*, Basingstoke: Macmillan.

McCabe, J. (2012) 'Staying afloat Inside Housing', *Inside Housing*, 13 July, http://www.insidehousing.co.uk/staying-afloat/6522720.article

McDonagh, T (2011) *Tackling homelessness and exclusion: Understanding complex lives*, York: Joseph Rowntree Foundation.

Oldman, C. (1997) 'Working together to help homeless people: an examination of inter-agency themes', in R. Burrows, N. Pleace and D. Quilgars (eds) *Homelessness and Social Policy*, London: Routledge, pp 229–42.

Padgett, D., Henwood, B.F. and Tsemberis, S. (2015) *Housing First: Ending Homelessness, Transforming Systems, and Changing Lives*, Oxford: Oxford University Press.

Roche, M. (2004) 'Complicated Problems, Complicated Solutions? Homelessness and Joined-up Policy Responses', *Social Policy and Administration*, 38(7): 758–74.

Scullion, L., Somerville, P., Brown, P. and Morris, G (2015) 'Changing homelessness services in Stoke-on-Trent: revanchism, 'professionalisation' and resistance', *Health and Social Care in the Community*, 23(4): 419–27.

Spicker, P. (2013) 'Personalisation Falls Short', *British Journal of Social Work*, 43(7): 1259–75.

Williams, P. and Sullivan, H. (2010) 'Despite all we know about collaborative working, why do we still get it wrong?', *Journal of Integrated Care*, 18(4): 4–15.

Witheridge T.F. (1989) 'The assertive Community Treatment Worker: An emerging role and its implications for professional training', *Hospital and Community Psychiatry* 40(6): 620–24.

ELEVEN

Personal health budgets: implementation and outcomes

Karen Jones, Julien Forder, James Caiels, Elizabeth Welch and Karen Windle

Introduction

The personalisation agenda in health and social care in England has focused on maximising choice and control over support and services. Since 2005, personal budgets have formed part of this agenda, with the aim of providing more choice and flexibility over how services are managed and delivered. The underlying assumption is that patients are in the best position to know what support would meet their desired social and health care outcomes. Over the past decade, the Department of Health in England has commissioned two national evaluations to run alongside pilot programmes of personal budgets in social and health care to explore the effectiveness and cost-effectiveness of the initiative for individuals, informal carers and the system. This chapter will initially provide a brief background to personal budgets in England. The main focus of this chapter will be to explore personal budgets in health care and the main findings from the national evaluation of the personal health budget pilot programme. This chapter will specifically focus on exploring the initial implementation process during the early stages of the pilot (Jones et al, 2010). We will then discuss whether the extent to which the implementation of personal health budgets was in accordance with the policy intentions underlying the initiative (as set by the Department of Health (2009)) and if it had an impact on outcomes and cost-effectiveness for patients with long-term health conditions (Forder et al, 2012).

Background

Personal budgets form one aspect of the personalisation agenda in England that aims to place individuals and their families at the heart of all decisions about their care. Within social care, the publication of the Care Act in 2014 represents a significant development for publicly-funded support in England, for the first time enshrining personal budgets into law. Individuals and informal carers now have a legal entitlement to a personal budget to help meet their eligible social care needs. There are three principles underlying personal budgets (Department of Health, 2009):

1. Individuals and informal carers should be informed of the level of the budget following an assessment.
2. Individuals and informal carers should be encouraged to develop a support/care plan that details how the resources will be used to meet identified outcomes.
3. There should be a choice of three deployment options: notionally, where the budget is held by the commissioner but the budget holder is aware of the service options and costs; managed by a third party; or as a direct payment where the budget holder receives a cash payment to purchase services/support.

The focus on personal budgets for individuals and informal carers within the Care Act followed a national pilot programme (2005–08) and a Department of Health-funded evaluation of 13 pilot sites (Glendinning et al, 2008). The evaluation aimed to explore whether individual budgets improved people's outcomes and, if so, how and for whom. A randomised controlled trial sat at the heart of the evaluation to compare the experiences of people who were offered an individual budget with the experiences of those receiving conventional services. A number of global measures of well-being were used, including the 12-item version of the General Health Questionnaire (GHQ-12) (Goldberg, 1992) that measures psychological wellbeing. The Adult Social Care Outcome Toolkit (ASCOT) was also included to explore the specific aspects of people's lives that are addressed by social care interventions (Netten et al, 2012). ASCOT aims to measure social care-related quality of life by exploring people's achievement of everyday activities, including: dressing and feeding, feeling safe, being occupied and having a sense of control.

Glendinning et al (2008) found some evidence to suggest that individual budgets were cost-effective in achieving social care-related quality of life (measured through the use of ASCOT) but not for psychological wellbeing (using GHQ-12). However, the impact of individual budgets varied between client groups. Individual budgets appeared to be cost-effective compared to conventional service delivery for both social care-related quality of life and psychological wellbeing among people who had used mental health services and for younger people with a physical disability. For people with learning disabilities, individual budgets were found to be cost-effective with respect to social care-related quality of life, but only when budget holders had a support/care plan in place. However, for this cohort, conventional service delivery appeared to be slightly more cost-effective compared to individual budgets with respect to psychological wellbeing. In addition, Glendinning et al (2008) found no evidence of cost-effectiveness differences between individual budgets and conventional service delivery for older people in terms of social care-related quality of life. Among older people, conventional support arrangements appeared to be marginally more cost-effective compared to individual budgets with respect to psychological wellbeing.

During this national evaluation, the government announced that personal budgets would be made available to all those eligible for publicly funded adult social care needs (HM Government, 2008). While individual budgets could include a number of funding streams (that is, social care funding, integrated community equipment services, access to work, Disabled Facilities Grants and the Independent Living Fund), personal budgets are limited to social care expenditure. The evaluation carried out by Glendinning et al (2008) found limited evidence to suggest that different funding streams were integrated into individual budgets during the Department of Health pilot programme.

A follow-on study carried out by Glendinning et al (2009) explored the impact of individual budgets on informal carers, building on the design and the data collected during the main evaluation (Glendinning et al, 2008). A total of 208 informal carers identified during the main evaluation were invited to take part in this follow-on study; 163 carers agreed. The study found that carers who provided assistance to service users who were randomised into the individual budget group during the main evaluation were significantly more likely to report higher quality of life compared with those assisting an individual randomised into the control group and receiving conventional services. While there was no statistical difference between the individual budget and control groups, outcomes measured by psychological wellbeing (GHQ-12), social care-related quality of life (ASCOT) and the Carers of Older People in Europe

(COPE) Index also appeared better for carers providing assistance to an individual budget holder.

In addition to the findings from Glendinning et al (2008; 2009), a number of reviews (Arksey and Kemp, 2008; Health Foundation, 2010; Glasby, 2013) have documented the development of self-directed support initiatives in various countries within the social and health care sectors. For example, the Health Foundation (2010) published a report that highlighted the main findings from a research scan involving 60 articles about personal health and social care budgets in the UK and internationally. This scan highlighted some evidence to suggest that taking control over service and treatments can have an impact on quality of life, confidence and empowerment (Health Foundation, 2010).

Personal health budgets

Following the social care experience in England, the process of personalisation was pioneered in health care to encourage clinicians and professionals in the NHS to become more responsive to the needs of patients with long-term health conditions or comorbidity (that is, one or more long-term health conditions). The personal health budget pilot programme was launched by the Department of Health in 2009, and an independent evaluation was commissioned to run alongside (Forder et al, 2012). Forder et al (2012) explored how personal health budgets are best implemented, where and when they are most appropriate, and what support is required for individuals in order to optimise outcomes. Twenty primary care trusts (PCTs) out of 70 sites participated in the in-depth evaluation with the remainder forming the wider cohort. Based on the plans submitted by pilot sites, the 20 in-depth pilot sites offered personal health budgets to individuals with the following health characteristics: long-term conditions (including chronic obstructive pulmonary disease, diabetes and long-term neurological conditions); mental health problems; NHS continuing healthcare; and stroke.

During this national evaluation carried out by Forder et al (2012), the Secretary of State for Health in England announced that by October 2014 everyone in receipt of NHS continuing healthcare will have the right to have a personal health budget, including a direct payment. During 2015, personal health budgets became available to other individuals with a long-term health condition (NHS England, 2014). However, the success of personal health budgets will be based not solely on the commitment from government but also on how effectively they are implemented (Alakeson and Rumbold, 2013). The implementation of a new initiative, such as personal health budgets, requires considerable organisational change with various models describing the change process (Kanter et al, 1992; Kotter, 1996; Luecke, 2003, cited in Todnem, 2007). Bamford and Daniel (2007) suggest that the development of a universal change model is proving elusive. However, Bamford and Daniel (2007) do highlight that lessons can be learnt from previous research that are relevant to the management of organisational change programmes, including:

• The reasons for the change should be clearly stated through effective and consistent communication channels.
• The organisation needs to become committed to the change process and develop a culture that is actively supportive of change, through effective and positive leadership.
• The organisational change process needs to be managed in a way that is sensitive to the impact of organisational change on the organisation and individuals.

Embedded through these three issues is the necessity for effective communication during the implementation phase of change. Drawing on the organisational change management literature and the social care experience, Jones et al (2010) initially explored the initial implementation process of personal health budgets during the set-up stages of the pilot programme. Subsequently, Forder et al (2012) explored the extent to which the implementation of personal health budgets, in accordance with the Department of Health policy intentions underlying the initiative, had an impact on outcomes and cost-effectiveness for patients with long-term health conditions.

Methods

The national evaluation of the personal health budget pilot programme took a mixed-methods longitudinal approach (Jones et al, 2010; Forder et al, 2012) to explore:

1. the implementation of personal health budgets within the 20 in-depth pilot sites;
2. the experiences of people selected to receive personal health budgets compared with the experiences of people continuing under current support arrangements for their condition.

Qualitative data collection

To explore the implementation process, Jones et al (2010) invited operational representatives working in the 20 in-depth pilot sites to participate in an interview between April and June 2010. A further round of interviews among operational staff, health professionals, third-party budget holders and commissioning managers was conducted between September and October 2010. Table 11.1 shows that a total of 43 semi-structured interviews were conducted with organisational representatives. The interviews were recorded and transcribed, and key themes were identified.

Table 11.1: Type and number of organisational representatives

Type of organisational representative	Number of interviews	Number of in-depth pilot sites involved
Operational staff	18	15
Health professionals (for example, community nurses and occupational therapists)	10	10
Commissioning leads	11	9
Third-party budget holders	4	3

Notes

Operational staff included those who were involved in the implementation and delivery of personal health budgets: for example, care navigators and frontline care staff.

Commissioning leads included managers involved in the piloting of new ways of contracting services purchased by the personal health budget.

Third-party budget holders included representatives of a voluntary organisation.

These data from the qualitative in-depth interviews were used, first, to explore the implementation process during the initial stages of the pilot programme; and second, to identify five implementation models to explore if particular configurations of personal health budgets had an impact on outcomes and cost-effectiveness. The implementation models were based on the degree to which pilot sites implemented personal health budgets in accordance with the policy intentions underlying the initiative, as set by the Department of Health (2009). The models varied according to: whether the budget was known before support planning; what flexibility there was in terms of the support that could be purchased; and the choice of deployment (including direct payment).

Table 11.2 shows how a range of specification options were condensed into five models by Forder et al (2012).

Table 11.2: Implementation models

Implementation models	In-depth pilot sites
Model 1 Personalised budget is known before support planning Flexibility in what help can be purchased Deployment choice (including Direct Payments)	8 pilot sites
Model 2 Budget is known before support planning (but may not be personalised – a set amount) Service directory Deployment choice (including Direct Payments)	4 pilot sites
Model 3 Budget is known before support planning (but may not be personalised – a set amount) Lack of flexibility in the help that can be purchased No deployment choice	3 pilot sites
Model 4 Budget is not known before support planning Flexibility in what help can be purchased Variation in the degree of deployment choice	4 pilot sites
Model 5 Model 1 and 2 combined	12 pilot sites

Model 1 could be regarded as the most 'pure', being nearest to policy intentions for the personal health budget initiative. Model 5 was a combination of models 1 and 2. The only difference between these models was the existence of a menu of services for the budget holder to choose from, which was as wide as possible to provide flexibility to the budget holder. Nineteen of the 20 in-depth pilot sites were classified within one of the models.

Quantitative data collection

Figure 11.1 outlines the main quantitative data collection that contributed to exploring the experiences of individuals selected to have a personal health budget compared with those receiving conventional services (Forder et al, 2012).

Figure 11.1: Main quantitative data collection sequence

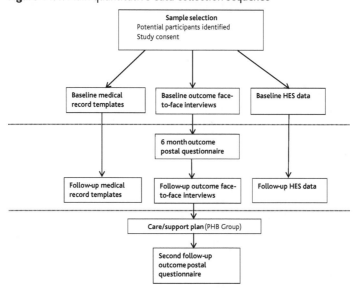

To investigate the impact of personal health budgets on outcomes, individuals selected to be in the personal health budget and control groups were invited to take part in a face-to-face interview within one month of giving informed consent and again 12 months later. Organisational representatives working within the pilot sites carried out the baseline outcome interviews between April 2010 and June 2011. The follow-up interviews began 12 months later, in April 2011, and continued until June 2012; these interviews were conducted by a research fieldwork agency. A postal outcome questionnaire was also sent to participants at two time-points during the study period: six months and up to 24 months following consent.

The baseline and follow-up interviews included a number of validated measures, including:

- *Health-related quality of life*: The EQ-5D measure was used to measure a person's quality of life in five domains (mobility, self-care, usual activities, pain/discomfort, anxiety/depression) that are likely to be related to their underlying health status.[1]
- *Care-related quality of life*: The Adult Social Care Outcomes Toolkit (ASCOT) was used to measure people's achievement of everyday activities, including basic capabilities such as dressing and feeding,

as well as more complex capabilities such as feeling safe, being occupied and having a sense of control (Netten et al, 2012).

- *Psychological wellbeing:* Psychological wellbeing was measured by the 12-item version of the General Health Questionnaire (Goldberg, 1992). The measure explores whether respondents have experienced a particular symptom or behaviour (for example, losing sleep over worry or feeling capable of making decisions about things) over the past few weeks.

The questionnaire also collected information around social care and primary care service use. In addition, demographic data, socioeconomic data and information on current circumstances were collected.

Information on participants' health condition and their use of primary healthcare services was gathered from GP records. Secondary care service use data were extracted from the Hospital Episodes Statistics (Health and Social Care Information Centre). Both sets of data were collected at two time points during the study period: first, around the time of consent to collect details of the previous 12 months' activity; second, around 12 months after recruitment to gather information for the year following consent (Forder et al, 2012).

Methods for assessing costs

Forder et al (2012) assigned a unit cost for each health and social care-related service. Primary and community health care services were costed using the values outlined in the unit costs for health and social care reports published by the Personal Social Services Research Unit at the University of Kent (Curtis, 2010; 2011). Social care services were given unit costs using the values outlined in the Personal Social Services Expenditure returns for 2009/2010 and 2010/2011.[2] Secondary care costs were calculated by applying the appropriate national tariff rates to episodes according to the health research group (HRG) classification of activity (inpatient, outpatient and A&E). The individual lengths of stay were also calculated for all episodes experienced by participants in order to apply the long-stay and zero-stay payment adjusters in the national tariffs (Forder et al, 2012).

Where consent was granted, support plans for the personal health budget holders were requested to be sent to the research team. The support plans included a breakdown of each service or support item and the corresponding cost included within the budget.

Multiple imputation

Following the multiple imputation methodology, Forder et al (2012) imputed missing data when considered to be random using the underlying patterns in the whole dataset. The study used a wide range of predictors in the statistical imputation models to estimate values for missing data.

Using the imputed datasets, multivariate difference-in-difference statistical techniques were employed to explore the relevant experiences of people in the personal health budget group between baseline and follow-up compared with those in the control group. The study used multiple regression with a range of control factors (that is, sociodemographic and socioeconomic factors, dependency level, specific health condition) to account for any differences between groups at baseline that might affect change over time in outcomes (for example, quality of life and wellbeing) and service utilisation costs beyond the impact of personal health budgets. Using the multivariate difference-in-difference approach, Forder et al (2012) were able to explore whether the implementation of personal health budgets had an impact on outcome change between follow-up and baseline and cost effectiveness. This method aimed to ensure that any remaining differences between the groups at follow-up were due to the use of personal health budgets.

Methods for assessing cost-effectiveness

Forder et al (2012) assessed the cost-effectiveness of personal budgets by calculating the net monetary benefit at baseline and follow-up for study participants in both the personal health budget and control groups. This approach calculates the value of any improvement in quality of life associated with personal health budgets relative to those in the control group less the difference in cost between the two groups. Personal health budgets were assessed as cost-effective relative to conventional service delivery if they produced greater net monetary benefits than the usual care comparator. Benefits are the £-value of improvements in quality of life. Following the approach used in England by the National Institute for Health and Care Excellence (NICE), an implicit value of between £20,000 and £30,000 was assessed for an improvement of one quality-adjusted year of life (QALY) (NICE, 2007; Raftery, 2009).

Sensitivity analysis

Sensitivity analysis was conducted to explore the assumptions made about the costing of services used by the personal health budget group and those underlying the multiple imputation procedure. The sensitivity of three types of assumptions was explored (Forder et al, 2012):

1. *Statistical assumptions.* For key analyses such as the cost-effectiveness estimates, both parametric and non-parametric (bootstrapping) methods were used, and found very little difference in the results.
2. *Costing assumptions.* On testing the sensitivity of the main results, there was not an impact until unrealistic assumptions were tried.
3. *Multiple imputation.* To test the sensitivity of the main results, an additional five imputations to the main dataset with a different randomly selected seed value, and second, variant imputation model were applied.

Forder et al (2012) explored the sensitivity of the main findings to changes in these assumptions by re-estimating net benefit differences with changes in assumptions as follows:

- using a different imputation dataset;
- using a different imputation model;
- selecting different sub-sample of the data for imputation;
- changing assumptions about which personal health budgets substitute for, rather than be provided in addition to, conventional services.

The NHS Research Ethics Committee conferred a favourable ethical opinion for the evaluation. Subsequently, the research was given research development management authorisation to commence the study in each pilot site.

Results

During the initial in-depth interviews with 43 organisational representatives, Jones et al (2010) found unanimous support for the overall aim of personal health budgets: 'A personal health budget helps people to get the services they need to achieve their health outcomes, by letting them take as much control over how money is spent on their care as is appropriate for them' (Department of Health, 2009). The positive impact seemed to be attributed to:

- *Increase in choice and control over services*: "Service users know what is good for them so they know what works and so I think it is a real positive in terms of control and choice and enabling them to stay in the community and enabling them to come to their own solutions." (Health professional)
- *Encouraging flexible and creative services*: It was perceived that increased choice and control could potentially encourage a greater number of flexible services that could fit better around an individual's lifestyle: "Younger people don't want to go to day care, they would prefer to use the direct payment system and choose to be with people they've got more in common with." (Operational staff)
- *Improvements in outcomes*: A consistent view was that the process has the potential to benefit both the budget holder and carer: "It can have a huge impact on mental or psychological health and I think that it will have an impact on keeping people healthy rather than this kind of dependency that people can get when they sit back and aren't involved [in their care]." (Health professional)
- *Improved relationships*: A number of organisational representatives thought that the personal health budget process could improve the relationship between the NHS and budget holders. It was thought that the care-planning process provides a way of finding out the real needs of budget holders and their preferences: "It's a process of working through what we need to do in terms of the planning and as a byproduct you get to know the person [budget holder] much better, which benefits both [care planner and budget holder]." (Operational staff)

However, it was consistently perceived that the implementation of personal health budgets was slow owing to the challenges that pilot sites faced during the early stages of the pilot programme: "Too slowly, too slowly, because of the challenges our PCT is having in terms of administering and assessing for the PHBs." (Operational staff)

It was thought, particularly among commissioning managers, that the commitment of managers and strong leadership would drive the required culture change. Furthermore, a number of organisational representatives highlighted that, to be able to work effectively, the implementation of personal health budgets had to be supported by staff: those who carry out assessments and agree the support plans and budgets, those who monitor the use of the budget and conditions of patients, and those who deliver services. Staff engagement and training to understand the process were viewed as important to realise the full potential of personal health budgets. It was thought that the purpose of training was to ensure that the frontline staff were in the best position to offer personal health budgets and to provide the necessary advice and support to the potential budget holder. To be able to set out conditions, or guide budget holders in terms of what would be considered a legitimate use of a budget, operational staff needed the appropriate information that at times was perceived to be missing (Jones et al, 2010).

> "From just working with people [service users] generally, they don't understand the system very well. So if they don't understand it and the person working with them [care navigator/health professional] doesn't understand it, then they won't get the best out of the system ... it's the process, what's involved and how to actually manage the situation once you've got the services you need." (Operational staff)

> "We need training about packages of choice, how to facilitate choice, we don't know this at the minute."(Health professional)

The delays in implementation had been attributed largely to the degree of culture change required within pilot sites, which seemed to be exacerbated by the climate of reducing resources and increasing uncertainty. Organisational representatives stressed that meeting need had to be balanced with resources and spending:

> "How do you square that with the resources that we have? Bear in mind that PCTs have a responsibility not to overspend work within their budget." (Operational staff)

The implementation challenges faced by pilot sites potentially would have had an impact on how personal health budgets were subsequently implemented during the pilot programme and the degree to which they were offering budgets in accordance with the Department of Health (2009) policy intentions. The findings from the in-depth interviews were used to explore the impact of the implementation process on outcomes and cost-effectiveness (Forder et al, 2012).

Outcomes

Figure 11.2 highlights that an active sample of 2,235 cases was included in the quantitative data analysis: 1,171 in the personal health budget group and 1064 in the control group. The active sample excluded participants for whom the research team did not receive baseline or follow-up outcome information, participants in residential care at baseline, participants under the age of 18 years of age or who had died before follow-up. Within the active study sample, 453 participants withdrew from the study. Of these, 158 (35%) participants died (Forder et al, 2012).

Forder et al, (2012) found relative improvements in care-related quality of life (ASCOT) and psychological wellbeing (GHQ-12) for individuals in the personal health budget group between follow-up and baseline compared to those in the control group, after controlling for confounding factors. Table 11.3 indicates that a positive impact on

Figure 11.2: Quantitative sample

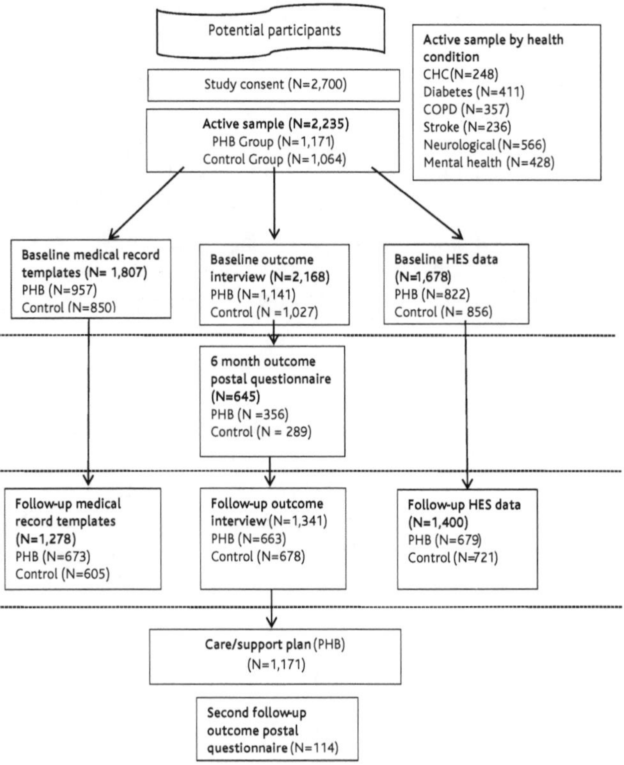

outcome-change between follow-up and baseline was also associated with pilot sites that offered greater choice and flexibility in the services that could be purchased using a personal health budget (implementation models 1, 2, 4 and 5 in Table 11.2, as previously reported).

Table 11.3: Outcome measures – impact of personal health budgets, by implementation model

	Coeff	Prob
Model 1		
ASCOT	0.039	0.026**
EQ-5D	-0.024	0.207
GHQ-12	-1.052	0.130
Subjective wellbeing	0.476	0.593
Model 2		
ASCOT	0.037	0.161
EQ-5D	-0.007	0.790
GHQ-12	-1.999	0.076*
Subjective wellbeing	0.816	0.367
Model 3		
ASCOT	-0.016	0.417
EQ-5D	-0.037	0.062*
GHQ-12	2.441	0.002**
Subjective wellbeing	-1.573	0.077*
Model 4		
ASCOT	0.044	0.027**
EQ-5D	0.010	0.670
GHQ-12	-2.445	0.001**
Subjective wellbeing	3.680	<0.001***
Model 5 (Models 1 and 2 together)		
ASCOT	0.037	0.028**
EQ-5D	-0.018	0.347
GHQ-12	-1.384	0.073*
Subjective wellbeing	0.623	0.396

Significance levels *p< 0.10 ** p< 0.05 ***p< 0.001

Table 11.3 indicates that the change in outcomes was significantly worse among Model 3 personal health budget holders than for people in the control group. This result indicates the positive impact of choice, as Model 3 had relatively little flexibility built into the process and was perhaps furthest away from the policy intentions.

Costs and cost-effectiveness

Table 11.4 shows the change in service costs between baseline and follow-up for both groups alongside the differences in these changes between groups over time. Overall, there was a total mean increase of £1,920 per person over the study period in the control group and by £800 in the personal health budget group (that is, a difference-in-difference of £1,120 less for the personal health budget group compared with the control group).

Table 11.4 highlights that the indirect costs fell significantly by £1,360 more in the personal health budget group (mainly due to inpatient care costs). By contrast, direct costs (that is, services covered by the personal health budget) grew at a slightly faster rate in the personal health budget group, with most of this cost growth-difference accounted for by wellbeing services. In the majority of cases, personal health budgets were provided in addition to usual services and so constituted an increase in expenditure of the group, other factors being equal.

Overall, personal health budgets were found to be cost-effective using the care-related quality of life (ASCOT) compared to conventional service delivery. Specifically, the personal health budget group showed greater benefit and less cost, on average, than the control group. The net benefit was between £1,520 and £2,690 greater for the personal health budget group than the control group after subtracting baseline differences. At the £30,000 threshold, the extra net benefit averaged £2,300 (£1,180 minus £1,120) more for the personal health budget group compared to the control group. For EQ-5D-measured benefits, personal health budgets showed greater net benefit than the control group, on average of between £1,020 and £700, though these were not statistically significant. The sensitivity analysis supported the main findings and in many cases the cost-effectiveness results were stronger, with personal health budgets showing cost-effectiveness (on the ASCOT scale) at the 95% confidence level (Forder et al, 2012).

Personal health budgets were shown to be cost-effective using the care-related quality of life measure (ASCOT) relative to conventional service delivery when implemented following the three main underlying principles and classified as Model 1 (see Table 11.2, as previously reported). However, when personal health budgets were implemented in the way that was least consistent with policy intentions (Model 3), it was found that personal health budgets were not cost-effective compared to conventional service delivery.

Table 11.4: Differences in service and support costs, by type – whole sample

	Change in cost between baseline and follow-up		Difference-in-difference	Significance probability
	PHB	Control		
Social care	2310	2720	-400	0.635
Wellbeing	500	0	510	<0.001***
Nursing and therapy services	80	-10	90	0.109
Other health services	120	70	50	0.003**
Subtotal: Direct costs	3020	2780	240	0.759
Primary care	60	70	-10	0.830
Inpatient care	-2150	-830	-1320	0.040**
Outpatient and A&E	-130	-100	-30	0.427
Subtotal: indirect costs	-2220	-860	-1360	0.042**
Total cost	800	1920	-1120	0.319

Significance levels: * p<0.10 ** p<0.05*** p< 0.001
N=2235

Discussion

There were two aims to this chapter:

1. to explore the implementation process during the initial stage of the personal health budget pilot programme;

2. to explore whether the extent to which the implementation of personal health budgets was in accordance with the Department of Health (2009) policy intentions, had an impact on outcomes and cost-effectiveness for patients with long-term health conditions.

To explore both aims, the study employed both qualitative and quantitative research methodologies to build up a comprehensive picture of the implementation process and the potential impact of personal health budgets.

The qualitative in-depth interviews with organisational representatives highlighted a number of positive views of personal health budgets. These included viewing the initiative as a potential mechanism for providing increased choice and control for patients, and encouraging the NHS to become more responsive to the needs of individuals who use the service. A number of challenges were also discussed around the implementation of the policy. Delays were largely felt to be due to the cultural change required within the organisation to make it a success, and how well this issue was managed and addressed within the sites. Mirroring the organisational change management literature (that is, Allen et al, 2007; Michaelis et al, 2009), communication and effective leadership seemed to be central to some of the reported challenges. Overall, organisational representatives thought that senior managers had a role to play during the early stages of implementation, which potentially was underestimated in some pilot sites, particularly around addressing the concerns of frontline staff and exploring the immediate impact on the workplace (Jones et al, 2010).

The extent to which organisational change was managed during the initial stages of the national pilot potentially had an impact on the degree to which personal health budgets were implemented in accordance with the Department of Health (2009) policy intentions underlying the initiative. The findings from the in-depth interviews allowed the research team to develop five implementation models. The results indicated that implementation adhering to the main underlying principles of personal health budgets had the potential to have a positive impact on outcomes for budget holders and whether they were cost-effective compared to conventional service delivery. Currently, the implementation models are being used by the Department of Health to guide the national roll-out of personal health budgets during 2015 and onwards.

Overall, these findings provided valuable information as to how personal health budgets should be effectively implemented; identifying those factors that could facilitate and inhibit the process during the current roll-out in England. The findings from this current study, previous research (that is, NHS Confederation and National Mental Health Development Unit, 2011) and the change management literature, all provide valuable guidance and information on how to manage the implementation of new initiatives, such as personal health budgets or the new Integrated Personal Commissioning pilot programme that began in April 2015.

While the evaluation carried out by Forder et al, (2012) has provided a direction for the national roll-out of personal health budgets, a number of limitations were acknowledged. In terms of the qualitative in-depth interviews (Jones et al, 2010), organisational representatives were interviewed during the early stages of the implementation process, while in the midst of structural change and financial challenges. The views are only those of the participants, and may not reflect the opinions of the wider organisations.

The main study (Forder et al, 2012) allowed 12 months between baseline and follow-up to enable the impact of receiving a personal health budget to be measured. This decision followed the experience from a similarly designed evaluation of the individual budgets pilots in social care (Glendinning et al, 2008) that incorporated a six-month follow-up period; a time frame found to be insufficient. The longer follow-up resulted in the final recruitment rates being sufficient, but with higher dropout rates, which may have had an impact on the robustness of the evaluation findings. There was a degree of missing data, which was addressed using the multiple imputation methods. Finally, in line with the ethos of the pilot, there were a wide range of services and support that could be purchased using the budget, as outlined within the personal health budget care/support plans. However, this meant that a number of assumptions had to be made to produce like-with-like cost estimates between the personal health budget and control groups.

Notwithstanding these identified limitations, the findings from the national evaluation (Forder et al, 2012) provided guidance and direction for the continued roll-out of personal health budgets, current programmes such as the Integrated Personal Commissioning pilots and within the international arena.

Acknowledgements

The chapter is based on the main findings from the national evaluation of the personal health budget pilot programme. The research was commissioned and funded by the Policy and Strategy Directorate in the

Department of Health. The views expressed are not necessarily those of the Department.

For the national evaluation, other team members contributed to the study design, data collection and final report, including: Kate Baxter, Jacqueline Davidson, Paul Dolan, Caroline Glendinning, Annie Irvine and Dominic King.

Notes

[1] © 1990 EuroQol Group. EQ-5D™ is a trademark of the EuroQol Group.

[2] http://www.ic.nhs.uk/services/social-care/social-care-collections

References

Alakeson, V. and Rumbold, B. (2013) *Personal health budgets: Challenges for commissioners and policy-makers*, London: Nuffield Trust.

Allen, J., Jimmieson, N.L., Bordia, P. and Irmer, V.E. (2007) 'Uncertainty during organizational change: Managing perceptions through communication', *Journal of Change Management*, 7(2): 187–210.

Arksey, H. and Kemp, P.A. (2008) *Dimensions of Choice: A narrative review of cash-for-care schemes*, York: Social Policy Research Unit, University of York.

Bamford, D. and Daniel, S. (2007) 'A case study of change management effectiveness within the NHS', *Journal of Change Management*, 5(4): 391–406.

Curtis, L. (2011) *Unit Costs of Health and Social Care*, Canterbury: Personal Social Services Research Unit, University of Kent.

Curtis, L. (2010) *Unit Costs of Health and Social Care*, Canterbury: Personal Social Services Research Unit, University of Kent.

Department of Health (2009) *Personal health budgets: first steps*, London: Department of Health.

Forder, J., Jones, K., Glendinning, C., Caiels, J., Welch, E., Baxter, K., Davidson, J., Windle, K., Irvin, A., King, D. and Dolan, P. (2012) *Evaluation of the personal health budget pilot programme*, Canterbury: Personal Social Services Research Unit, University of Kent.

Glasby, E.W. (2013) *Personal budgets and Health: a review of evidence*, London: Policy Research in Commissioning and the Healthcare System.

Glendinning, C., Arksey, H., Jones, K., Moran, N., Netten, A. and Rabiee, P. (2009) *Individual budgets: Impact and outcomes for carers*, York: Social Policy Research Unit, University of York.

Glendinning, C., Challis, D., Fernandez, J., Jacobs, S., Jones, K., Knapp, M., Manthorpe, J., Moran, N., Netten, A., Stevens, M. and Wilberforce, M. (2008) *Evaluation of the Individual Budgets Pilot Programme: Final Report*, York: Social Policy Research Unit, University of York.

Goldberg, D. (1992) *General Health Questionnaire*, Windsor: NFER Nelson.

Health Foundation (2010) *Personal health budgets: Research scan*, London: Health Foundation.

Jones, K., Welch, E., Caiels, J., Windle, K., Forder, J., Davidson, J., Dolan, P., Glendinning, C., Irvine, A. and King, D. (2010) *Experiences of implementing personal health budgets: 2nd interim report*, Canterbury: Personal Social Services Research Unit, University of Kent.

Michaelis, B., Stegmaier, R. and Sonntag, K. (2009) 'Affective commitment to change and innovation implementation behaviour: The role of charismatic leadership and employees trust to top management', *Journal of Change Management*, 9(4): 399–417.

Netten, A., Burge, P., Malley, J., Potoglou, D., Towers, A-M., Brazier, J., Flynn, T., Forder, J. and Wall, B. (2012) 'Outcomes of social care for adults: developing a preference-weighted measure', *Health Technology Assessment,* 16(16): 1-165.

NICE (2007) *Briefing paper for the methods working party on the cost effectiveness threshold*, London: National Institute for Health and Clinical Excellence.

NHS Confederation and National Mental Health Development Unit (2011) *Facing up to the challenge of personal health budgets: The view of fontline professionals*, London: NHS Confederation and National Mental Health Development Unit.

NHS England (2014) *Personal health budgets: Update*, London: NHS England.

Raftery, J. (2009) 'NICE and the challenge of cancer drugs', *British Medical Journal*, 338: b67.

Todnem, R. (2005) 'Organisational change management: A critical review', *Journal of Change Management*, 5(4): 369–80.

TWELVE

Personalised care funding in Norway: a case of gradual co-production

Karen Christensen

Introduction

Currently, many European welfare states are searching for ways of meeting the future's increasing demand for long-term care services (EU, 2012). One of the central ways of meeting that demand is about changing the role of the welfare service recipient from a passive receiver of welfare state services to an active social citizen directly involved in and participating in the production of services (Johansson and Hvinden, 2007). Two key theoretical concepts applied for analysing this involvement and participation currently are 'personalisation', meaning personalising the services (see for example, Leadbeater, 2004; Christensen and Pilling, 2014) and 'co-production', primarily between the user and local authorities (for example, Hunter and Richie, 2007; Needham and Carr, 2009; Scourfield, 2015). In this article, using a case analysis, the author will show that it is fruitful to combine these two concepts, this being further explored below. Co-production represents a stronger version of personalisation, but there are also different strengths of co-production. This implies gradual manifestations of user involvement and participation. However, any critical case analysis in this matter requires the researcher to reflect on these different manifestations to see if modifications of the strength of user involvement and participation have to be made at the different levels. The aim of this chapter is to present a case of gradual manifestation of co-production, simultaneously looking at the nuances within this. Intentionally, a Scandinavian case is used, as Scandinavian countries in general are known for their generous welfare services (Esping-Andersen, 1999) and therefore often are presented as examples to follow.

The Norwegian case of BPA

The case that will be used here is the user-controlled personal assistance scheme in Norway (Brukerstyrt Personlig Assistanse, BPA). This is a welfare arrangement that, based on legislation-based assessments, allocates a budget (here called personalised care funding) to disabled people; they can then employ their own care workers – called personal assistants – to assist them with the help they need in everyday life. In the UK, similar arrangements are direct payments, and later personal budgets (see for example, Land and Himmelweit, 2010). Although this arrangement based on a personalised care funding is not confined to disabled people, in practice this is most usually the case in Norway, with eight out of 10 users being physically disabled people (Johansen et al, 2010: 16). BPA in Norway provides a central example of the policies of personalisation in the social care sector (Christensen and Pilling, 2014). Although 'personalisation' is a complex concept (discussed more below), in general this is about 'tailoring services to individuals' needs and preferences rather than ... fitting individuals into existing service provision' (Christensen and Pilling, 2014: 480). This is a way of trying to personalise, or individualise, the services to the user with the aim of giving them more choice and control. Very much central to this personalisation is the budget that enables the user to employ personal assistants him/herself (possibly with support); these schemes are therefore usually called cash-for-care in the international literature.

A growing body of literature has had a focus on cash-for-care in Europe (for example, Ungerson, 2004; Ungerson and Yeandle, 2007; Da Roit and Le Bihan, 2010), including Norway (for example, Andersen et al, 2006; Johansen et al, 2010; Guldvik and Andersen, 2013). The literature has covered different issues, such as implementation and policy development (for example, Pearson, 2000; Boxall et al, 2009; Askheim et al, 2014), the search for disabled people's independence and empowerment (for example, Morris, 1993; Christensen, 2009), the potentially subordinated position of assistants (for example, Guldvik, 2003; Guldvik et al, 2014), and user/care worker relationships (for example, Glendinning et al, 2006; Christensen, 2012). Rather than contributing to these broader topics, this chapter will make a narrower but specific policy analysis of care funding related to the personal assistance model (BPA). The analysis will be based on critical questions regarding the extent of user involvement and participation.

In the following, the author introduces the history of BPA. She then explores further the concepts of personalisation and co-production, and also briefly presents the sources and method of the analysis. Finally, the chapter provides a policy analysis of personalised care funding related to BPA in Norway. This analysis points out four key areas to be explored and discussed: muddling of user-control, rights boundaries, negotiating the user role in assessment, and user role duties.

From pilot project to welfare user rights – the history of BPA

The history of the Norwegian personal assistance model, BPA, started in 1991 with a three-year pilot project financed by the Department of Health and Care and organised by the Norwegian disability association (Norges Handicapforbund). Related to this project were two factors important for the future of personal assistance in Norway. One was the establishment of a cooperative ULOBA, an organisation run and controlled by disabled people themselves, actively involved in the whole process. BPA was introduced as an alternative to traditional home care services, giving the possibility of also obtaining assistance outside the home and with user control as the key characteristic: 'What is particularly characteristic of this scheme is the user's control of the organisation and content of the service' (St.meld. 34, 1996-97: 34). The other factor was the way disabled people in the pilot project could choose between different ways of organising personal assistance: with themselves as employer and manager, with the municipality as the employer and themselves as manager or with a user-controlled cooperative as the employer and themselves as manager. The pilot project was positively evaluated due to the possibility of more flexible services (Norges Handicapforbund, 1994). The department then made this scheme a priority area in their action plan towards disabled people in Norway, including in this a plan for future legislation (St.meld. 34, 1996-97).

The ideology behind BPA was inspired particularly by the US rooted Independent Living (IL) movement, which encouraged disabled people's active participation in society and opposed institutional care (residential homes) for disabled people, and the dominating role of professionals, including the biomedical view of disability (Andersen et al, 2006). At the time of the personal assistance pilot project in Norway, this IL movement had already inspired several other Nordic countries (Finland, Sweden and Denmark) to introduce legislation for some disabled people to manage their own personal assistance (St.meld. 34, 1996-97).

BPA became legalised in 2000 by the Social Services Act, in § 4-2, stating that these services include 'practical support and training, including user-controlled personal assistance, to those with special needs of assistance due to illness, impairment, age or for other reasons'. Since then all Norwegian municipalities have been obliged to offer BPA as an alternative to traditional social services such as home care. However, there was an important change in 2006 regarding the criterion for allocating BPA. Where earlier the requirement for BPA was that the disabled person should be able to act as a manager of his/her personal assistants, it now became an option to let another person (parent or trust) take over this manager role (Rundskriv I-15/2005). And while physically disabled people aged 18+ were seen as the main group of BPA participants when it was legalised in 2000, these limitations were later also removed. The main issue after these expansions was a discussion about making BPA a right. However, before that, in 2011, when a new Health and Social Care Act was passed, BPA got its own article (§ 3-8) further obliging Norwegian municipalities to offer BPA, and generalising also the idea to future social services by calling them all home based personal assistance services, BPA being one of them. It took 15 years to develop a right to BPA, this being a plan since 2000: by 1 January 2015, the article § 2-1d about the right to BPA was added to the Patients' and Users' Rights Act (Prop. 86 L, 2013-2014). The government saw this right as part of their follow up to the United Nations Convention on the Rights of Persons with Disabilities.

Since 2000 the number of BPA users has risen sharply. Starting with around 686 in 2000, to 2,268 in 2010 and 3,007 users in 2014, represents a rise of 438% over 14 years (Andersen et al, 2006: 42, Johansen et al, 2010: 10, Otnes and Haugstveit, 2015). With about three personal assistants employed per BPA user, the figure for assistants can be estimated as around 9,000 employees today with one third of them being employed by private providers (Guldvik and Andersen, 2013: 27), among them ULOBA.

In the 1990s, when the social care sector was impacted by new public management ideas, some municipalities implemented the purchaser-provider model. This model contributed to marketisation, for example by giving the option of contracting private for-profit actors to provide services (Vabø et al, 2013), including BPA. Comparing 2002 with 2010 indicates that the group of users being employers themselves increased from 9% to 11%, those choosing ULOBA increased from 26% to 33% and those using the municipality decreased from 65% to 54% (Johansen et al, 2010: 28). Today (non-profit) ULOBA shares the position as an alternative to the user-employer and the municipality-employer with a range of for-profit companies (Guldvik and Andersen, 2013), but a large group is still using the municipality-employer organisation.

The concepts of personalisation and co-production

The national document that suggests making BPA a priority area for the future social care services in Norway starts with a poem by Kuan-Tzy (600 BC). The last part of this poem says: 'If you give a man a fish, he will have food this time only. If you teach him fishing, he will have food for the rest of his life.' (St.meld. 34, 1996-97). It can be said that this is the simple idea behind the political agenda of personalisation: a partnership based on co-production.

On a very general theoretical level the concepts of personalisation and co-production, are inspired by theories about a shift from government to governance (Stoker, 1998; Enroth, 2011). While government is based on a traditional hierarchical top down organisation of the public sector with a clear separation of the public and private sector, 'governance' rather represents a network based organisation where the fulfilling of the public sector's social objectives includes a range of different non-public actors. This implies a decentralisation of the governing functions and involves new actors such as voluntary organisations, for-profit actors, but also users taking part in decision-making processes. Here in particular, user involvement is important. The relation to the theory of governance makes it clear that this is part of a broader public sector change.

The policies of personalisation fit into this because they are generally aiming at this user-involvement/user-control (Leadbeater, 2004; Christensen and Pilling, 2014). Exploring further the concept of personalisation, Leadbeater (2004) takes as his starting point an example similar to the 'teach a man to fish' example mentioned earlier, but then points to five levels of personalisation.

At the first level, services are more available, accessible and user-friendly; at the second level users are given more information and guidelines about how to choose the services they need; at the third level users are giving influence on how to spend the money they are allocated (Leadbeater uses the example of disabled people commissioning their care packages); at a fourth level users are co-producers of a service by actively participating in the design of it; and at the highest level, users would be self-organised, with public professionals only providing an environment conducive to this self-organisation (Leadbeater, 2004: 21-3). Moving from the first to the highest level, an increasingly radical shift in the user role is taking place: from a dependent user to the role of a consumer, and finally to a co-designer of the services. Following this presentation, Leadbeater asks the question: 'How far does the government want to go?' This is also an important question here: how far does the

Norwegian government go with their care funding of BPA? However, applying the concept of co-production needs additional explanation.

Scourfield (2015) offers a further differentiation of Leadbeater's fourth (co-production) level, after pointing out the fact that 'Co-production is a slippery concept' (Scourfield, 2015: 544, referring to the Social Care Institute for Excellence's guide (Needham and Carr, 2009)). The original idea of co-production is from the US in the 1970s and was used for example in community policing, based on the assumption that outcomes will be qualitatively better if they involve those who will be users of the policy objectives (Needham and Carr, 2009). Transferred later to the public sector, it reached social care and was here defined, for example, by Hunter and Richie (2007: 9) as 'a particular form of partnership between people who use social care services and the people and agencies who provide them'. And later in their same argument: 'In the co-production model, the state has an important role in creating the conditions for productive partnership between professionals and 'problem-owners' (Hunter and Richie, 2007: 15). In order to unpick the concept further, Scourfield's differentiation is useful. He distinguishes between three different levels:

- At a descriptive level, users are not real co-producers but are doing what they are told to do.
- At an intermediate level the users are recognised as people who can supplement the services, they are invited and to some degree also required to make their contribution to the services.
- At the transformative level, the users are empowered in terms of operating within structural conditions that give them some kind of 'genuine control over the production process' (Scourfield, 2015: 549).

What can be learned from this differentiation is, that there may be co-production examples that have nothing to do with power transformation, or as expressed by Hunter and Richie (2007: 15): 'Co-production is not a magic fix. It does not dispense with the need for promoting equality, enforcing standards or improving delivery. However, it offers a different way to think about the relationship between the state, service providers and service users.'

According to Hunter and Richie (2007), co-production is different from the traditional model with professional experts and dependent users as well as from the consumer model with users as consumers in a market. In the following section, the author briefly presents the material to which this conceptual framework and its critical questions will be applied.

The policy analysis – sources and method

The sources of the chapter's policy analysis first of all comprise texts providing information about national policy relating to BPA. These texts consist of BPA legislation texts (the Health and Care Services Act of 2012; and the Patient and User Right Act of 1999, including its relevant change in 2015) and important and related national documents. These are primarily national circular letters (Rundskriv I-/20/2000; Rundskriv I-15/2005; Rundskriv I-9/2015) but also a handbook with guidelines for those allocated BPA funding (Helsedirektoratet, 2015a). Regarding the circular letters, the one from 2015 is based on those from 2000 and 2005, implying here that rather than the new one replacing the older ones, they are consecutive policy documents and all need to be analysed.

The texts are official open-published state documents and are here subject to qualitative analysis (Scott, 1990: 14). Following Scott's point of understanding such documents, as shaped by a specific policy context with implicit assumptions and orientations, the analysis is guided by questions such as: What does BPA's position and presentation in legislation reveal about options for strengthening user -control? How strong is the right to BPA when looking more closely at the official guidelines for practising it? What characterises the role of the user in the assessment of allocating BPA, when including both explicit and implicit parts? And if the user at some stage is allocated a co-producing partnership role, what does this actually mean?

For corroboratory purposes and to deepen the arguments from the document analysis the author includes some secondary data, in particular from a research report, specifically about the allocation process, the assessments these allocations are based upon and the user's role. The research report is written by two BPA experts (Guldvik and Andersen, 2013). It is based on data from 10 selected municipalities in Norway, the data being collected through qualitative interviews with employees, administrative municipality representatives, and leaders of private for-providers of BPA. Particularly relevant here is the municipal government's assessment of needs in terms of hours for the BPA funding. It should be mentioned that this report was written before BPA became rights-based. However, there is so far no material available about the implications of this current change. Furthermore, I argue that this policy change to BPA may not represent a significant change, although clearly this was the wish of the Norwegian disability movement (Andersen et al, 2006). When relevant, some of the earlier empirical research mentioned will be included in the arguments of the analysis.

Muddled user-control of BPA policy

Before 2012, Norwegian health care services had separate legislation, one for health services (nursing home care and so on) and one for social care services (home help and so on). The Health and Social Care Act implemented in 2012 represented a policy shift in this matter. It gathered together the legislation for these services. This merging of legislation is important for the analysis of how far BPA could become personalised. Being part of this broader law in fact means that BPA is not manifested separately, but is seen as part of a broader range of services that Norwegian municipalities are obliged to offer to their inhabitants. These other kinds of services are not based on the same type of ideology relating to user-control, which can imply a weakness of the user-control argument. Thus, since the development of BPA in the early 1990s, this welfare scheme has been (and, based on the 2012 legislation, is even more today) represented as an alternative service, outside of the service mainstream: 'User-controlled personal assistance is an alternative way of organising practical and personal help for severely impaired people who need assistance in their daily life, within and outside their home' (Rundskriv I-20/2000: 2).

Being an alternative implies not only that BPA is a non-traditional welfare scheme, but more importantly here, that BPA is offered alongside non-user-controlled services. A disabled person could, for example, be a user of BPA, but simultaneously receive home nursing every night. According to research based figures, in fact two out of five BPA users in 2010 received additional (traditional) municipal services, with, for example, 29% receiving home nursing services (Johansen et al, 2010: 20). This way, traditional services for many are integrated in the total care package for a user of BPA, thereby muddling the user-control by mixing the user roles of dependency and independence. Potentially, this implies watering down the policy strength of personalisation.

The boundaries of BPA rights

As mentioned earlier, it took 15 years to establish a right to BPA. Central discussions in this period were about the costs and who this right should be for. When BPA finally became a right on 1 January

2015, it was limited to some of the people entitled to health and care services according to §3-2, 1st part, no 6b in the Health and Social Care Act. BPA was limited to people below the age of 67; it could not include services that would require two workers at the same time; it could not include night services; and the user had to have long-term and comprehensive needs for assistance. 'Long-term' was defined as two years, and 'comprehensive' was defined as a minimum of 32 hours help per week. Users who would need a minimum of 25 hours per week would have a right to BPA too. However, the condition for this right would be that the municipality could document that this arrangement would be of lower cost than other types of (read: non-user-controlled) services. According to the latest figures regarding BPA users over the age of 67 (11% in 2014, see Otnes and Haugstveit, 2015: 74), one may say that a limit at this age would not exclude many people from this group. In policy terms, however, this is different. It sends the signal that user-controlled services are not for older people and that the policies of personalisation are not directed at them. However, the circular letter of 2015 seems to anticipate a future policy shift here by saying that BPA could be 'an appropriate way of organising the services also for users above 67' (Rundskriv I-9/2015: 3).

According to the distribution of BPA hours allocated (Johansen et al, 2010), this policy of BPA rights gives below half of the current group of disabled people with BPA a right to it. And with a tendency over time for more people having a small number of allocated hours (1-15 hours/ week rising from 27% in 2002 to 38% in 2010, see Johansen et al, 2010: 14), rather more people could be excluded. Furthermore, this policy creates a new dividing line between those needing 25+/32+ hours and those below this line, also making the assessment of hours more sensitive.

According to the same User and Patient Rights Law (2015), article §3-1, the service offer should, as far as possible, be figured out in cooperation with the user (or patient). It is additionally stressed that it is very important to let the user have a say when the service offer is worked out, also according to the Health and Social Care Act. This is also explicitly stressed in the circular letter of 2015 (Rundskriv I-9/2015: 2). However, this stress on the involvement of the user, when the service offer is worked out, was also included in the earlier Social Services Act of 2000, in its article § 8-4, not least also due to its ambitious aim, stating that this is to '... contribute to the individual's possibility of being and living independently and have an active and meaningful life together with others' (Rundskriv I-20/2000: 2). In general, therefore, and from a policy perspective, one might conclude here, that there has been no major policy change following the right to BPA regarding the user's role during the assessment process of allocating a certain number of hours to the individual user. But what characterises this process?

The user role in the assessment – a negotiating role

An important policy issue regarding the process of allocating hours for BPA has so far – and before the right – been related to the paternalistic way that this allocation process has been organised: 'It is the municipality which as the point of departure shall decide what kind of services are suitable' (Rundskriv I-20/2000: 2). So although the users should be involved, the municipality through its representatives has the final say. But what criteria are they using? According to the research by Guldvik and Andersen (2013), the amount of hours needed for assistance has been crucial in the decision to allocate BPA (and will be more so now with the right). Some municipalities only allocated BPA when the hours needed were high. However, this research also found municipalities allocating BPA when the need for hours was as low as 5–6 hours. The new right to BPA directed at those with a high number of hours may therefore have a negative impact on these 'small-users'. But this will also depend on the general municipal view of BPA. BPA can still be chosen if found relevant by the municipality, although the user will need 25+/32+ hours to have a right to BPA. The same research found that some municipalities are unenthusiastic about BPA and that they do not even present information on their websites about this option (Guldvik and Andersen, 2013: 18). Such municipal differences have been stressed in the earlier BPA literature too (see for example, Andersen et al, 2006: 132). This thinking behind the concrete assessments carried out will therefore most likely continue to be a factor directing the assessments in different municipalities. In other words, the municipal representatives would sometimes have as their norm in the procedure to allocate traditional services, or a combination of different traditional services, but BPA only when this is strongly wished for by the user. With a right to BPA for some, the argument in the dialogue (or one may better call this negotiation (Guldvik and Andersen, 2013: 19)) with the municipality, may be stronger for those knowing about BPA, wanting it and being assessed as eligible for enough hours to get it. For others the negotiation will be weaker.

While earlier research into BPA suggested that people who were assessed as potential BPA users would normally get more hours than before, this direction more recently has declined. In 2002 90% of those who either got their traditional services replaced totally by BPA or got BPA as a supplement to their services, were allocated a higher amount of hours through this shift. In 2010, this was decreased to 62% (Johansen et al, 2010: 21). Related to this change, and important here, is also that those disabled people who said that they had a major influence on the determination of the amount of hours, decreased from 43% in 2002 to 30% in 2010 (Johansen et al, 2010: 22). The right to BPA will most likely not bring this flexibility back, for various reasons. One is that the circular letter of 2015 now explicitly says that the municipalities should assess the need for services independently of whether this is later organised as BPA. This implies that the right to BPA should not change the assessment (Rundskriv I-9/2015: 3). Another reason is that the conditions for the right are so clearly restricted, by law. And finally, a tendency towards more equal procedures for all (that is user-controlled and traditional services) seems to have increased, due to the organisation in many Norwegian municipalities of the purchaser-and-provider model (see Vabø et al, 2013). With this organisation, all assessments regarding social care services are carried out by professionals from the same municipal purchase unit. This will most likely contribute to maintaining paternalistic ways of measuring out the number of hours, although it is required that users are involved.

Interestingly, and supporting this assumption, is the fact that early research found that the users had more influence on the amount of hours than the content of hours allocated (Andersen et al, 2006: 69). This is also mentioned in a national guideline document of 2015 (Helsedirektoratet, 2015a: 10): 'It should clearly be stated [by the municipality] … what kind of assistance needs should be covered in the actual BPA-arrangement'. But this does not harmonise with the policy about what is supposed to happen when the hours are allocated.

The duties of the user role

'*Within the hours* allocated by the municipality and stated in the legally binding resolution about personal assistance, the user can, in principle, control who he/she wants to have as helper(s), what the assistant(s) shall do, where and at what times the help shall be given.' (Helsedirektoratet, 2015b, emphasis added).

As can be seen from this piece of text published by the Norwegian Directorate of Health, responsible for providing information about welfare services, there is a dividing line between what is going on in the process of assessment and at the stage when BPA has been allocated (a similar formulation is used in Rundskriv I-20/2000). 'Within the hours' implies in policy terms, that the municipality has made a decision, and within this decided framework, the user is given almost full user-control. There is, however, one important duty, which has been central in the Norwegian model (Christensen and Pilling, 2014) and since the beginning has also functioned as a decisive criterion for being assessed as eligible to BPA: the role of manager towards the assistants, taken by the user him/herself or by another person (Rundskriv I-20/2000; Rundskriv I-15/2005; Rundskriv I-9/2015). The manager role is different from the employer role. The employer, whether this is the municipality, a BPA provider, or the user him/herself (see earlier) – again decided by the municipality with the user involved in the decision process – holds the traditional employer duties. This includes providing a contract, payments, employment and terminating employment and so on.

Although the different employer models are important, even more important here is the policy concerning the manager role, as this role cannot be given to anybody else, unless the reason is, for example, cognitive impairments (since 2006, see earlier). This is why the Norwegian Directorate of Health (Helsedirektoratet, 2015a) has produced a handbook particularly directed at managers of BPA, see its foreword. In this, it is clarified that there is a role division related to BPA, between the municipality, the employer, the manager, the possible co-manager and the assistant.

Crucial to the discussion here is the work division between the municipality and manager. The municipality has the general responsibility of offering BPA and safeguarding all responsibilities for the employment of workers and their working conditions, regardless of whether the municipality itself is the employer, or this is outsourced to a private actor or the user. On the other hand, independently of these arrangements, the user (or a co-user) should always be the manager. The handbook (Helsedirektoratet 2015a: 12-13) says that this role requires the following daily day-to-day routines: follow laws and agreements like other personal coordinators/managers, organise the assistants' working hours, keep an account of the working hours, fulfil a professional not personal role in relation to the assistants, be active in acquiring relevant knowledge about leader competence by taking courses. It is furthermore the responsibility of the manager to guide the assistants in their work by providing a job description, teaching the assistants and giving them the option of further development, giving them a work timetable and providing a safe and reasonable work environment. This range of duties points to the broad daily responsibilities involved in the user's part when choosing and being allowed by the municipality to choose BPA. These duties have to be taken into account by the municipal government, when making the final decision about organising the services as BPA or not. However, when this is the decision, the municipality then requires the user to act as a professional, not only in regard to the management of the assistants, but even in the relationship with them. There should be 'a professional distance between user and assistant' (see Rundskriv I-9/2015: 8). This way, the user – at this stage – is made a co-producer, in policy terms, by the municipality.

Concluding discussion

The advantage of combining the concepts of personalisation and co-production when looking at how services are fitted to users (and not the other way around), is that this reveals the gradual manifestation of co-production; this being placed at a higher level of personalisation when requiring, for example, a partnership between equal partners. But analysing further the policy around a specific case then also gives the opportunity of discussing this upwards movement and adding nuances.

Crucial in this matter regarding BPA are primarily three aspects. The first one concerns the information (see Leadbeater's second level of personalisation) about BPA, very important for users in order to make informed choices about their wishes for help needed. Here the BPA case shows that while policy can require all Norwegian municipalities to offer BPA, it cannot control the way and the extent to which information is given, because this is within the authority of the municipality. In other words, there is always a way to avoid this, if this is the dominant attitude towards BPA in a municipality; typically this would include smaller Norwegian municipalities. The way BPA is muddled into other services not based on the ideology of user-control contributes to these information issues as the professionals may concentrate on information and guidelines about the major services rather than the BPA-alternative that both locally and nationally represents a few percentages of all services (SSB, 2015).

The second aspect found in the chapter's analysis is about the important negotiating process taking place right before and at Leadbeater's third level of giving the users influence on the money, using Scourfield's two types of co-production: doing what one is told to do, and supplementing or contributing to services, because these are found as part of the same negotiating process between the municipality/their professionals and the user. In other words, the case of BPA policy shows that there is a kind of double-edged sword in the policy directed at the decision about what kind of and what amount of services (in hours) to allocate and formalise legally. On one hand, the users should always be involved, on the other it is always the municipality that makes the final decision. The strongest type of personalisation therefore at this stage of BPA is supplementing this decision. However, stressing the negotiation part prior to the formal decision (Guldvik and Andersen, 2013) also is a suggestion here of adding a stronger user agency (see also Johansson and Hvinden, 2007) to this part of the policy of the personalisation process: although only making a contribution, this should still be considered an active and important moment.

The third aspect is related to the stage where BPA is allocated and where a type of co-production is taking place. The nuances of co-production can here be revealed by using Leadbeater's fourth level and Scourfield's second and third level about supplementing services and being empowered at the transformative highest level. Regarding first the employer choice and manager role, the level of co-production is higher if the user is the employer him/herself and if the user, not a possible co-user, is the manager. Looking then at the municipality-user relationship, one has to understand a possible transformative level only within the structural framework that the municipality governs. In this sense, the municipality and the user are not equal partners. Rather the analysis shows that a work division is taking place, where the user – after the formalised BPA decision – is obliged to carry out a range of duties related to the manager role guided by the municipality. The user's co-production therefore very much is about duty and responsibility towards the municipal authorities.

Finally, there is the highest level of personalisation (Leadbeater, 2004), where the professionals are no longer directly involved because the users are self-organised. While this obviously is the future policy aim of some users, this will not be an option for others. The right to BPA will provide a future dividing line between those who possibly will be viewed as able to reach this self-organising level, and those for whom the welfare state will still be very important. In this sense, further policy developments following the right to BPA in Norway will be extremely important to follow.

References

Andersen, J., Askheim, O.P., Begg, I.S. and Guldvik I. (2006) *Brukerstyrt personlig assistance: Kunnskap og praksis*, Oslo: Gyldendal Akademisk.

Askheim, O.P., Bengtsson, H. and Bjelke, B.R. (2014) 'Personal assistance in a Scandinavian context: similarities, differences and developmental traits', *Scandinavian Journal of Disability Research*, 16(1): 3–18.

Boxall, K., Dawson, S. and Beresford, P. (2009) 'Selling individual budgets, choice and control: local and global influences on UK social care policy for people with learning difficulties', *Policy and Politics*, 37(4): 499–515.

Christensen, K. (2009) 'In(ter)dependent lives', *Scandinavian Journal of Disability Research*, 11(2): 117–30.

Christensen, K. (2012) 'Towards sustainable hybrid relationships in cash-for-care systems', *Disability and Society*, 27(3): 399–412.

Christensen, K. and Pilling, D. (2014) 'Policies of personalisation in Norway and England: On the impact of political context', *Journal of Social Policy*, 43(3): 479–96.

Da Roit, B. and Le Bihan, B. (2010) 'Similar and yet so different: cash-for-care in six European countries' long-term care policies', *The Milbank Quarterly*, 88(3): 286–309.

Enroth, H. (2011) 'Policy network theory', in M. Bevir (ed) *The Sage handbook of governance*, London: Sage, pp 19–35.

Esping-Andersen, G. (1999) *Social foundations of post-industrial economies*, Oxford: Oxford University Press.

EU (European Commission) (2012) *Greying Europe – we need to prepare now* – European Commission, 5 May, http://ec.europa.eu/news/economy/120515_en.htm

Glendinning, C., Halliwell, S., Jacobs, S., Rummery, K. and Tyrer, J. (2006) 'New kinds of care, new kinds of relationships: How purchasing services affects relationships in giving and receiving personal assistance', *Health and Social Care in the Community*, 8(3): 201–11.

Guldvik, I. (2003) 'Personal assistants: Ideals of social care work and consequences for the Norwegian personal assistance scheme', *Scandinavian Journal of Disability Research*, 5(2): 122–39.

Guldvik, I. and Andersen, J. (2013) 'BPA – trekk ved kommunal saksbehandling, arbeidsgivernes tilrettelegging og assistentenes arbeidsbetingelser', *Research report 156/2013*, Lillehammer: Lillehammer University College.

Guldvik, I., Christensen, K. and Larsson, M. (2014) 'Towards solidarity: working relations in personal assistance', *Scandinavian Journal of Disability Research*, 16(1): 48–61.

Helsedirektoratet (2015a) *Opplæringshåndbok brukerstyrt personlig assistanse BPA*.

Helsedirektoratet (2015b) *Brukerstyrt personlig assistanse (BPA). Kommunens plikter og brukernes rettigheter. Søk om tilskudd til opplæring av assistenter,* https://helsedirektoratet.hn.qa.nhn.no/sykehjem-og-hjemmetjenester/brukerstyrt-personlig-assistanse-bpa

Hunter, S. and Richie, P. (2007) *Co-production and personalisation in social care. Changing relationships in the provision of social care,* London: Jessica Kingsley Publishers.

Johansen,V.,Askheim, O.P.,Andersen,J. and Guldvik, I. (2010) 'Stabilitet og endring – Utviklingen av brukerstyrt personlig assistanse', *Research Report 143/2010,* Lillehammer: Høgskolen i Lillehammer.

Johansson, H. and Hvinden, B. (2007) 'What do we mean by active citizenship?' in B. Hvinden and H.Johansson (eds) (2007) *Citizenship in Nordic welfare states: Dynamics of choice, duties and participation in a changing Europe,* London and NewYork: Routledge, pp 32–49.

Land, H. and Himmelweit, S. (2010) 'Who cares:Who pays? A report on personalisation in social care prepared for UNISON', *UNISON,* http://docplayer.net/228573-Who-cares-who-pays-a-report-on-personalisation-in-social-care-prepared-for-unison.html

Leadbeater, C. (2004) *Personalisation through participation. A new script for public services,* London: Demos.

Morris, J. (1993), *Independent lives? Community care and disabled people,* Basingstoke: Macmillan.

Needham, C. and Carr, S. (2009) 'Co-production: an emerging evidence base for adult social care transformation'. *Research Briefing 31,* London: Social Care Institute for Excellence.

Norges Handicapforbund (1994) *Brukerstyrt personlig assistance. Erfaringer fra et forsøksprosjekt,* Oslo.

Otnes, B. and Haugstveit, F. V. (2015. 'Kommunal variasjon i omsorgstjenester', Statistisk sentralbyrå/Statistics Norway, SSB Report 2015/44.

Pearson, C. (2000) 'Money talks? Competing discourses in the implementation of direct payments', *Critical Social Policy,* 20(4): 459–77.

Prop. 86 L, 2013–2014, https//www.stortinget.no/Saker-og-publikasjoner/Saker/Sak/?p=59833.

Rundskriv I-20/2000. Brukerstyrt personlig assistanse. Sosial- og helsedepartementet, Helse- og omsorgsdepartementet.

Rundskriv I-15/2005.Brukerstyrt personlig assistanse (BPA) – utvidelse av målgruppen.

Rundskriv I-9/2015.Rettighetsfesting av brukerstyrt personlig assistanse (BPA). Helse- og omsorgsdepartementet.

Scott, J. (1990) *A matter of record: Documentary sources in social research*, Cambridge: Polity Press.

Scourfield, P. (2015) 'Implementing co-production in adult social care: an example of meta-governance failure?' *Social Policy and Society*, 14(4): 541–54.

SSB, 2015. Statistics Norway. Available at:: https://www.ssb.no

St.meld. 34 (1996-97) *Resultater og erfaringer fra Regjeringens handlingsplaner for funksjonshemmede og veien videre*. Sosial- og helsedepartementet.

Stoker, G. (1998) 'Governance as theory: five positions', *International Social Science Journal*, 50(155): 17–28.

Ungerson, C. (2004) 'Whose empowerment and independence? A cross-national perspective on 'cash for care' schemes', *Ageing & Society*, 24: 189–212.

Ungerson, C. and Yeandle, S. (eds) (2007) *Cash for care in developed welfare states*, Basingstoke: Palgrave Macmillan.

Vabø, M., Christensen, K., Jacobsen, F.F. and Trætteberg. H.D. (2013) 'Marketisation in Norwegian eldercare: preconditions, trends and resistance', in G. Meagher and M. Szebehely (eds) *Marketisation in Nordic eldercare: A research report on legislation, oversight, extent and* consequences, Stockholm Studies in Social Work 30, Stockholm: Stockholm University, Department of Social Work, pp 163–202.

THIRTEEN

Individualised funding for older people and the ethic of care

Philippa Locke and Karen West

Introduction

Personal budgets (PBs) have been described as the highest profile strand of the personalisation agenda (Needham and Glasby, 2014: 12). PBs aim to provide service users with control over their care by providing them with choices over the type of care they receive as well as choices over who provides that care. Their introduction was the result of a sustained disability rights campaign, but the extent to which they are appropriate for all social care users has been questioned. Older people, in particular, as a group have been problematically situated in this policy shift to self-directed support. Where older people have money for self-directed support, this is far more likely to be as a budget managed by the local authority (Age UK, 2013). An evaluation of the early implementation of PBs suggested a substantial proportion of older people were likely to experience personal budgets as a burden rather than as leading to improved control over their care (Glendinning et al, 2008: 44) and more recent assessments continue to highlight problems for older service users (Lymbery, 2010; Woolham and Benton, 2013; Moran et al, 2013; Age UK, 2013).

This chapter examines the position of older people in relation to the move to personal budgets for social care from the perspective of the feminist ethic of care as articulated by Gilligan (1982) and Tronto (1993), which emphasises the fundamentally relational and contextual nature of care. Our overarching argument is that when it comes to the care of older people, the stark 'line in the sand' between autonomy and paternalism that the current discourse of rights-based personalisation and individualised funding marks out, is hard to discern and, therefore, an inadequate basis for care policy for people in later life. First, we briefly set out the emergence and intentions of personalisation and personal budgets. We then contrast the rights-based nature of personalisation, self-directed support and personal budgets, contrasting this with the ethic of care perspective. We then draw briefly on original research on care relationships in later life to illustrate the unavoidably relational nature of need and care. Finally, we argue that it is not simply a matter of ensuring that personal budgets deliver 'real choice and control' (Age UK, 2013: 3) for older people, but also one of enabling responsive caring relationships.

Individual rights versus relational care

The overarching aim of personalisation has been to provide service users with control over their care by selecting the elements that most closely meet their personal preferences (Needham, 2011: 54). One of the central means by which policy has sought to achieve this has been through the extension of choice and the provision of personal budgets, which allow service users to purchase the type of support that they deem to be most appropriate to them. Ostensibly, the turn towards individualised funding responds to the disability rights movement, which campaigned for disabled people to move away from institutionalised care. An early success is seen to be the NHS and Community Care Act 1990, which is perceived as bringing care closer to the individual and the community and is based on a philosophy of 'choices and rights' (Roulstone and Morgan, 2009: 334). While it is difficult to summarise the achievements of campaigns over several decades it can be argued that the disability rights movement played a crucial role in personalisation becoming a mainstream approach (Needham, 2011: 70). The disability rights movement essentially sought the provision of social care with an emphasis on individual choices, maintaining independence and support tailored to individual needs (Roulstone and Morgan, 2009: 336). From the perspective of disability rights, it is the assertion of autonomy that is the central objective. Care, from this perspective is equated with charity, obligation and paternalism, and, above all, a denial of autonomy. Purchased support, on the other hand, is thought to put the user in control. Users and supporters are brought into a market-based relation of exchange – cash for support – rather than a kin relation, based upon duty or kindness.

From the perspective of a feminist ethic of care, on the other hand, care is not something that is given to those who lack the means to be autonomous. Rather it is a core element of humanity and concerns any activity to 'maintain, continue, and repair our *world* so that we can live in it as well as possible' (Tronto, 1993: 103; emphasis in original).

The feminist ethic of care claims to be a moral theory (Tronto, 1993). It stems from the seminal work of Carol Gilligan's (1982) *In a different voice: Psychological theory and women's development* ,which argues for an 'ethic of care' rather than an 'ethic of rights'. Tronto (1993) identifies three major distinctions between these two ethics: first, the ethic of care is based on relationships and responsibilities, while the ethic of rights is based on rights and rules; second, the ethic of care stems from concrete circumstances, rather than abstract situations and third, the ethic of care depends on activity while the ethic of rights depends on principles (Shakespeare, 2000: 73).

The ethic of care takes the view that care is not something that one person does to another rather it is a relational activity that impacts on both the care giver and the care recipient. Tronto (1993: 127) outlines four specific elements that encompass the relations between care giver and care recipient: attentiveness, responsibility, competence and responsiveness of the care receiver. In addition to these, further discussions on the ethic of care have included the elements of trust and respect (Barnes, 2012: 19). The practice of care comprises these elements. If we are not attentive to the needs of others we cannot address those needs but, equally, we must be attentive to our own care needs (Tronto, 1993: 130). Care involves skill and knowledge and so competence is essential to the provision of good care (Tronto, 1993: 133). Tronto (1993: 131) argues that the notion of responsibility offers a more flexible perspective than obligation for understanding what people should do for each other. Responsibility in moral theory differs from the concept in political theory where it is often viewed as the need to conform to obligations, which usually arise from promises that have been made. In the ethic of care, responsibility emanates from implicit practices rather than from promises or formal rules (Tronto, 1993: 131). Responsibilities may stem from something we did or did not do, for example, by becoming parents we take on the responsibility of caring for our children, or we might assume a responsibility because we recognise a need for care and there is no other way that the need will be met except by our meeting it. Finally, responsiveness addresses the issue of dependency and challenges the view of the autonomous and self-supporting individual. It considers the relationship between the care recipient and the care giver and the way in which that relationship unfolds. Responsiveness requires that awareness of vulnerability within the care relationship and the possibilities of abuse that arise with such vulnerability. It also suggests a need to keep a balance between the needs of care givers and care recipients. Responsiveness requires attentiveness and, as such, emphasises the way in which these elements of the ethic of care are intertwined (Tronto, 1993: 136). In essence, to use the ethic of care requires a careful consideration of the situation in which care is taking place as well as the needs and competencies of all the individuals involved (Tronto, 1993: 136).

Shakespeare (2000: 73) puts forward the argument that an 'ethic of rights' should be applied to the provision of care. He argues that because, from an ethic of care perspective, we are all dependent on each other to varying degrees, then 'disabled people's limitations are not qualitatively different from others' (Shakespeare, 2000: 77). As such, they should be able to assert their rights in the same way that others do. Morris (2013: 2) is critical of this view and suggests that in many situations people require additional resources to be made available to allow them to access their human and civil rights. She argues that an ethic of care starts from the position that everyone has the same human rights, but also recognises the additional requirements that some people have in order to access those human rights (Morris 2013: 15). Caring relationships, in some situations, are unavoidably the primary means by which people even have the possibility of being connected to the external world of human rights. The danger that Morris (2013) draws attention to is that by focusing exclusively on the means by which care is provided, either by PBs or collective services, we may fail to give sufficient consideration to the quality of caring relationships and the ways in which they promote and protect human rights. As Lloyd (2010: 191) has suggested, the ethic of care and Tronto's concept of responsiveness in particular, is (or ought to be) at the heart of the personalisation agenda, since enabling those using services to define their needs and how they should be met is what personalisation is (or should be) all about. So, while the ethic of rights was instrumental in the introduction of PBs (Lloyd 2010: 191), an ethic of care and responsiveness is key to understanding how the turn to individualised funding supports and respects personhood. This is critical, since, in practice, and in a context of public service austerity, individualised funding seems to have become a key mechanism for withdrawing state sponsored welfare (West, 2013), leaving those in need of support even more dependent on the kindness of others. In the following section, we examine how individualised funding is shaping up in practice and, drawing on the prescient work of Marian Barnes (2011), and show how the rhetoric in personalisation's founding document – *Putting people first* (HM Government, 2007) – made it clear that it was never really about people who do not already have access to a network of support outside of primary, familial relations.

Putting the autonomous individual first

The expansion of choice of services, while intended to 'empower' the individual has correspondingly led to an increase in individual responsibility, with an expectation that care recipients will make good choices that promote their own health and wellbeing (Clarke, 2005: p 451). Critiques of this approach to service provision suggest that a focus on individual control over services values independence, self-sufficiency, and separation from others, at the expense of recognising the merit of relationships and interconnections (MacKenzie and Stoljar 2000: 8). Indeed, as foreseen personalisation has promoted individualism and isolation as community services such as day centres, branded as outmoded, were closed to make way for alternative, and more efficient, individualised forms of support (Needham, 2013: 94-7). This reduction of community services and the subsequent move towards individualisation has been argued to lead to 'the withering of social bonds' (Fine, 2013: 423) in the name of a neo-liberal agenda of moving responsibility from the state to the individual (Needham and Glasby, 2014: 21).

The neo-liberalisation of social policy implies a fundamental shift in the relationships between the state and the individual (Lemke, 2001: 200). This takes place in two ways: first, the market becomes the organising principle underlying the state. Second, the social domain becomes part of the economic domain so that cost-benefit calculations and market criteria can be applied to decision making processes within the family, married life, professional life and so on (Lemke, 2001: 200). Those in need of support become rational agents making cost-benefit calculations regarding their support needs. This relies on a conception of individuals as autonomous agents that are causally isolated from other agents, independent of the family and community relationships and other social relations in which they exist (MacKenzie and Stoljar, 2000: 7). However, this positioning of the individual is challenged by perspectives that emphasise the relational nature of social life, in particular the perspective of relational autonomy that regards agents' identities as formed within the context of social relationships and actions that impact on the lives of those around them (MacKenzie and Stoljar, 2000: 4). This view forms a fundamental part of the ethic of care's relational approach to choice. In this perspective, individuals are conceptualised as emotional, embodied, desiring, creative, and feeling, as well as rational, creatures (MacKenzie and Stoljar, 2000: 21). Choice is not always, or even often, the result of reasoned deliberation, but rather a consequence of impulse in urgent and contingent encounters requiring on-the-spot decisions as our own

255

and others' needs, expectations and feelings shape our thoughts (Hoggett, 2001: 40). This is particularly important in the context of care for older people where the fear of deep old age may additionally limit people's willingness to plan for future care needs (Price et al, 2012). In these situations, Mol (2008: 7) suggests that: 'it is difficult to weigh up the advantages and disadvantages of one uncertain future against another. We use fear as our advisor, or let other emotions cloud our judgements.'

Drawing on the ethic of care perspective, Barnes (2011) analysed the way in which the founding rhetoric of the turn to individualised funding made it clear that it was not so much a case of putting people first, as claimed, but rather of placing the rational, independent and fully connected individual at the centre of social policy reform. PBs and personalisation were first formalised in the policy concordat *Putting people first* (PPF) (HM Gov, 2007). Barnes (2011) undertook an analysis of this document from an ethic of care perspective in order to identify the way in which it perceived the individuals who were the centre of the discussion and who would benefit from the personalisation agenda. Barnes (2011: 159) states that PPF is suffused with explicit statements of the values that shape the policy. She found that there were assumptions about older and disabled people that indicated that the policy approach failed to engage with the wide range of circumstances in which older and disabled people live their lives. Rather, PPF constructs two groups of people, the first, the mainstream majority, capable of and willing to embody values of independence and self-determination, who have no need of 'care' and would find this restrictive and possibly oppressive. The second is a marginal group comprised of people unable to live up to the autonomous expectations of policy and thus for whom paternalism is acceptable. In particular, the position of isolated older people experiencing chronic mental or physical ill health was not distinguished from that of a disabled adult who is in paid employment and has a significant social network (Barnes, 2011: 157). For example, there was an assumption that people are not socially isolated, and that many are in paid work: 'interdependent on family members, work colleagues, friends and social networks' (HM Gov, 2007: 3).

Barnes (2011) argues that her analysis shows that the personalisation agenda appears to offer a perspective that instead of empowering those in need of care instead provides an approach that could reinforce the marginalisation of those that are most vulnerable and that 'personalisation is in danger of prioritising service models that relate emotionality and messy moral dilemmas to the private sphere from which public decision making is excluded' (Barnes, 2011: 165). Many of the 'emotional and messy dilemmas' relating to care are found within the relationship between care givers and care recipients. The understanding of the importance of care givers is reflected in the increase of carer rights over recent years but these have developed separately from the rights of the individual care recipient (Mitchell et al, 2014: 1434).

The following section explores how the context of older people's care needs connects with the individualised approaches of personalisation and how the relational perspective of the ethic of care highlights the difficulties of connecting the needs of care givers and care recipients in practice.

Personal budgets and older people

Those in favour of personalisation argue that it is appropriate to offer everyone personalised services, as the aim is to provide a service based on an individual's needs and no one has a greater understanding of those needs than the individual themselves (Needham, 2011: 52). It could be argued that although the circumstances of older people are common within their age group, they are not familiar to the individual and they don't 'know' how to manage the changes they experience, particularly in the context of the crisis and shock that accompany the loss of mobility or bereavement (Lloyd, 2014: 62).

Research into the implementation of personal budgets and the subsequent outcomes for service users suggests that there are particular challenges for older people who are allocated personal budgets (Glendinning et al, 2008; Netten et al, 2012: 1570; Moran et al, 2013; Age UK, 2013). These challenges could be explained by the policy emphasis on individual choice, which can be problematic for older people who approach social care services for the first time when they are at a point of crisis (Glendinning et al, 2008: 43). The reasons that older people delay approaching social services were explored by Themessl-Huber et al (2007: 226-8) who found that older people were reluctant to activate formal services or carers, even in emergency situations, because they preferred to wait for a familiar person, such as a relative or a GP to provide the care. Older people were reluctant to 'bother people' that they perceived as being busy and under time pressures and instead, people preferred to wait until a relative or other familiar person was available (Themessl-Huber et al, 2007). This appears to be in contrast to the ethic of rights put forward by the disability movement, where care is a right to be demanded. Seeking help may be delayed because of the fear of losing independence and a concern for some older people that by activating formal care services they will be perceived as frail and no longer able to continue living independently. These fears of losing independence can also lead to older people refusing services altogether and denying that anything is wrong or that external help is needed (Arksey and Glendinning, 2007: 18). This denial may mean that older people do not have time to collate information about the choices available to them and so are left having to make urgent decisions with little understanding of the options that exist.

The Social Care Institute of Excellence's (2012) 'Rough guide to personalisation' talks about people needing 'access to information, advocacy and advice so they can make informed decisions'. It is recognised there will always be some older people who will require support to make decisions (Broome et al, 2012: 27), yet evidence suggests that resources for this vital support are lacking, since budget allocations tend to be set at a level that covers little more than basic personal care and maintenance (Age UK, 2013). In health care situations, the source of information is often easily identifiable, for example, a GP, consultant or specialist nurse. In social care, however, the sources of information are not so obvious. For people whose needs arise from an accident or sudden illness, access to information regarding social care may be facilitated by the care teams involved in managing the crisis, whereas people with a fluctuating or gradual onset of needs generally have to seek information about services themselves (Baxter and Glendinning, 2011).

The expectation that older people are expected to navigate the market of care services is argued to go against the realities of frailty in old age that are well known within social work practice (Ward and Barnes, 2015: 14). The positing of choice as a single independent event is also called into question. For older people the need for care is not always consistent and as conditions change there is the additional challenge of fluctuating needs where it may be necessary to make repeated choices (Glendinning, 2008: 462). Because of this, Glendinning (2008: 465) suggests that choice may need to be 'reconceptualised as a dynamic process in which decisions are constantly reviewed' rather than the current rhetoric where it is portrayed as a single event that produces a positive outcome. Mol (2008) compares the role of the consumer in choosing a product with the way that care is delivered, contrasting the logic of choice with the logic of care. In Mol's (2008) logic of care, care is an interactive, open-ended process that may be shaped and reshaped depending on its results. This view is echoed by Winance (2010: 111) who suggests that '[t]o care is to tinker', to test, touch, adapt, adjust, pay attention to details and change them and continue to do this until a suitable arrangement is reached. These approaches to care, which emphasise the fluid nature of choice, challenge the view of an individualist process and are echoed in the debates surrounding the personalisation of care where it is recognised that there is a shift from concerns about individual choice and responsibility towards a greater awareness of the role of trusted and meaningful relationships (Glasby and Needham, 2014: 190).

Choice may become overwhelming when facing difficult decisions about an uncertain future. In these situations, choice may be more about care givers and care professionals picking up cues and ensuring that the care recipient feels listened to and understood (Ward and Barnes, 2015: 8). In these situations, it is the nature of the interaction that is key, rather than the imperative of choice (Ward and Barnes, 2015: 8). From an ethic of care perspective this is the responsiveness of the care relationship where the care recipient's needs must be considered and attended to (Tronto, 1993: 136).

In addition to an assessment to identify the needs of the older person, local authorities now have a duty to offer carers assessments of their own. Evidence suggests that carers are seldom offered a carer's assessment, with one study suggesting that this was less than one fifth (Woolham et al, 2014). Even where needs are separately assessed, there are questions about how best to assess the needs of, and deliver support to, older people and their care-giving relatives and friends in the context of the often close and interdependent relationships between them (Glendinning et al, 2015: 24). A study by Glendinning et al (2015: 27) suggests that the most common way in which carers' needs were assessed was to ask the carer if they were 'willing and able' to continue providing support and about any help they may need to do this. This was often done in front of the person for whom care was being provided, which made it difficult for the carers to answer negatively. In other cases, there was an expectation by care professionals that the carer would continue to provide support (Glendinning et al, 2015: 27). In terms of the feminist ethic of care, the question of whether someone is 'willing' to provide support is problematic as to suggest that you are unwilling to care is to position oneself as morally lacking (Tronto, 1993). This demonstrates that despite the understanding that carers play an important role, the assessment of the needs of older people and their carers continues to underestimate the nuances and implications of care relationships.

The vital role of families in arranging support

This section draws on data from a doctoral study that explored the experiences of older people's social care choices beginning with identifying the needs of older people and how they, and their informal/ family carers, defined those needs. Ethical approval was granted by the research committee of the School of Languages and Social Sciences at Aston University. The research explored the way in which care responsibilities were negotiated between older people and their families. The participants were recruited using purposive sampling and one to one interviews were undertaken with 19 individuals who were either care givers, care recipients or both. The interviews ranged in length from one to three hours and were analysed using narrative analysis. Names used here are pseudonyms to preserve the anonymity of the participants.

The need to make care choices can arise as a result of a crisis situation or may be planned in light of increasing care needs. The discourse around care focuses on individual control and would suggest that the older person would be at the centre of the process of arranging care and be involved in the final decision. However, rather than the older person actively considering the 'options', several participants describe making choices on behalf of a relative who was either not well enough to make decisions about their care or who trusted their relative to make the decision on their behalf. The data presented here seek to add to the discussion of the roles of carer and care recipient in the care relationship and how individual situations result in different approaches to the definition or identification of care needs.

In exploring the relational nature of care it is possible to see how the care needs of the different family members become intertwined. Andy and Maggie were both in their late 70s. Andy had recently recovered from stomach cancer and Maggie was living with advanced dementia. Their adult son and daughter lived nearby but their daughter, Sue, visited most often to check that her parents' needs were being met, demonstrating the elements of both attentiveness and responsiveness:

'I tend to spend an hour or two with them every day … it's been gradual really … you just become aware that they're doing less and whereas Dad used to come and help me do DIY around the house suddenly he can't lift things so much or his eyesight's not so good so I start helping them… I mean it would be very easy just to take over and say right I'm moving in … but I don't think that would be right … I want him to feel independent and be independent as much as he can without running himself into the ground.'

Sue asserted that her father was the carer for her mother and that Sue had very little to do with care. This was contradicted by her comment that she spends an hour or two each day helping her parents with various needs sometimes, which was simply taking them out for a coffee to ensure that they had a change of scenery. The role of carer within family relationships is difficult to define and some care givers do not recognise or accept the label of carer (Larkin and Milne, 2014: 27). Although many of Sue's activities with her parents could be categorised as care giving, she did not recognise that the label could apply to her.

Andy began to have problems with his knee and as his mobility was impaired, it was arranged that carers would visit twice a day to wash and dress Maggie; however, Andy made sure that all the care tasks were completed before their visit. He argued that the carers were a waste of money and were not needed:

> "Now it's just, it's getting ready in the morning, up and showered and dressed, getting Maggie up and dressed and I just feel it would be an intrusion in our life to get anybody else to do that when I can do it. Fair enough if I fall over or can't then I think Sue would take over but I just feel I wouldn't like a stranger, maybe it wouldn't be a stranger for long, a stranger coming in and doing that."

Although the external carers were employed to undertake the physical tasks of caring for Maggie, their purpose was also to provide support, and so also care for Andy. His resistance to this arrangement had implications for his daughter, as there was an expectation that she would take over the role. Mol's (2008) logic of choice emphasises that the options that are available to choose are limited and the requirement to negotiate with older people in order for them to accept that some care relationships are not an available choice is not something that is considered within the discussions of empowerment and choice.

Making arrangements after a hospital stay may be facilitated by healthcare professionals and, for some older people in these situations, care relationships may play an important role in communicating the needs and preferences of the older person. An example of this is provided by Mrs Cole, carer for her husband who had advanced Parkinson's disease. Mrs Cole suffered a heart attack and shortly thereafter a stroke, yet when she was due to be discharged from the hospital she was not deemed to be eligible for convalescent care in a nursing home:

"She was in hospital after her first heart attack. She was then under the care of the hospital social work team, which is different to the community social work team … We spent a huge amount of time, my mum did, I did, liaising between hospital social worker and community social worker to get them to talk to each other about the various issues that were going on, they never really did."

The family were aware that Mrs Cole needed time to recover and attempted to communicate her needs to the care professionals as she was not able to do so. From the professional's perspective, Mrs Cole's role as carer for her husband was not part of the assessment as to whether she was fit to be discharged from hospital. This highlights the difficulty in assessing the needs of care givers and the importance of taking into account care relationships from the perspective of both care giver and care recipient.

While informal care by family members is an important part of the care of older people, as the older person's needs increase, the family may no longer be able to provide good quality care. Jerry and his wife had cared for his mother, Mabel, at home but had agreed that when Mabel was no longer able to stand unaided then they would no longer be able to care for her. Jerry undertook the decision to change the care arrangements, and together with his brother, visited local care homes and selected one that was close and where they felt Mabel would be comfortable. Jerry described how he was finding it increasingly difficult to cope:

"The only problem was mum's knees … she was falling… I was strong enough to lift her when she'd fallen down … but even getting into bed, getting up in the night, that was getting more difficult. In the end we got a baby monitor, one that you could listen to… I could have it by the bed upstairs and we could hear if she was moving about or trying to or had a fall or anything you know if she called out … but it did mean in the end that I was getting up several times a night every night and that's seven days a week because there's nobody else.'"

Here Jerry is making it clear that he is unable to continue the care role and not unwilling. As discussed previously, Jerry would appear to be uncaring if he were to simply say that he was no longer willing to care for Mabel. Instead, he emphasises the difficulties that he faces in providing the care without the proper equipment and support. Jerry undertook the decision to change the care arrangements and visited local care homes. The important aspect in the nursing home that he selected was that each room was equipped with a hoist over the bed. This would mean that Mabel could be comfortably and safely moved from the bed to a chair. Although she had not been involved in the selection of the home, the brothers were seeking to protect their mother's right to be cared for in a dignified and safe manner rather than Jerry continuing to cope alone, which carried the risk of poor care as he became increasingly tired.

These narratives show the importance of care relations and the way that care choices are part of ongoing care relationships, rather than individual decisions made by isolated individuals. In order for older people to be able to receive good care, they are at times necessarily dependent on the choices made by their families and significant others. The data shows how some of the elements of the feminist ethic of care, in particular Tronto's (1993) concept of responsiveness in care relationships plays an instrumental role in the day to day care of older people.

Conclusion

The ethic of care emphasises the relational nature of care and the importance of considering the needs of both care recipients and care givers. The introduction of PBs was perceived as meeting the requirement for responsiveness as it enabled service users to define their needs and how those needs should be met. However, the policy documents such as PPF suggest that there is a lack of understanding of the circumstances of social care users. Instead of care being viewed as part of daily life, it is portrayed as something that is evoked only in exceptional circumstances and only for those who are unable to exercise control.

There is an expectation that people would both want to and are capable of managing PBs, whereas for older people this is not the case. Older people often have fluctuating needs leading to the requirement that choices may need to be constantly reviewed so that the language of choice as a single, problem-solving event is not appropriate, but rather choice is an ongoing dynamic process. In order to make choices, each individual must face costs, in terms of time, effort and resources in order to collate information that is relevant to their particular needs. The relational elements of the ethic of care allow for the understanding that carers are often involved in making decisions regarding care. The rights of carers have developed separately from those of service users and while it is understood that carers' rights should be considered, the practice of questioning whether they are willing to continue in the care role raises problems, as people may not want to position themselves as unwilling to care for another person as this would make them appear to lack moral integrity.

The examples of care relationships within families shows that rather than making choices about care provision, older people may assume that family members will be willing and able to step in and provide care when the need arises. In situations where this is not possible, then care decisions may not be made by the older person but by their family members who, rather than avoiding care responsibilities, are seeking to ensure that the older person is cared for in the best way possible. In terms of the feminist ethic of care, this is an illustration of responsiveness, the consideration of the needs of both the care giver and the care recipient. For some, the care choice that they want to make is to rely on others to make decisions about their care.

The ethic of care perspective draws attention to the ways in which the personalisation agenda, instead of placing the care needs of the individual in the centre of the discussion, continues to marginalise care and instead emphasises independence and self-determination. The idea of responsiveness in the feminist ethic of care is crucial for examining the ways in which individualised funding impacts on care relationships.

References

Age UK (2013) 'Personal budgets in social care', http://www.ageuk.org.uk/brandpartnerglobal/plymouthvpp/publication%20and%20leaflets/ageukig26_personal_budgets_inf.pdf

Arksey, H. and Glendinning, C. (2007) 'Choice in the context of informal care-giving', *Health and Social Care in the Community*, 15(2): 165–75.

Barnes, M. (2011) 'Abandoning Care? A Critical Perspective on Personalisation from an Ethic of Care', *Ethics and Social Welfare*, 5(2): 153–67.

Barnes, M. (2012) *Care in Everyday Life*, Bristol: Policy Press.

Baxter, K. and Glendinning, C. (2011) 'Making choices about support services: Disabled adults' and older people's use of information', *Health and Social Care in the Community*, 19(3): 272–79.

Broome, S. et al. (2012) *Improving decision-making in the care of older people, Exploring the decision ecology*, York: The Joseph Rowntree Foundation, www.jrf.org.uk

Clarke, J. (2005) 'New Labour's citizens, activated, empowered, responsibilized, abandoned?' *Critical Social Policy*, 25(4): 447–63.

Fine, M.D. (2013) 'Individualising care. The transformation of personal support in old age', *Ageing and Society*, 33(3): 421–36.

Gilligan, C. (1982) *In A Different Voice: Psychological Theory and Women's Development*, Cambridge, MA: Harvard University Press.

Glasby, J. and Needham, C. (2014) 'Glass half full or glass half empty', in C. Nicholson and J. Glasby (eds) *Debates in Personalisation*, Bristol: Policy Press, pp 185–91.

Glendinning, C. et al (2008) *Evaluation of the Individual Budgets Pilot Programme Final Report*, York: Social Policy Research Unit, University of York, http://eprints.whiterose.ac.uk/73483/.

Glendinning, C. (2008) 'Increasing choice and control for older and disabled people: A critical review of new developments in England', *Social Policy and Administration*, 42(5): 451–69.

Glendinning, C., Mitchell, W. and Brooks, J. (2015) 'Ambiguity in practice? Carers' roles in personalised social care in England', *Health and social care in the community*, 23(1): 23–32, http://www.ncbi.nlm. nih.gov/pubmed/25332011.

HM Government (2007) *Putting people first: A shared vision and commitment to the transformation of adult social care,* London: HM Government, p 8. Available at webarchive.nationalarchives.gov.uk/20130107105354/ http://www.dh.gov.uk/en/Publicationsandstatistics/Publications/ PublicationsPolicyAndGuidance/DH_081118.

Hoggett, P. (2001) 'Agency, rationality and social policy', *Journal of Social Policy*, 30(1): 37–56, http://journals.cambridge.org/production/ action/cjoGetFulltext?fulltextid=73582

Larkin, M. and Milne, A. (2014) 'Carers and Empowerment in the UK: A Critical Reflection', *Social Policy and Society*, 13(1): 25–38, http:// www.journals.cambridge.org/abstract_S1474746413000262

Lemke, T. (2001) '"The birth of bio-politics': Michel Foucault's lecture at the Collège de France on neo-liberal governmentality', *Economy and Society*, 30(2): 190–207.

Lloyd, L. (2014) 'Can personalisation work for older people?' in C. Needham and J. Glasby (eds) *Debates in Personalisation*, Bristol: Policy Press, pp 55–64.

Lloyd, L. (2010) 'The Individual in Social Care: The Ethics of Care and the 'Personalisation Agenda' in Services for Older People in England', *Ethics and Social Welfare*, 4(2): 188–200.

Lymbery, M. (2010) 'A new vision for adult social care? Continuities and change in the care of older people', Critical Social Policy, 30(1): 5–26, http://csp.sagepub.com/cgi/doi/10.1177/0261018309350806

Mackenzie, C. and Stoljar, N. (2000) Relational Autonomy: Feminist Perspectives on Autonomy, Agency and the Social Self, Oxford: Oxford University Press.

Mitchell, W., Brooks, J. and Glendinning, C. (2014) 'Carers' Roles in Personal Budgets: Tensions and Dilemmas in Front Line Practice', British Journal of Social Work, 45(5): 1–18, http://bjsw.oxfordjournals. org/content/early/2014/03/30/bjsw.bcu018.abstract

Mol, A. (2008) The logic of care: Health and the problem of patient choice, London: Routledge.

Moran, N. et al (2013) 'Older people's experiences of cash-for-care schemes: Evidence from the English Individual Budget pilot projects', Ageing and Society, 33(5): 826–51.

Morris, J. (2013) 'Impairment and Disability: Constructing an Ethics of Care That Promotes Human Rights', Hypatia, 16(4): 1–16.

Needham, C. (2011) Personalising Public Services: Understanding the personalisation narrative, Bristol: Policy Press.

Needham, C. (2013) 'Personalization: From day centres to community hubs?' Critical Social Policy, 34(1): 90–108, http://csp.sagepub.com/ cgi/doi/10.1177/0261018313483492.

Needham, C. and Glasby, J. (eds) (2014) Debates in Personalisation, Bristol: Policy Press.

Netten, A. et al (2012) 'Personalisation through individual budgets: Does it work and for whom?' British Journal of Social Work, 42(8): 1556–73.

Price, D. et al (2012) 'Financial planning for social care in later life: The 'shadow' of fourth age dependency', Ageing and Society, 34(3): 388–410, http://www.journals.cambridge.org/abstract_S0144686X12001018

Roulstone, A. and Morgan, H. (2009) 'Neo-Liberal Individualism or Self-Directed Support. Are We All Speaking the Same Language on Modernising Adult Social Care?' Social Policy and Society, 8(3): p 333, http://www.journals.cambridge.org/abstract_S1474746409004886.

Shakespeare, T. (2000) Help, Birmingham: Venture Press.

Social Care Institute for Excellence (2012) 'Personalisation: A rough guide', SCIE Guide 47, London: Social Care Institute for Excellence, www.scie.org.uk/publications/guides/guide47/files/guide47.pdf.

Themessl-Huber, M., Hubbard, G. and Munro, P. (2007) 'Frail older people's experiences and use of health and social care services', Journal of nursing management, 15(2): 222–29, http://doi.wiley.com/10.1111/ j.1365-2834.2007.00726.x

Tronto, J. (1993) *Moral Boundaries: A Political Argument for an Ethic of Care*, London: Routledge.

Ward, L. and Barnes, M. (2015) 'Transforming Practice with Older People through an Ethic of Care', *British Journal of Social Work*, 1–17, http://bjsw.oxfordjournals.org/content/early/2015/04/07/bjsw.bcv029.abstract

West, K. (2013) 'The grip of personalization in adult social care: Between managerial domination and fantasy', *Critical Social Policy*, 33(4): 638–57, http://WOS, p 000326043900003

Winance, M. (2010) 'Care and disability: Practices of experimenting, tinkering with, and arranging people and technical aids', in A.M. Mol, I. Moser and J. Pols (eds) *Care in Practice: On Tinkering in Clinics, Homes and Farms*:Verlag, Bielefeld, pp 93–118.

Woolham, J. and Benton, C. (2013) 'The costs and benefits of personal budgets for older people: Evidence from a single local authority', *British Journal of Social Work*, 43(8): 1472–91.

Woolham, J. Ritters, K., Steils, N. and Daly, G. (2014) 'Do personal budgets for older people live up to expectations?' *The Guardian*, 9 May.

Index